THE AQUARIAN TEACHER

KRI
International Teacher Training in Kundalini Yoga as taught by Yogi Bhajan®

LEVEL ONE INSTRUCTOR YOGA MANUAL

This KRI INTERNATIONAL KUNDALINI YOGA TEACHER TRAINING LEVEL ONE YOGA MANUAL is designed to be used in conjunction with the LEVEL ONE TEXTBOOK.

YOGI BHAJAN, PhD
MASTER OF KUNDALINI YOGA

The Aquarian Teacher: KRI International Teacher Training in Kundalini Yoga
as taught by Yogi Bhajan® Level One Instructor by Yogi Bhajan, Ph.D.

FIRST EDITION ©2003 Kundalini Research Institute
SECOND EDITION ©2004 Kundalini Research Institute
THIRD EDITION ©2005 Kundalini Research Institute
FOURTH EDITION ©2007 Kundalini Research Institute
FIFTH EDITION ©2010 Kundalini Research Institute

ISBN 978-1-934532-37-9

MANAGING & CONTRIBUTING EDITOR
Guru Raj Kaur Khalsa

SENIOR CONSULTING EDITOR
Gurucharan Singh Khalsa

CONSULTING EDITOR
Shakti Parwha Kaur Khalsa

BOOK DESIGN
Guru Raj Kaur Khalsa

ILLUSTRATIONS
Ong Kar Kaur Khalsa

COPY EDITORS
Pranpati Singh (John Ricker)
Guruka Singh Khalsa

PRODUCER & PUBLISHER
Kundalini Research Institute

PROJECT COORDINATOR
Nam Kaur Khalsa

The diet, exercise and lifestyle suggestions in this book come from ancient yogic traditions. Nothing in this book should be construed as medical advice. Any recipes mentioned herein may contain potent herbs, botanicals and naturally occurring ingredients which have traditionally been used to support the structure and function of the human body. Always check with your personal physician or licensed health care practitioner before making any significant modification in your diet or lifestyle, to insure that the ingredients or lifestyle changes are appropriate for your personal health condition and consistent with any medication you may be taking. For more information about Kundalini Yoga as taught by Yogi Bhajan® please see www.yogibhajan.org and www.kundaliniresearchinstitute.org.

©2013 Kundalini Research Institute. All teachings, yoga sets, techniques, kriyas and meditations courtesy of The Teachings of Yogi Bhajan. Reprinted with permission. Unauthorized duplication is a violation of applicable laws. ALL RIGHTS RESERVED. No part of these Teachings may be reproduced or transmitted in any form by any means, electronic or mechanical, including photocopying and recording, or by any information storage and retrieval system, except as may be expressly permitted in writing by the The Teachings of Yogi Bhajan. To request permission, please write to KRI at PO Box 1819, Santa Cruz, NM 87567 or see www.kundaliniresearchinstitute.org.

COVER PHOTO of Yogi Bhajan in Rome, courtesy of Sadhu Singh Khalsa—all rights reserved. For permission to reproduce this photograph for any purpose, contact Sadhu Singh, at yogitea@libero.it. For purchase of the photograph in the U.S., contact yogiemporium@yahoo.com.

A Note to All From Yogi Bhajan

"THERE IS NO IDENTITY FOR YOU, EXCEPT YOUR SPIRITUAL IDENTITY. There's no grace in you but to learn. There is no achievement other than to become learned. There's no power but to share what you have learned with all and everyone. Share with compassion—you will be compensated, and you shall have no complex. Then all that there is shall come to you, and you will not have to go after anyone."

THESE DAYS EVERY HUMAN BEING FEELS THEY ARE PERFECT, they are righteous, they know it all; and they are judgemental of the world around them. In yoga a person has to be humble, have the power to merge, and to be spiritually, mentally, and physically committed for exalted experiences.

The Master can share the knowledge, but the experiences belong to the student. Therefore, we do not claim any result or effect or guarantee any result or achievement because the experience belongs to the individual student individually, his or her consciousness, and his or her power to practice.

We are not a commercial organization and we are not a business. We are just sharing the knowledge and technology that have been passed down to us. You are our students. We don't initiate students, because we believe that each student must initiate himself or herself. According to our definition, a student is the one who studies from the Master to become the Master.

We advise that you consult your physician before beginning this program. Then freely decide whether to participate in these teachings.

The Age of Aquarius is on our head whether we feel, know or understand or not. Past is going to become obsolete, and teachers of the Age of Aquarius are going to help humanity. This is your chance to be leaders with love and affection. We wish you the best of luck.

Yogi Bhajan

From KRI Director of Training

BY THE KINDNESS OF MY TEACHER, YOGI BHAJAN, I have witnessed his vision grow. From his first few words declaring his purpose, to create teachers, to a robust global network of teachers dedicated to live with awareness and uplift each person. From the first kundalini yoga Teacher Training in the western hemisphere with a dozen students crammed cozily together in a small house in 1970 Los Angeles to our most recent IKYTA meeting in New Mexico with hundreds of active teachers serving students in every country.

From the first he would say, "You do not know me, I know you. I accept none of you as my students. Accept your Self first and show me your grace and caliber by your service and compassion. Compassion is the language of the Aquarian Age. You want flesh and bones and a personality, I want nothing. You will know me by my words and teachings."

Most of you will in fact know him through the teachings. And when you practice the teachings and link to the Golden Chain of teaching energy, you will also know Yogi Bhajan by his subtle presence. Practice brings awareness, awareness brings subtlety, subtlety brings depth, depth brings dedication, dedication brings humility, humility brings grace, and grace brings you the master's touch, which is that presence of spirit that is timeless, without ego and without any boundaries—pure and infinite.

That domain of the Infinite, the *anahat*, is always present and accessible. It is as intimate as your breath. Yogi Bhajan is a master of the time. He has merged into the Infinite consciously in the House of Guru Ram Das, which holds the space of Kundalini Raj Yoga for the Aquarian Age.

I encourage each of you to read the words of these teachings, then be silent and listen to the heart within them. Watch the video records of Yogi Bhajan teaching to get a sense of his clarity, directness, compassion and attitude of service. It is rare to even glimpse someone who has mastered themselves to share mastery. No words or descriptions can convey the impact of participating in his classes, virtually or otherwise. Confirm by experience your own connection to the Teacher, the teachings and the inner teacher within you. Practice the *kriyas* to energize, awaken, purify and heal yourself. Then you can experience teaching with the constant capacity to commit to the integrity of the Self, to commit to stillness and listen, and commit to fearless, compassionate action to serve all.

There is nothing more powerful than Kundalini Yoga to awaken your consciousness, to confront your ego and drop your fears. There is nothing more elegant, to build the strength of your nervous system and character. There is nothing more effective to develop the caliber to be happy in the midst of challenge, and grateful each moment of life. And there is nothing more profound that takes you to the core of your being to listen deeply and hear the pulse of the Creator, the *naad* and *shabd guru*, in all people and all things.

The journey has many steps, abounds with insight and inspiration, invites deep companionship and calls on your body, mind and spirit to work together. At each step the hand of the Teacher is there to help guide you, the teachings are there with flawless energy and technique. My prayer is that each of you realizes your potential and role as an Aquarian Teacher of Kundalini Yoga and awareness.

This manual (along with its companion textbook) stems from our efforts to provide a systematic introduction to the vast teaching materials given by Yogi Bhajan. It is the effort of many people. Our vision is to establish a clear standard for the concept of a teacher, the technology of Kundalini Yoga and a discipline to train yourself in both.

My gratitude to Yogi Bhajan for sharing the teachings and directing this effort. My gratitude to Shakti Parwha Kaur Khalsa who has held the standard steadily from the beginning. And my gratitude to the many teachers who have given comments, ideas, critiques and countless hours of time to realize this series of training manuals. And lastly, my appreciation to Guru Raj Kaur Khalsa who has patiently compiled, designed, and structured the Textbook and Manual coordinating the pieces by meetings, calls and emails to reach the final product.

Gurucharan Singh Khalsa, Ph.D.
Director of Training, Kundalini Research Institute
July 2002

From the Mother of 3HO

By luck or by chance, by the grace of God, I was the first woman in the United States to study with Yogi Bhajan. He told me, "You've been a student long enough; you should be a teacher." And so within two months of attending his classes, I was teaching. That was in 1969. I'm still teaching, and still learning. The more I teach, the more I learn.

In 1970, when Yogi Bhajan started traveling and I heard he was teaching new kriyas in various cities (nobody was tape recording), I felt insecure not knowing all the latest techniques. He said, "Just teach what you know, and teach people to relax." This is still important advice for any teacher. By all means, learn as much of the technology as you can, but realize basically that you don't have to know "everything" to help people to help themselves.

When you affirm the Oath of a Teacher before each class, and when you tune in to the Golden Chain with *Ong Namo Guru Dev Namo*, be aware these are not just rituals, they are real and effective means to help you avoid what Yogi Bhajan warned us was the "one incurable disease." That disease is an occupational hazard for teachers, it's called "Spiritual Ego." No matter how much your students appreciate you (and they will), for your own spiritual health, remember that you are not the Doer. It is only by the grace of God and the generosity of our spiritual Teacher (with a capital "T") that any one of us is able to share the magnificent technology of Kundalini Yoga.

In 1969 when Yogi Bhajan taught his first class in Kundalini Yoga in the United States, hardly anyone had accurate information about this ancient, sacred, and up until then, secret, science. Its technology for transformation and empowering of the individual human being had been given only to those students who could prove their devotion, dedication, self-discipline, humility, and obedience to the Teacher. Despite scriptural warnings that whoever taught Kundalini Yoga publicly would not live to see his next birthday, Yogi Bhajan flaunted tradition. He saw that it was the very thing that was desperately needed at this time of the dawning of the Aquarian Age. The time to bring The Yoga of Awareness to the world had come.

He made it clear from the beginning that he had come to train teachers, not to gather disciples, and he emphasized, "Don't love me, love my teachings." But, as students flocked to him, we were enveloped in his absolute, unconditional, amazing loving presence, and love him we did—and still do. It has been his mission to enable us to become "ten times greater than him." To me that means ten times more kind, compassionate, patient, and selfless. (Not to mention wise and graceful.) It's a big order.

His quotable quotes, the "clichés" that have become a part of our 3HO vocabulary can fill volumes. "Keep up, and you'll be kept up." Of course he shared knowledge about the healing, therapeutic benefits of Kundalini Yoga, but he stressed that "Doing is believing." So, when you teach, he said, "Give people an experience."

As you are about to become Kundalini Yoga teachers, I offer my heartfelt welcome to this family of beings who truly want to live, be, and share the technology to be Healthy, Happy, and Holy. It is, after all, your birthright. Teach it, claim it, and the world will be a better place for your having lived and breathed on it.

Humbly yours,
Shakti Parwha Kaur Khalsa
July 2002

From the Editor

THIS AQUARIAN TEACHER MANUAL (and its companion Textbook) are the efforts of many people to codify the great body of teachings brought down through the ages and the ethers by Yogi Bhajan. And at this point in time, these Volumes represents the unity of the pioneers who carried these teachings forward, to stand together as one, as Aquarian Teachers, and present in a simple form, the basic teachings of Kundalini Yoga as taught by Yogi Bhajan.

Over the last thirty-three years, thousands of pages of material have been created and collected, as those whose lives have been changed by this miraculous science have endeavored to document and share these teachings with others. The Aquarian Teacher represents the distillation of those thousands of pages into an essential, basic format, to serve as a beginning for the first Level of KRI Training in becoming a Kundalini Yoga Teacher.

These Volumes, in their simplicity, are meant to be part of a three-fold process in your Training. The technology and wisdom contained in its pages will serve as a resource for years to come.

The second in the trinity are The Master's Touch lectures, in book and video form. In 1996 and 1997, Yogi Bhajan taught the first Master's Touch course in Espanola, New Mexico, and Assisi, Italy. He asked that these lectures be transcribed and made into a book. These lectures form a great legacy. They embody the spark of the Golden Chain and are an invaluable tool for developing your personal relationship with Yogi Bhajan and the Golden Chain.

The third is your Teacher Trainer, whose dedication to these teachings and to his or her beloved Teacher Yogi Bhajan, and to you and your destiny, will pass these teachings to you purely and selflessly.

THANKS AND ACKNOWLEDGEMENT are in order. Particular acknowledgment to Gurucharan Singh Khalsa and Satya Singh Khalsa, whose original Teacher Training Manuals formed the foundation of these Volumes, and to Tarn Tarn Singh Khalsa, Hari Kaur Khalsa, and Dharm Kaur Khalsa who began the process of forming an outline. Thanks to Pranpati Singh who helped to add structure and continuity, and to Guruka Singh Khalsa, who added helpful finishing touches.

Deep appreciation to my daughter Ong Kar Kaur, for her tireless work on the hundreds of drawings—a seemingly never-ending task. And to my young daughter, a young yogini, Nirinjan Kaur, who was our model for the meditations. Both completed their Teacher Training in 2002 and were eager to contribute to this important project. Thanks are also due to Naseem Gulamhusein of Vancouver and Sat Dharm Singh of Mexico for modeling posture.

And for material appearing in the Textbook, thanks to Guruchander Singh Khalsa and Nirvair Singh Khalsa for their work developing the teachings on the Ten Bodies. Thanks to Guru Prem Singh and Simran Kaur for their dedication to perfecting posture, one of the great limbs of yoga, to Shakta Kaur and Gurumukh for their work with children and pre-natal yoga, respectively. And to Darshan Kaur for contribution to the list of mantras.

Thanks to Shakti Parwha Kaur and Gurucharan Singh who are like philosopher stones for the accuracy and integrity of these teachings.

Thanks to Darshan Kaur Khalsa, Dharm Kaur Khalsa, and Hari Kaur Khalsa for helpful review, and to Nam Kaur Khalsa and Satya Kaur Khalsa to whom this project was so precious.

I humbly bow to the efforts of the many pioneers in Teacher Training worldwide, particularly all those who have pioneered Teacher Training in Europe and other parts of the world.

All contributed to this work out of their love of and desire to serve these teachings, and out of their love for and gratitude to their Teacher, Yogi Bhajan.

It was my personal privilege to serve my Teacher, and the great House of Guru Ram Das. I worked on it with personal and impersonal dedication. I humbly present it, on behalf of my Teacher, and ask forgiveness for any shortcomings. Any shortcomings are mine, not his.

MAY YOUR HUMBLE PRAYER to serve be fulfilled through these teachings and through the course on which you are embarking. May the touch of Guru Ram Das soothe and make fruitful your longing to serve these times, and to uplift every heart.

Humbly,
Guru Raj Kaur Khalsa
May 1, 2003

Sets & Meditations

Chapter 1
SETS & KRIYAS   *9*

Chapter 2
MEDITATIONS & PRANAYAMS WITHOUT MANTRA   *57*

Chapter 3
MEDITATIONS WITH MANTRA   *85*

Pronunciation Guide

This simple guide to the vowel sounds in transliteration is for your convenience. More commonly used words are often spelled traditionally, for example, Sat Nam, Wahe Guru, or pranayam, even though you'll often see them written Sat Naam, Whaa-hay Guroo, and praanayaam, in order to clarify the pronunciation, especially in mantras. Gurbani is a very sophisticated sound system, and there are many other guidelines regarding consonant sounds and other rules of the language that are best conveyed through a direct student-teacher relationship. Further guidelines regarding pronunciation are available at www.kundaliniresearchinstitute.org.

a	hut
aa	mom
u	put, soot
oo	pool
i	fin
ee	feet
ai	let
ay	hay, rain
r	flick tongue on upper palate

CHAPTER 1

Sets & Kriyas

WARM UP
Surya Namaskar (Sun Salutation) — 10

TEACHERS' FAVORITE SETS
Awakening Yourself to Your Ten Bodies — 12
Basic Spinal Energy Series — 13
Flexibility and the Spine — 14
Kriya for Elevation — 17
Nabhi Kriya — 19
Nabhi Kriya for Prana-Apana — 20
Sat Kriya — 22
Strengthening the Aura — 23
Stress Set for Adrenals & Kidneys — 24
Surya Kriya — 26

MORE GREAT SETS
Disease Resistance and Heart Helper — 28
Exercise Set for the Kidneys — 29
Foundation for Infinity — 31
Healthy Bowel System — 33
Kriya for Disease Resistance — 34
Kriya for Morning Sadhana — 36
Preparatory Exercises for Lungs, Magnetic Field & Deep Meditation — 40
Navel Adjustment Kriya — 42
Magnetic Field and Heart Center — 43
New Lungs and Circulation — 45
Pituitary Gland Series — 47
Prana-Apana Balance — 48
Releasing Premenstrual Tension & Balancing Sexual Energy — 49
Transforming the Lower Triangle to the Higher Triangle — 51
Sat Kriya Workout — 53
Wahe Guru Kriya (Trikuti Kriya) — 54

Examples of Sets Focusing on each Chakra — 55
Examples of Appropriate Sets for Beginners — 55
Examples of Good Warm-up Sets — 55

Surya Namaskara – THE SUN SALUTATION

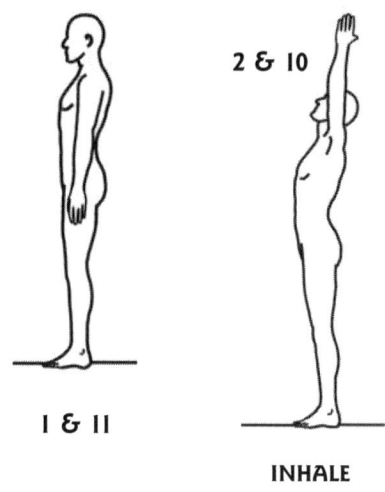

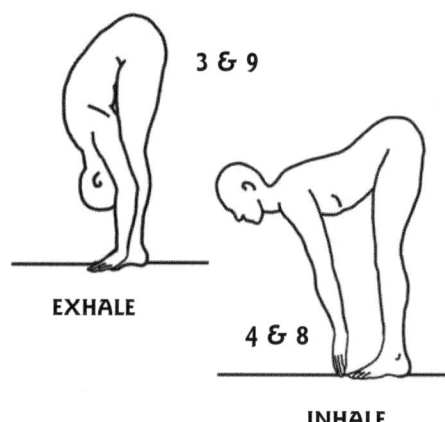

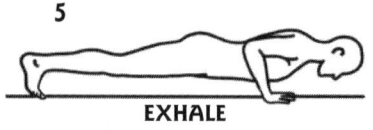

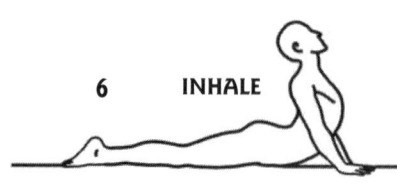

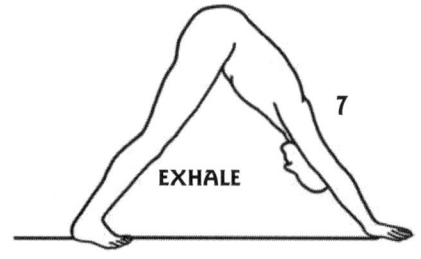

1) **Standing Straight (Samasthiti).** Stand up straight, feet together, toes and heels touching, weight evenly distributed between both feet. Find your balance. The arms are by your sides, fingers together.

2) **Stretching Up.** Inhale, bring your arms up over your head, palms touching. Elongate the spine, lifting the chest and relaxing your shoulders. Be sure not to compress the vertebrae of the neck and lower back. Look up at the thumbs.

3) **Front Bend (Uttanasana).** Exhale and bend your torso forward. As you bend forward, keep your spine straight, elongating it as if reaching forward with the top of the head. When the spine can no longer be held straight, relax the head as close to the knees as possible. Ideally, the chin will be brought to the shins. Keep knees straight and place hands on the floor on either side of the feet, with fingertips and tips of the toes in line. Gaze at the tip of the nose.

4) Inhale, raise the head up, straighten the spine, keeping the hands or fingertips on the floor. Gaze at the Third Eye Point.

5) **Push-up (Chaturanga Dandasana).** Exhale and bend the knees, stepping or jumping back so that the legs are straight out behind, balancing on the bottoms of the bent toes. Elbows are bent, hugging the rib cage, and palms are flat on the the floor under the shoulders, with fingers spread wide apart. The body is in a straight line from forehead to ankles. Keep yourself equally balanced between hands and feet. Do not push forward with the toes.

6) **Cobra Pose. (Bhujangasana).** From this position, inhale, straighten the elbows and arch the back. Stretch through the upper back so that there is no pressure on the lower spine. Point the forehead at the sky and gaze at the tip of the nose. Fingers are spread wide apart.

7) **Triangle Pose. (Adho Mukha Svanasana).** Exhale, lift the hips up so that the body is balanced in an inverted v-shape. Feet and palms are flat on the floor; elbows and knees straight. Fingers are spread wide apart. Gaze toward the navel and hold this position for **five breaths**.

8) Inhale and jump or step back into position #4.

9) **Front Bend (Uttanasana).** Exhale and bend forward into position #3.

10) **Stretching up.** Inhale and come all the way up into position #2..

11) **Standing up. (Samasthiti).** Exhale and return to the starting position with arms by the sides.

COMMENTS:

When Yogi Bhajan was studying with his Teacher, the Sun Salutation was used as a warm-up exercise before starting the Kundalini Yoga Kriyas. This is an excellent warm-up and is beneficial as an exercise in its own right. It increases cardiac activity and circulation, stretches and bends the spine, massages the inner organs, aids the digestive system, exercises the lungs, and oxygenates the blood. Synchronize your breath with the movements to create an uninterrupted rhythm throughout the sequence of positions. Start by practising three rounds and then gradually increase to five or six. When practiced with awareness, this improves one's ability to maximize performance and enjoyment of all yoga postures.

Awakening to Your Ten Bodies

The Ten Bodies are:
Soul Body
Negative Mind
Positive Mind
Neutral Mind
Physical Body
Arc Line
Auric Body
Pranic Body
Subtle Body
Radiant Body

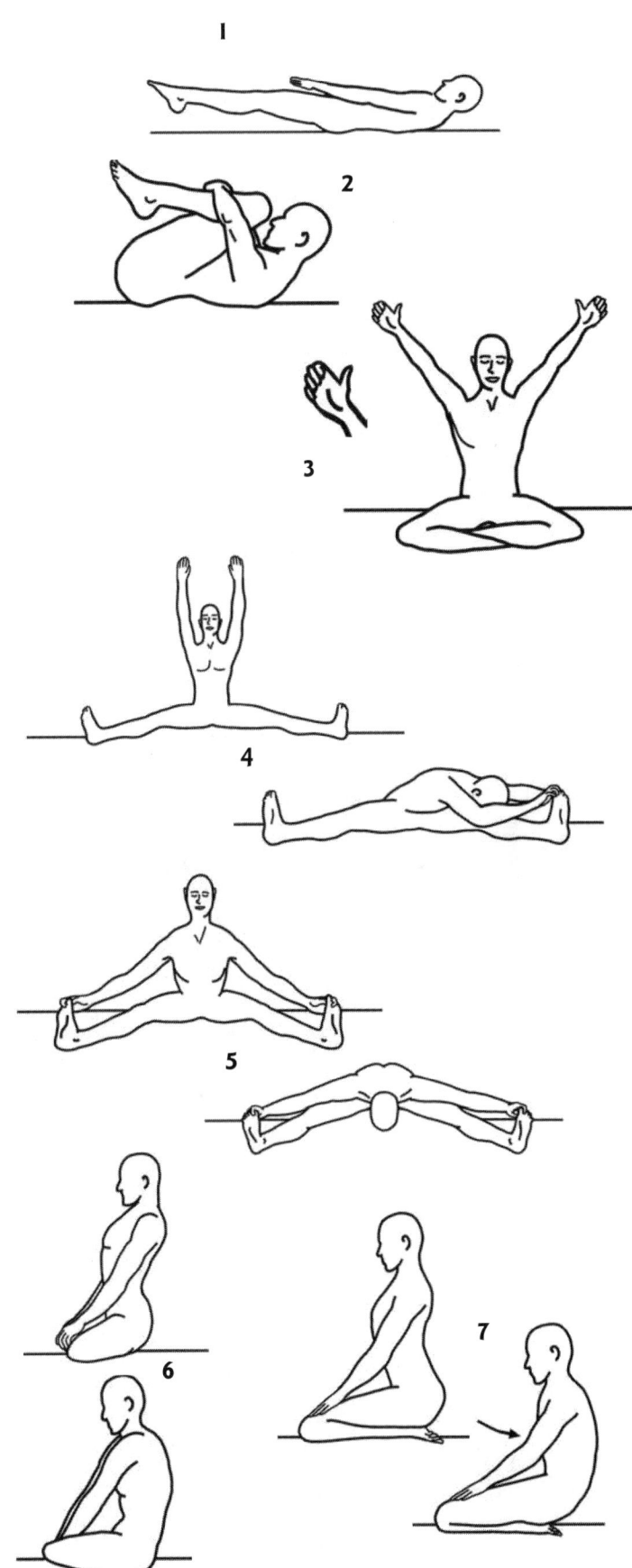

1) **Stretch Pose.** Lie on the back with the arms at your sides. Raise the head and the legs six inches, and the hands six inches with the palms facing each other slightly over the hips to build energy across the Navel Point. Point the toes, keep your eyes focused on the tips of the toes and do Breath of Fire. **1-3 minutes**.

2) **Nose to Knees.** Bring the knees to the chest, with the arms wrapped around the knees. Tuck the nose between the knees, and begin Breath of Fire. **1-3 minutes.**

3) **Ego Eradicator.** Sit in Celibate Pose or Easy Pose. Raise the arms to a 60° angle. Curl the fingertips onto the pads at the base of the fingers. Plug the thumbs into the sky. With eyes closed, concentrate above the head, and do Breath of Fire. **1-3 minutes.** To end, inhale, touch the thumbtips together overhead. Exhale and apply *mulbandh*. Inhale and relax.

4) **Life Nerve Stretch.** Sit with the legs stretched wide apart. With arms overhead, inhale. Then exhale, stretch down and grab the toes of the left foot. Inhale, come straight up; then exhale and stretch down over the right leg and grab the toes. Continue **1-3 minutes.**

5) **Life Nerve Stretch.** Continue to sit with the legs stretched wide apart. Hold onto the toes of both feet, exhale as you stretch down bringing the forehead to the floor, then inhale as you come sitting up. **1-3 minutes.**

6) **Spinal Flex (Camel Ride).** Sit in Easy Pose. Grab the shins in front with both hands. Inhale. Flex the spine forward and rock forward on buttocks. Then exhale, flex the spine backwards and roll back on buttocks. Keep the head level and arms fairly straight and relaxed. **1-3 minutes.**

7) **Spinal Flex (Camel Ride).** Sit on the heels. Place the hands flat on the thighs. Flex the spine forward on the inhale, backward on the exhale. Focus at the Third Eye Point. **1-3 minutes.**

Awakening to Your Ten Bodies

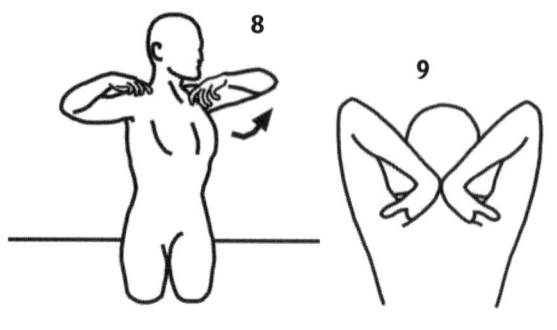

8) **Spinal Twist.** Still on the heels, grasp the shoulders with the fingers in front, thumbs in back. Inhale and twist to the left, exhale and twist to the right. Keep the elbows high, and parallel to the floor. (Do not reverse.)
1-3 minutes.

9) Grasp the shoulders as in the previous exercise. Inhale and raise the elbows up so that the backs of the wrists touch behind the neck. Exhale and lower the elbows to shoulder height, and repeat.
1-3 minutes.

10) **Arm Pumps.** Interlace the fingers in Venus lock. Inhale and stretch the arms up over the head, then exhale and bring the hands back to the lap.
1-3 minutes.

11) **Alternate Shoulder Shrugs.** Sit in Easy Pose with the hands resting on the knees. Inhale and shrug the left shoulder up. Exhale and raise the right shoulder up as you lower the left shoulder. Continue for **1 minute**. Then, reverse the breath so that you inhale as you shrug the right shoulder up, exhale as you shrug the left shoulder and lower the right shoulder. Continue for **1 minute**.

12) **Shoulder Shrugs.** Inhale and shrug both shoulders up, exhale down.
1 minute.

13) **Neck Turns.** Remain sitting in Easy Pose hands on the knees. Inhale, and twist your head to the left, and exhale and twist it to the right, like shaking your head "no". Continue for **1 minute**. Then reverse your breath, so that you inhale and twist to the right; exhale and twist to the left. Continue for **1 minute**. Inhale deeply, concentrate at the Third Eye, and slowly exhale.

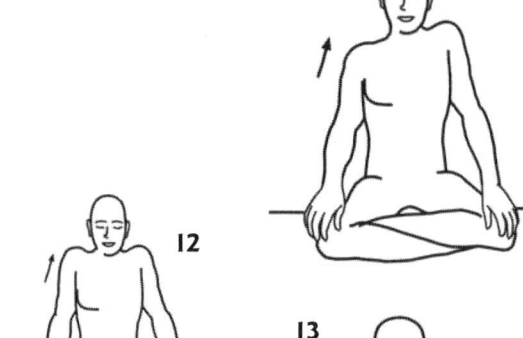

14) **Frog Pose.** Squat down so the buttocks are on the heels. The heels are touching, and off the ground. Put the fingertips on the ground between the knees. Keep the head up. Inhale, straighten legs up, keeping the fingers on the ground. Exhale and come back squatting down, face forward. The inhale and exhale should be strong. Continue this cycle **54 times.**

15) *Deeply relax on the back.*

Laya Yoga Meditation
Sit in Easy Pose with the hands on the knees in Gyan Mudra (thumb and index finger together.) Chant *Ek Ong Kaar(uh) Saa-Taa-Naa-Maa(uh) Siree Wha(uh) Hay Guroo*. On *Ek* pull the navel. On each final "uh" lift the diaphragm up firmly. The "uh" sound is more of a powerful movement of the diaphragm than a pronounced purposeful projected sound. Relax the navel and abdomen on *Hay Guroo*. This is a 3-1/2 cycle meditation. With the breath, visualize the sound spiralling up from the base of the spine to the top of the head in 3-1/2 circles. **11-31 minutes.**

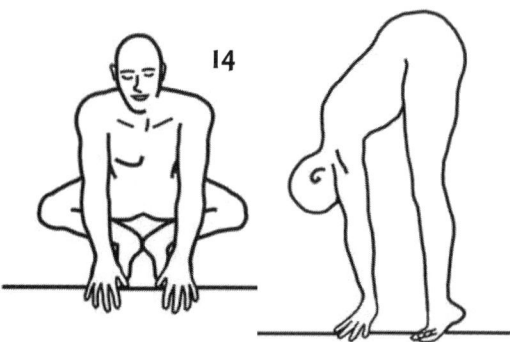

This set is from *Owners Manual for the Human Body.*

Teachers' Favorite Sets
Sets & Meditations
Basic Spinal Energy Series

1) **Spinal Flex.** Sit in Easy Pose. Grab the ankles with both hands and deeply inhale. Flex the spine forward and lift the chest up. On the exhale, flex the spine backwards. Keep the head level so it does not "flip-flop." Repeat **108 times,** then inhale. *Rest 1 minute. Spinal flexes have a "multi-stage reaction pattern" that greatly alters the proportions and strengths of alpha, theta and delta waves.*

2) **Spinal Flex.** Sit on the heels. Place the hands flat on the thighs. Flex spine forward with the inhale, backward with the exhale. Mentally vibrate *Sat* on the inhale, *Nam* on the exhale. Repeat **108 times.** *Rest 2 minutes.*

3) **Spinal Twist.** In Easy Pose, grasp the shoulders with fingers in front, thumbs in back. Inhale and twist to the left, exhale and twist to the right. Breathing is long and deep. Continue **26 times** and inhale facing forward. *Rest 1 minute.*

4) **Bear Grip.** Lock the fingers in Bear Grip at the heart center. Move the elbows in a see-saw motion, breathing deeply with the motion. Continue **26 times** and inhale, exhale, pull the lock. *Relax 30 seconds.*

5) **Spinal Flex.** In Easy Pose, grasp the knees firmly. Keeping the elbows straight, begin to flex the upper spine. Inhale forward, exhale back. Repeat **108 times.** *Rest 1 minute.*

6) **Shoulder Shrugs.** Shrug both shoulders up on the inhale, down on the exhale. Do this for less than **2 minutes.** Inhale and hold 15 seconds with shoulders pressed up. Relax the shoulders.

7) **Neck Rolls.** Roll the neck slowly to the right **5 times,** then to the left **5 times.** Inhale, and pull the neck straight.

8) **Bear Grip.** Lock the fingers in Bear Grip at the throat level. Inhale—apply *mulbandh.* Exhale—apply *mulbandh.* Then raise the hands above the top of the head. Inhale—apply *mulbandh.* Exhale—apply *mulbandh.* Repeat the cycle **2 more times.**

9) **Sat Kriya.** Sit on the heels with the arms overhead and palms together. Interlace the fingers except for the index fingers, which point straight up. Men cross the right thumb over the left thumb; women cross the left thumb over the right. Chant *SAT* and pull the Navel Point in; chant *NAAM* and relax it. Continue powerfully with a steady rhythm for at least **3 minutes,** then inhale, apply Root Lock and squeeze the energy from the base of the spine to the top of the skull. Exhale, hold the breath out and apply all the locks. Inhale and relax.

10) *Relax completely on your back for* **15 minutes.**

COMMENTS:
Age is measured by the flexibility of the spine: to stay young, stay flexible. This series works systematically from the base of the spine to the top. All 26 vertebrae receive stimulation and all the chakras receive a burst of energy. This makes it a good series to do before meditation. Many people report greater mental clarity after regular practice of this *kriya*. A contributing factor is the increased circulation of the spinal fluid, which is crucially linked to having a good memory.

In a beginner's class, each exercise that lists 108 repetitions can be done **24 times.** The rest periods are then extended from **1 to 2 minutes.**

COPYRIGHT YOGI BHAJAN 2003

Flexibility & the Spine 1 OF 3

1) **Archer Pose.** Stand with the right leg bent forward so the knee is over the toes. The left leg is straight back with the foot flat on the ground, at a 45° angle to the front foot. Raise the right arm straight in front, parallel to the ground and make a fist as if grasping a bow. Stretch thumbs up and back. Pull the left arm back with elbow high, as if pulling the bowstring back to the shoulder. Feel a tension across the chest. Face forward; apply Neck Lock, and project the gaze of the eyes as if through the thumbnail. Hold the position **3 to 5 minutes**, switch legs and arms, and repeat.

2) **Leg Lifts.** Immediately lie on the back. Put the heels together and lift both legs **two feet** from the ground. Hold the position **1 to 3 minutes** with Long Deep Breathing.

3) **Locust Pose.** Lie on the stomach. Make fists with the hands and put them on the lower abdomen inside the front hip bones near the groin. Keeping the heels together and the legs straight, lift them up as high as possible. Hold for **3 minutes.**

4) **Bow Pose.** Still on the stomach, reach back and firmly grasp the ankles. Lift the chest up off the ground, and balance by pulling the ankles. Hold for **2 to 3 minutes.**

5) **Windmill.** Stand up straight and spread the legs **two feet apart**. Turn to the left and reach down with your right hand to touch the outside of the left ankle. The left arm is pointing up. Inhale to the center and switch sides, turning to the right and reaching down with the left hand to touch the outside of the right ankle. Continue this alternate motion. On the inhale, rise up completely; on the exhale reach for the ankle. Repeat **25 times.**

6) **Forward Bend.** Stand up with the legs **6 inches apart**. Bend forward and place the palms flat on the ground and exhale. Inhale and rise up, stretching backwards with the arms over the head. Continue **25 times**.

7) **Sidebends.** Stand with the legs **6 inches apart**. Bend sideways stretching the arm over the head. Alternate smoothly from side to side, inhaling as you bend and stretch exhaling up. Do not let the body bend forward or backward. Continue **25 times**.

Flexibility & the Spine

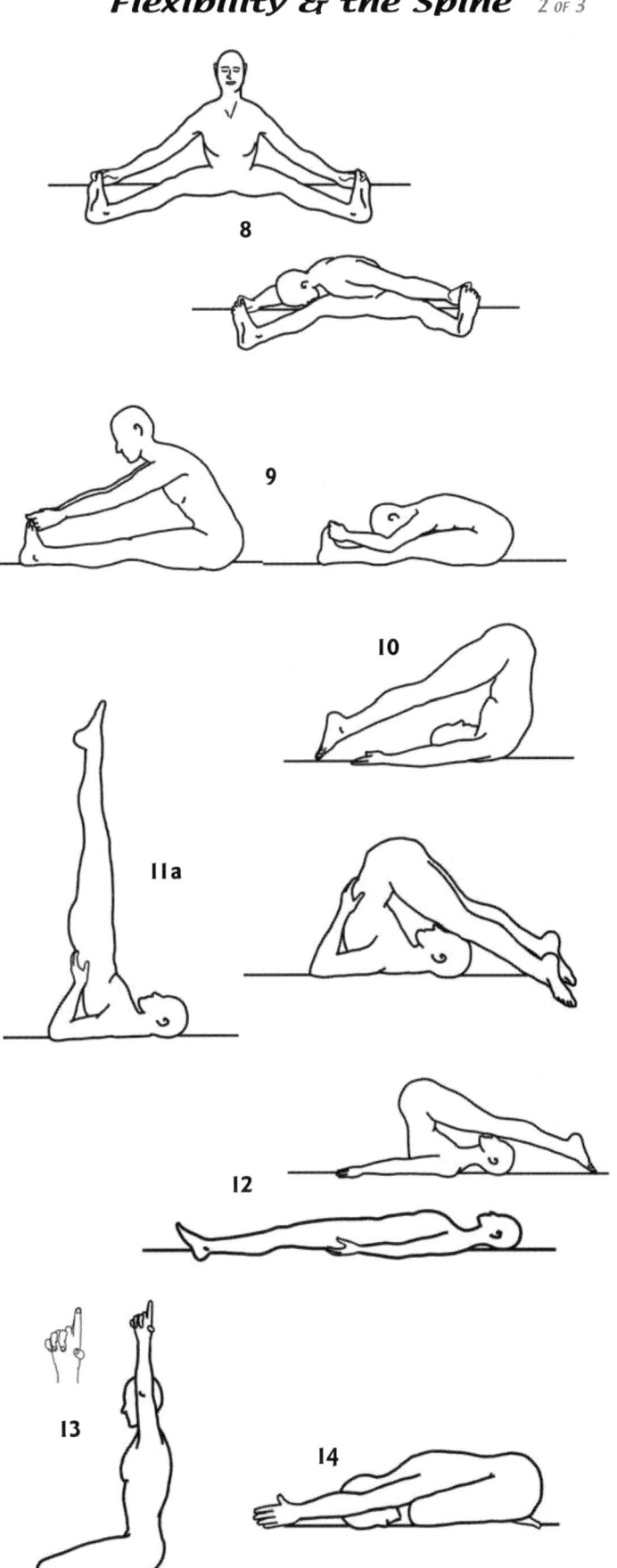

8) **Life Nerve Stretch.** Sit down and extend the legs out in front, spreading them wide. Grab the big toe of each foot by locking the Jupiter and Saturn Fingers around the toe, the thumb pressing the toenail. Keeping a firm grip on both toes, inhale the spine up straight. Exhale and touch the head to the right knee. Inhale center, and exhale down to the left knee. Continue to alternate toe touches **25 times** on each side. Inhale, hold the breath and exhale.

9) **Front Stretch.** Still sitting, bring the legs together while still holding onto the toes. Inhale up, exhale, elongate the spine, bend forward from the navel. Head follows last. Continue this pumping motion **25 times.**

10) **Plow Pose**. Lie flat on the back. Slowly raise the legs over the head until they touch the floor. The arms are over the head pointing towards the toes. Keep the knees straight. *Relax* in this position for **5 minutes.** Slowly lower the legs back down to the ground.

11) a) Come into **Shoulder Stand** by raising the legs straight up towards the ceiling. Support the spine perpendicular to the ground with the hands. Let most of the weight be on the elbows. Hold for **3 to 5 minutes**.

   b) Then bring the legs down in back of the head in **Plow Pose,** but spread the legs wide apart. Slowly go from this position to shoulder stand **4 times.** Lower the legs and spine and rest on the back.

12) Come into **Plow Pose** with the arms along the ground in back of the spine. Alternate from Plow Pose to lying flat on the back. Continue **50 complete times**. The hands may be used to lift the legs up and back. *Relax for 3 minutes.*

13) **Sat Kriya**. Sit on the heels with the arms overhead and the palms together. Interlace the fingers except for the index fingers, which point straight up. Men cross the right thumb over the left thumb; women cross the left thumb over the right. Chant *SAT* and pull the Navel Point in; chant *NAAM* and relax it. Continue powerfully with a steady rhythm for **5 minutes**, then inhale, apply Root Lock and squeeze the energy from the base of the spine to the top of the skull. Exhale, hold the breath out and apply all the locks. Inhale and relax.

14) **Guru Pranaam.** Immediately bend forward in *Guru Pranaam.* Place the forehead on the ground and stretch the arms overhead, keeping the palms together. Meditate at the Brow Point by silently projecting the primal sounds, *Saa Taa Naa Maa.* Continue for **31 minutes**.

This set is from *Sadhana Guidelines.*

Flexibility & the Spine 3 OF 3

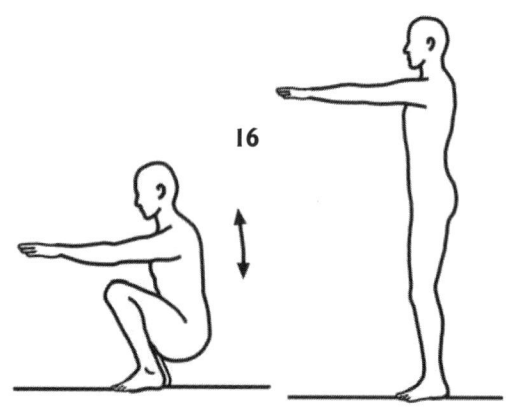

15) Sit in Easy Pose. Inhale and raise both arms over the head bringing the backs of the hands together. Exhale and lower the arms letting just the fingertips touch the floor. Continue this motion for **5 minutes**.

16) **Crow Pose Knee-bends.** Stand up and extend the arms straight forward parallel to the ground. Begin **25** deep knee-bends into Crow Pose, keeping the spine straight and the feet flat.

17) **Cat-Cow.** Come onto the hands and knees. Arch the spine down and raise the head with the inhale. With the knees hip-width apart and the heels together behind you, exhale and arch the spine up and lower the head. Continue for **5 minutes.**

18) Deeply relax for **15 to 30 minutes** on the back. Cover the body with a blanket to keep from getting cold.

COMMENTS:
This set is an example of a series which would not be given in a routine Kundalini Yoga class. It is for students who have attained a moderate degree of flexibility and coordination in regular classes and *sadhana*, and who want to eject residual poisons and drugs from the muscle tissue. If the set is done every morning for six months, it adjusts the spine so well that many chiropractic bills will be unnecessary. Before attempting this set under guidance, be sure you have no major physical problems that will prevent you from doing any of the exercises. Unlike most Kundalini Yoga *kriyas*, you do not take a 2-3 minute rest between each exercise unless it is explicitly stated. It could be adapted to a regular class by keeping the time of the exercises to **1-2 minutes** and by adding rest periods between the exercises.

This set is from *Sadhana Guidelines*.

Kriya for Elevation

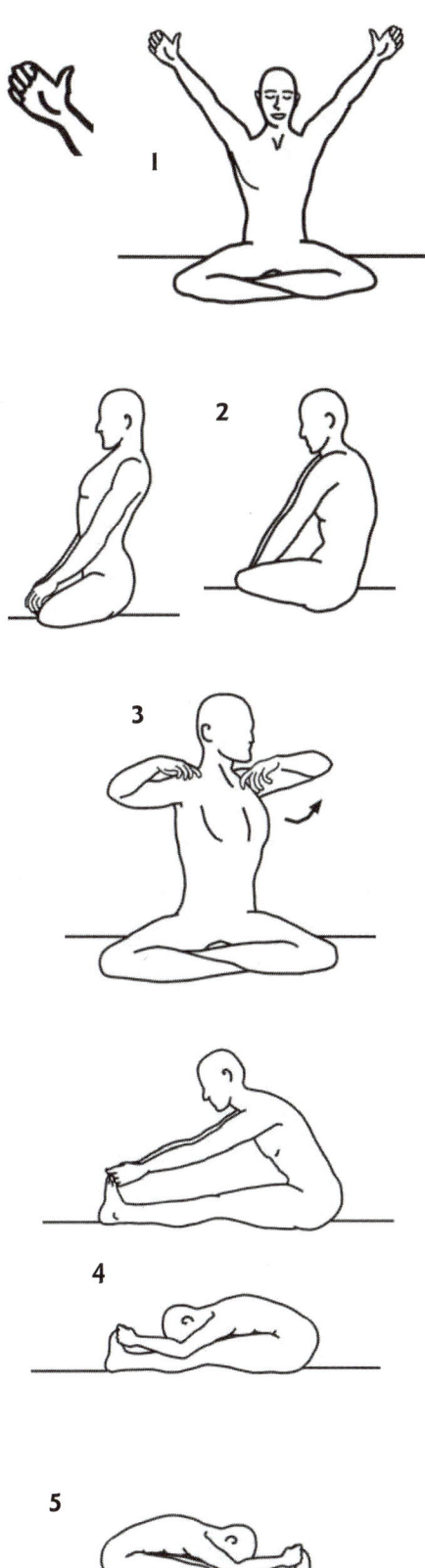

This easy set of exercises is excellent as a tune-up. It systematically exercises the spine and aids in the circulation of prana to balance the chakras.

1) **Ego Eradicator.** Sit in Easy Pose. Raise the arms to a 60 degree angle. Curl the fingertips onto the pads at the base of the fingers. Plug the thumbs into the sky. Eyes closed, concentrate above the head, and do Breath of Fire. **1-3 minutes.** To end, inhale and touch the thumbtips together overhead. Exhale and apply *mulbandh*. Inhale and relax.
This exercise opens the lungs, brings the hemispheres of the brain to a state of alertness, and consolidates the magnetic field.

2) **Spinal Flex.** Sitting in Easy Pose, grasp the shins with both hands. As you inhale, flex the spine forward and lift the chest. As you exhale, flex the spine back, keeping the shoulders relaxed and the head straight. Continue rhythmically with deep breaths for **1-3 minutes**. Then inhale, exhale, relax. *This exercise stimulates and stretches the lower and mid-spine.*

3) **Spinal Twist.** In Easy Pose, grab the shoulders, with the thumbs in back and the fingers in front. Keep the elbows high, with the arms parallel to the ground. Inhale as you twist the head and torso to the left. Exhale as you twist to the right. Continue for **1-4 minutes**. To end, inhale, facing straight forward. Exhale and relax.
This exercise stimulates and stretches the lower and mid-spine.

4) **Front Life Nerve Stretch.** Stretch both legs straight out in front. Grab the toes in finger lock. (Index finger and middle finger pull the toe, and the thumb presses the nail of the big toe.) Exhale, as you lengthen the core of the spine, bending forward from the navel, continuing to lengthen the spine. The head follows, last. Inhale, use the legs to push up. The head comes up last. Continue with deep, powerful breathing for **1-3 minutes**. Inhale up and hold the breath briefly. Stay up and exhale completely, holding the breath out briefly. Inhale and relax.
This exercise works on the lower and upper spine.

5) **Modified Maha Mudra.** Sit with the right heel tucked into the perineum and the left leg extended forward. Grasp the big toe of the left foot with both hands, applying a pressure against the toenail. Pull Neck Lock. Exhale, bring the elbows to the ground as you lengthen the spine, bending forward from the navel, continuing to lengthen the spine, bringing the head to the knee. Spine stays straight. Hold, with Breath of Fire for **1-2 minutes**. Inhale. Exhale and stretch the head and torso forward and down. Hold the breath out briefly. Inhale, switch legs and repeat the exercise. Relax.
This exercise helps elimination, stretches the sciatic nerve and brings circulation to the upper torso.

Real maha mudra (great lock)
Only on left heel
All bandhas
Tongue to roof of mouth
Eyes focus at top of head

Bend knee if necessary

Kriya for Elevation

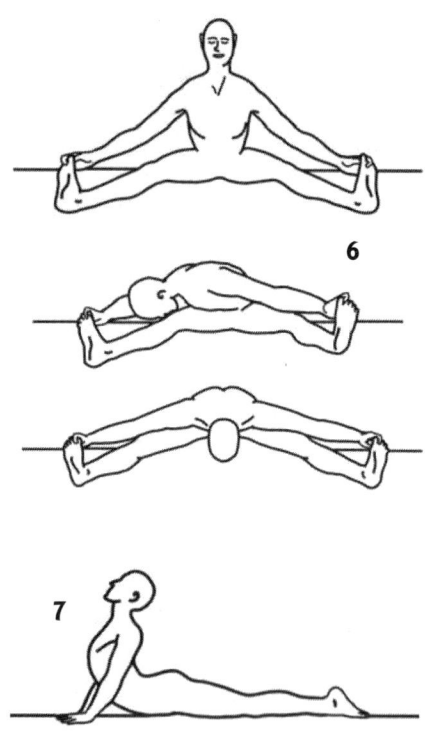

6) **Life Nerve Stretch.** Spread the legs wide, grasping the toes as in Exercise 4. Inhale and stretch the spine straight, pulling back on the toes. Exhale and, bending at the waist, bring the head down to the left knee. Inhale up in the center position and exhale down, bringing up the head to the right knee. Continue with powerful breathing for **1-2 minutes.** Then inhale up in the center position and exhale, bending straight forward from the waist touching the forehead to the floor. Continue this up and down motion for **1 minute**, then inhale up stretching the spine straight. Exhale, bringing the forehead to the floor. Hold the breath out briefly as you stretch forward and down. Inhale and relax.
This exercise develops flexibility of the lower spine and sacrum and charges the magnetic field.

7) **Cobra Pose.** Lie on the stomach with the palms flat on the floor under the shoulders. The heels are together with the soles of the feet facing up. Inhale into Cobra Pose, arching the spine, vertebra by vertebra, from the neck to the base of the spine until the arms are straight. Begin Breath of Fire. Continue for **1-3 minutes.** Then inhale, arching the spine to the maximum. Exhale and hold the breath out briefly, apply *mulbandh*. Inhale. Exhaling slowly, lower the arms and relax the spine, vertebra by vertebra, from the base of the spine to the top. *Relax*, lying on the stomach with the chin in the floor and the arms by the sides.
This exercise balances the sexual energy and draws the prana to balance apana so that the kundalini energy can circulate to the higher centers in the following exercises.

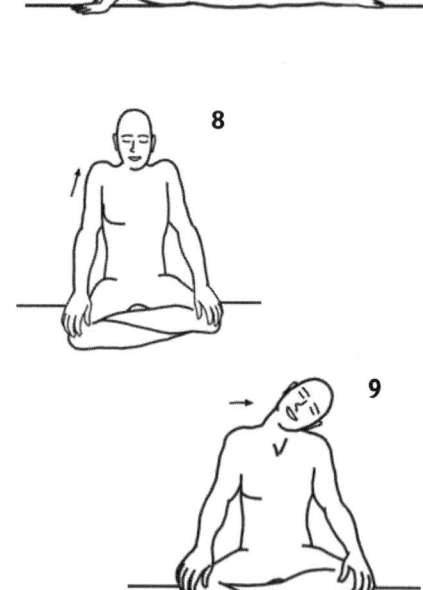

8) **Shoulder Shrugs.** Sit in Easy Pose. Place the hands on the knees. Inhale and shrug the shoulders up toward the ears. Exhale and drop the shoulders down. Continue rhythmically with powerful breathing for **1-2 minutes.** Inhale. Exhale and relax.
This exercise balances the upper chakras and opens the hormonal gate to the higher brain centers.

9) **Neck Rolls.** Sit in Easy Pose. Begin rolling the neck clockwise in a circular motion, bringing the right ear toward the right shoulder, the back of the head toward the back of the neck, the left ear toward the left shoulder and the chin toward the chest. The shoulders remain relaxed and motionless. The neck should be allowed to gently stretch as the head circles around. Continue for **1-2 minutes**, then reverse the direction and continue for **1-2 minutes** more. Bring the head to a central position and relax.

10) **Sat Kriya.** Sit on the heels with the arms overhead and the palms together. Interlace the fingers except for the index fingers, which point straight up. Men cross the right thumb over the left thumb; women cross the left thumb over the right. Begin to chant *Sat Naam* emphatically in a constant rhythm about 8 times per 10 seconds. Chant the sound *Sat* from the navel point and solar plexus, and pull the navel all the way in and up. On *Naam* relax the navel. Continue for **3-7 minutes,** then inhale and squeeze the muscles tight from the buttocks all the way up the back past the shoulders. Mentally allow the energy to flow through the top of the skull. Exhale. Inhale deeply. Exhale completely and apply the *mulbandh* with the breath held out. Inhale and relax.
Sat Kriya circulates the kundalini energy through the cycle of the chakras, aids in digestion and strengthens the nervous system.

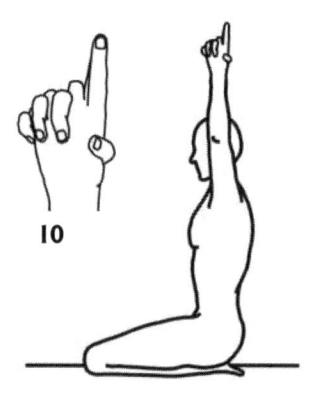

11) *Relax in Easy Pose or on the back with the arms at the sides, palms up. Deep relaxation allows you to enjoy and consciously integrate the mind/body changes which have been brought about during the practice of this kriya. It allows you to sense the extension of the self through the magnetic field and the aura and allows the physical body to deeply relax.*

This set is from *Keeping Up with Kundalini Yoga.*

Teachers' Favorite Sets

Sets & Meditations

Nabhi Kriya

1) **Alternate Leg Lifts.** On back, inhale and lift right leg up to 90 degrees. Exhale and lower it. Repeat with left leg. Continue alternate leg lifts with deep, powerful breathing for **10 minutes.**
This is for the lower digestive area.

2) **Leg Lifts.** Without pause, inhale and lift both legs up to 90 degrees, exhale as you lower them. For balance and energy, have the arms stretched straight up, palms facing each other.
5 minutes.
This is for the upper digestion and solar plexus.

3) **Knees to chest.** Bend knees and clasp them to chest with the arms, allowing the head to relax back. Rest in this position for **5 minutes.**
This eliminates gas and relaxes the heart.

4) *Exercises 4-6 flow from one to the other without any break.* Beginning in position 3, inhale, open the arms straight out to the sides on the ground and extend the legs straight out to 60 degrees. Exhale and return to original position. Repeat and continue for **15 minutes.**
This charges the magnetic field and opens the navel center.

5) **Leg Lift.** On back, bring left knee to the chest, hold it there with both hands and rapidly raise the right leg up to 90 degrees and down, inhaling up, exhaling down for **1 minute.** Switch legs and repeat for **1 minute.** Repeat the complete cycle once more.
This sets the hips and lower spine.

6) **Front Bends.** Stand up straight, raising arms overhead, hugging ears, and press fingers back so that palms face the sky or ceiling. Exhale as you bend forward to touch the ground, keeping the arms straight and hugging ears, and inhale up, very slowly with deep breathing. On exhale, apply *mulbandh*. Continue at a slow pace for **2 minutes,** then rapidly for **1 more minute.**
This is for the entire spinal fluid and the aura.

7) Totally relax or meditate for **10-15 minutes.**

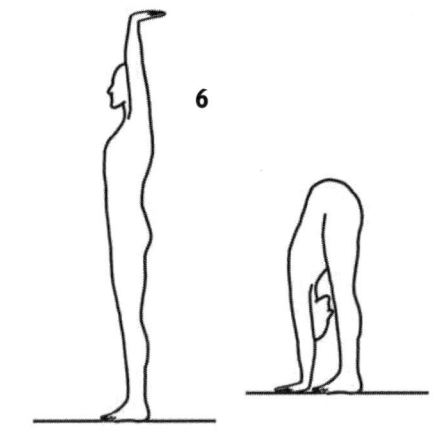

COMMENTS:
Nabhi refers to the nerve plexus around the navel point. This set focuses on developing the strength of the navel point. Times indicated are for advanced students. To begin practice, start with 3-5 minutes on the longer exercises. Together, these exercises get the abdominal area in shape quickly, and activate the power of the Third Chakra.

COPYRIGHT YOGI BHAJAN 2003

Nabhi Kriya for Prana-Apana

1) **Life Nerve Stretch Variation.** Sit with the right leg straight out and the left foot on the right thigh. Grab the big toe of the right foot with the thumbs of both hands, pressing against the toenail and the first two fingers of both hands applying a pressure against the soft part of the toe. Pull back on the big toe. Stretch the spine straight and apply Neck Lock. Begin Breath of Fire. Continue for **1-2 minutes**. Then inhale, change legs, and continue for **1-2 minutes** more. Inhale and relax.
This exercise opens the lungs, balances the polarity of the aura, and stimulates the pituitary.

2) **Kicking Buttocks.** Lie on your back with your arms at your sides. Bring the knees into the chest and begin alternately kicking the buttocks with the heels. Inhale as you raise each leg, exhale as you strike the buttocks. Continue **1-3 minutes**. Inhale and relax.
This exercise is an aid to digestion.

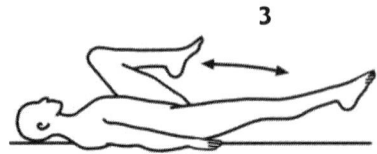

3) **Leg Pistoning.** Remaining on the back, raise both legs to 18 inches. Inhale and draw the left knee to the chest. Exhale as you extend the left leg and simultaneously draw the right knee to the chest, keeping the lower legs parallel to the floor. Continue this push-pull motion with powerful breathing for **1-3 minutes**. Inhale and extend both legs out. Exhale and relax.
This exercise aids in digestion.

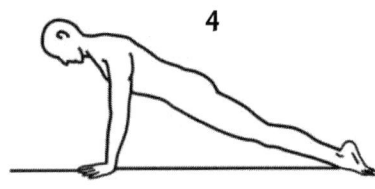

4) **Front Platform.** Lie on the stomach. Place the hands under the shoulders and raise the body until the elbows lock. The weight of the body is supported by either the palms or the fingertips, and the tops of the feet. The body, from the head to the toes forms a straight line. Begin Breath of Fire. Continue for **1-3 minutes.** Inhale and hold the breath briefly. Exhale. Inhale. Then exhale completely and hold the breath out briefly. Inhale and relax.
This exercise gives strength to the lower back and stimulates the brain.

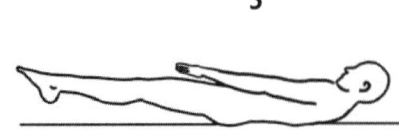

5) **Stretch Pose.** Lie on the back, push the base of the spine into the ground, bring the feet together, and raise the heels 6 inches. Raise the head and shoulders 6 inches and stare at your toes with the arms stretched out, pointing at the toes. In this position inhale and hold briefly. Exhale. Inhale. Exhale completely and apply *mulbandh*. Inhale and relax.
This exercise activates and balances the Third Chakra, sets the Navel Point and aids in digestion.

Nabhi Kriya for Prana-Apana

6) **Heart Center Stretch for Healing.** Sit in Easy Pose.

6a) Spread the arms at an angle of 60 degrees, parallel to the ground, as if to receive someone. The arms create a large V, with the Heart Center being the point of the V. Spread and tense all fingers. Take a few long, deep breaths.

6b) Inhale, and bring the fingers into tight fists. Slowly bring the fists to the center of the chest as if bringing in a great weight. When they reach the center of the chest exhale forcefully. Repeat this procedure **2 or 3 times**.

6c) Spreading the arms at an angle of **60 degrees** or more, tense the fingers and breathe long and deep. The arms create a large V, with the Heart Center being the point of the V. **1 minute.**

6d) Slowly bring the hands to a position 4 inches apart in front of the chest with the palms facing each other, fingers pointing up. Staring at the space between the palms, feel the energy flow between the hands. Continue long deep breathing in this position for **1-2 minutes**.

6e) Bring the palms together at the center of the chest into Prayer Pose. Meditate at the Brow Point for **1 minute.**

6f) Keeping the hands at the Heart Center, bend forward from the waste and bring the forehead to the floor. Relax in this position for **1-2 minutes**.
This exercise brings mental and physical focus to the hands and opens the Heart Center.

7) **Meditation**. Return to a cross-legged sitting position. Meditate.

8) *Deeply relax.*

COMMENTS:
This *kriya* balances *prana* and *apana* by focusing on the Third Chakra at the Navel Point and then at the Heart Center. It is good for general strength, for digestion, for abdominal toning, for alleviating mild depression and for developing the healing flow of *prana* through the hands.

This set is from *Keeping Up With Kundalini Yoga.*

Sat Kriya

HOW TO DO SAT KRIYA

Sit on the heels with the arms overhead and palms together. Interlace the fingers except for the index fingers, which point straight up. Men cross the right thumb over the left thumb; women cross the left thumb over the right. Chant *SAT* and pull the Navel Point in; chant *NAAM* and relax it.

Continue at least **3 minutes** (or whatever time is specified in the *kriya*.) Then inhale, apply Root Lock (*mulbandh*) and squeeze the muscles tightly from the buttocks all the way up the back, past the shoulders. Mentally allow the energy to flow through the top of the skull. Exhale, hold the breath out and apply all the locks (*mahabandh*). Inhale and relax.

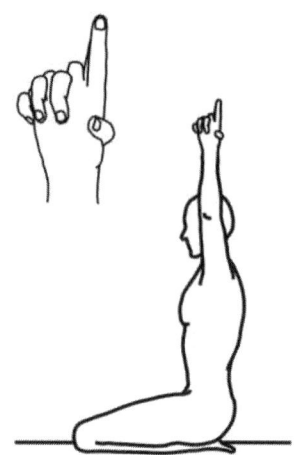

▸ You may build the time of the *kriya* to **31 minutes**, but remember to have a long, deep relaxation immediately afterwards. A good way to build the time up is to do the kriya for **3 minutes**, then rest **2 minutes.** Repeat this cycle until you have completed **15 minutes** of Sat Kriya and **10 minutes** of rest. Finish the required relaxation by resting an additional **15-20 minutes**. Do not try to jump to 31 minutes because you feel you are strong, virile or happen to be a yoga teacher. Respect the inherent power of the technique. Let the kriya prepare the ground of your body properly to plant the seed of higher experience. It is not just an exercise, it is a *kriya* that works on all levels of your being—known and unknown. You might block the more subtle experiences of higher energies by pushing the physical body too much. You could have a huge rush of energy. You may have an experience of higher consciousness, but not be able to integrate the experience into your psyche. So prepare yourself with constancy, patience and moderation. The end result is assured.

▸ If you have not taken drugs or have cleared your system of all their effects, you may choose to practice this *kriya* with the palms open, pressing flat against each other. This releases more energy than the other method. It is generally not taught this way in a public class because someone in the class may have weak nerves from drug use.

▸ Notice that you emphasize pulling the Navel Point in. Don't try to apply *mulbandh*. *Mulbandh* happens automatically if the navel is pulled. Consequently, the hips and lumbar spine do not rotate or flex. Your spine stays straight and the only motion your arms make is a slight up-and-down stretch with each *Sat Naam* as your chest lifts.

COMMENTS:
▸ Sat Kriya is fundamental to Kundalini yoga and should be practiced every day for at least 3 minutes. Its effects are numerous.
▸ This exercise works directly on stimulating and channelizing the kundalini energy, so it must always be practiced with the mantra *Sat Naam*.
▸ Sat Kriya strengthens the entire sexual system and stimulates its natural flow of energy. This relaxes phobias about sexuality. It allows you to control the insistent sexual impulse by rechannelizing sexual energy to creative and healing activities in the body.
▸ People who are severely maladjusted or who have mental problems benefit from this *kriya* since these disturbances are always connected with an imbalance in the energies of the lower three chakras.
▸ General physical health is improved since all the internal organs receive a gentle rhythmic massage from this exercise.
▸ The heart gets stronger from the rhythmic up-and-down of blood pressure you generate from the pumping motion of the Navel Point.

If you have time for nothing else, make this *kriya* part of your daily promise to yourself to keep the body a clean and vital temple of God.

Strengthening the Aura

1) **Triangle Push-Ups.** Come into Cow Pose and lift the hips. The body forms a triangle. Raise the right leg up with the knee straight. Exhale, bend the arms and bring the head toward the ground. Inhale, raise up to the original Triangle Pose. The body moves in one line, from the head to the toes, forward and down. Continue this Triangle Push-up for **1-1/2 minutes.** Switch legs and continue for another **1-1/2 minutes.**

2) Sit in Easy Pose. Extend the left hand forward as if grasping a pole so the palm faces to the right. Cross the right hand beneath the left, palm down. Drop the thumb so that the palm faces the the right. Grasp the left hand (the right fingers over the left hand) then lock the thumbs. Inhale, raise the arms to 60°. Exhale, bring the arms down to shoulder level. Keep the elbows straight. Breathe deeply for **2 to 3 minutes.** Then inhale, stretch the arms up. *Relax.*

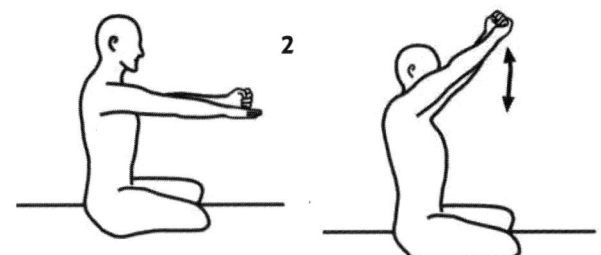

3) Bring the arms out in front with the hands at the level of the face, palms facing each other about 6 inches apart. As you inhale, swing the arms down and back. Exhale, bring them forward to the original position. Continue **3 minutes** with deep rhythmic breaths.

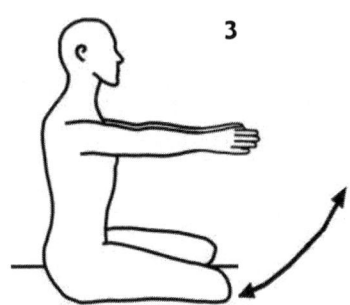

COMMENTS:
This is a great *kriya* for keeping disease away and developing your aura. The time can be build up to 7-1/2 minutes for each side in Exercise 1, and 15 minutes each for Exercise 2 and 3. That will create a tremendous sweat. It will rid almost any digestive problem. It gives strength to the arms and it extends the power of protection and projection in the personality.

This set is from *Sadhana Guidelines.*

Stress Set for Adrenals & Kidneys 1 OF 2

Note to the Teacher: This exercise set is done with very little rest between the exercises.

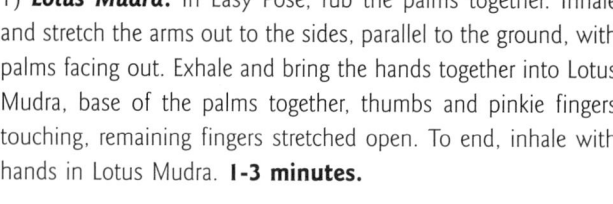
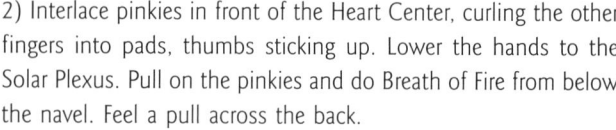
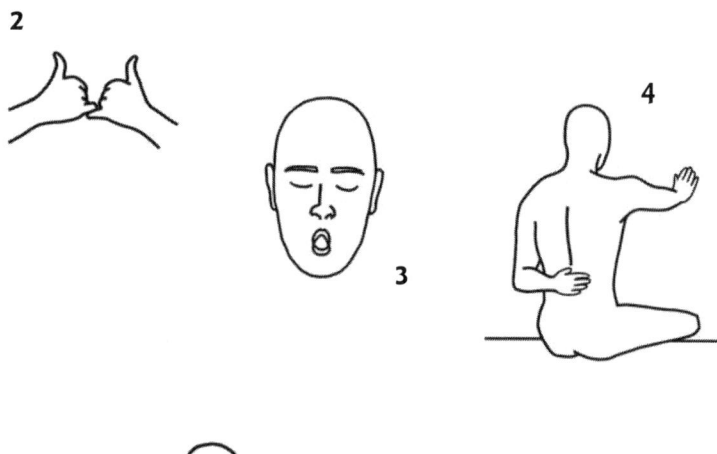
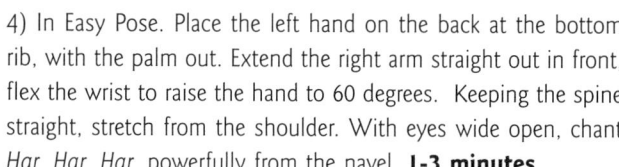
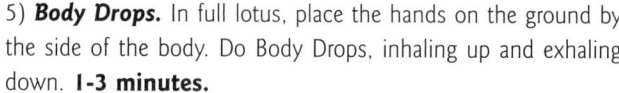

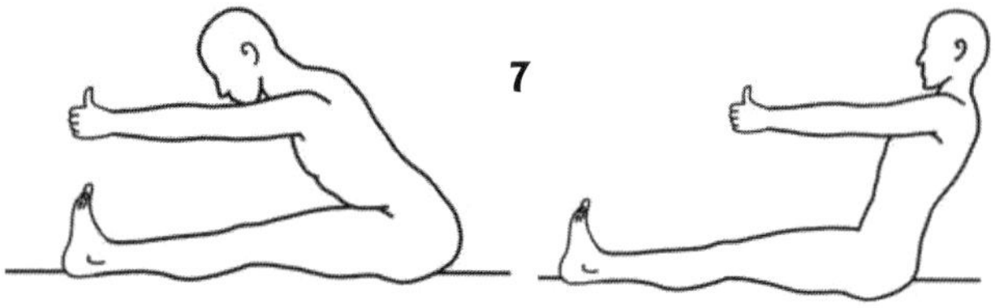

1) **Lotus Mudra.** In Easy Pose, rub the palms together. Inhale and stretch the arms out to the sides, parallel to the ground, with palms facing out. Exhale and bring the hands together into Lotus Mudra, base of the palms together, thumbs and pinkie fingers touching, remaining fingers stretched open. To end, inhale with hands in Lotus Mudra. **1-3 minutes.**

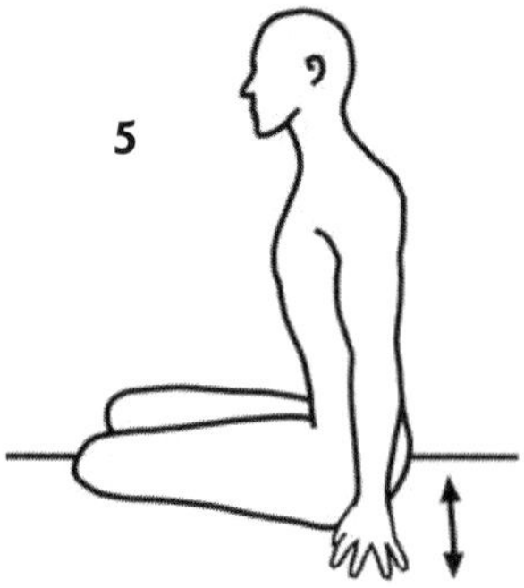

2) Interlace pinkies in front of the Heart Center, curling the other fingers into pads, thumbs sticking up. Lower the hands to the Solar Plexus. Pull on the pinkies and do Breath of Fire from below the navel. Feel a pull across the back.
1-3 minutes.
Note: It's common for the hands to drift up. Make sure the hands are in front of the Solar Plexus.
This generates heat and works on one side of the adrenals.

3) **Cannon Breath.** Still in Easy Pose with straight spine. Relax the hands and begin Cannon Breath. (Breath of Fire through a firm O-shaped mouth; don't allow the cheeks to move.) Inhale and concentrate on the spine. **1-3 minutes.**
This works on the other side of the adrenals.

4) In Easy Pose. Place the left hand on the back at the bottom rib, with the palm out. Extend the right arm straight out in front, flex the wrist to raise the hand to 60 degrees. Keeping the spine straight, stretch from the shoulder. With eyes wide open, chant *Har, Har, Har,* powerfully from the navel. **1-3 minutes.**

5) **Body Drops.** In full lotus, place the hands on the ground by the side of the body. Do Body Drops, inhaling up and exhaling down. **1-3 minutes.**
Note: Spinal alignment is very important here. Keep Neck Lock applied and spine erect. Keep the back molars together to protect the tongue.

6) In Easy Pose, place the hands in front of the solar plexus, left hand facing body, right hand pressing left wrist with the base of the palm. With the head in Neck Lock, look down with powerful, long, deep breathing. **1-3 minutes.**
The power of the breath is the depth to which you will cleanse.

7) **Front Stretch with Spine Straight.** Sit with legs stretched out in front, arms out parallel to the ground, hands in fists, thumbs pointing up. Inhale stretching forward, exhale leaning back. Powerful breath. Keep arms parallel to the ground on the inhale and the exhale. **1-3 minutes.**
Note: It is common to see the arms drop on the forward motion and lift on the backward motion.

Stress Set for Adrenals & Kidneys

8) **Pelvic Lift.** Lying on the back, bend the knees, bringing the soles of the feet flat onto the ground, heels at the buttocks. Grab the ankles. Inhale, lift the pelvis up; exhale down. **1-3 minutes.**

9) **Modified Cat-Cow.** In cat-cow position, exhale as you bring the left knee to the forehead, and inhale as you stretch the leg out and up in back. Do not over-extend. **1-3 minutes.** Switch legs. **1-3 minutes.**

10) Sitting on the heels, bring the forearms to the ground in front of knees, palms together, thumbs pointing up. Inhale as you stretch over the palms, and exhale back. Keep the chin up to create pressure at the lower back. **1-3 minutes.**

11) **Back Rolls.** Lay on the back. Bring the knees to the chest, nose between the knees, breathing normally, and roll back and forth on the spine. **1-3 minutes.**

12) *Totally relax.* Corpse Pose is recommended for one full hour. Have a glass of water.

COMMENTS:
Do we have a reserve capacity to get to our destination despite the snowstorm? Our energy can be flowing, we can be eating well, sleeping enough, but if our adrenals fail, it is hard to keep up. We get tired and snappy. Glandular balance, and in particular, strong adrenals and kidneys are important to have that extra edge, to control anger and hypoglycemia. Without strong adrenals and kidneys, the heart can't function well.

Surya Kriya 1 of 2

1) **Breathing through the Right Nostril.** Sit in Easy Pose with a straight spine. Rest the right hand in Gyan Mudra on the knee. Block the left nostril with the thumb of the left hand. The other fingers point straight up. Begin long, deep, powerful breaths in and out of the right nostril. Focus on the flow of breath. Continue for **3 to 5 minutes**. Inhale and relax.
This exercise draws on the "sun" breath and gives you a clear, focused mind.

2) **Sat Kriya.** Sit on the heels with the arms overhead and the palms together. Interlace the fingers except for the index fingers, which point straight up. Men cross the right thumb over the left thumb; women cross the left thumb over the right. To do Sat Kriya begin rhythmically chanting *Sat Naam*, emphasizing *Sat* as you pull the navel in. On *Naam* release the lock. Focus at the brow point. Continue for **3 minutes**. Then inhale, suspend the breath, apply *mulbandh* and imagine your energy radiating from the Navel Point and circulating throughout the body. Relax. Repeat the exercise for **3 minutes.** Then inhale, apply *mulbandh*, and mentally draw all the energy to the top of the fingertips. *Relax.*
This exercise releases energy stored at the Navel Point.

3) **Spinal Flex**. Sit in Easy Pose. Grasp the shins with both hands. Inhale, stretch the spine forward and lift the chest. Exhale, let the spine flex backwards. Keep the head level during the movements. On each inhale mentally vibrate the mantra *Sat*, on the exhale vibrate *Naam*. On each exhale apply *mulbandh*. Continue rhythmically with deep breaths **108 times**. Then inhale, hold briefly with the spine perfectly straight. Exhale. *Relax.*
This exercise brings the released kundalini energy along the path of the spine and aids its flexibility.

4) **Frog Pose.** Place the toes on the ground, heels together off the ground, fingers on the ground between the knees, and lift the head up. Inhale, raise the buttocks high. Lower the forehead towards the knees and keep the heels off the ground. Exhale, come back to the original squatting position, face forward. Continue with deep breaths **26 times**. Inhale up, then relax down onto the heels.
This transforms the sexual energy.

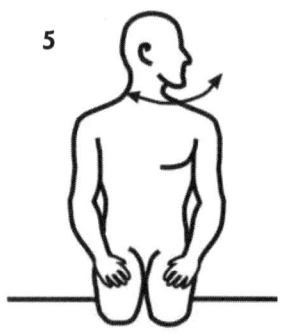

5) **Neck Turns.** Sitting on the heels, place the hands on the thighs. With the spine very straight, inhale deeply as you turn the head to the left. Mentally vibrate *Sat*. Exhale completely as you turn the head to the right. Mentally vibrate *Nam*. Continue inhaling and exhaling for **3 minutes**. Inhale with the head straight forward. *Relax.*
This opens the throat chakra, stimulates circulation to the head and works on the thyroid and parathyroid glands.

Surya Kriya 2 of 2

6) **Spinal Bend.** Sit in Easy Pose. Grab the shoulders with the fingers in front and the thumbs in back. The upper arms and elbows are parallel to the ground. Inhale as you bend to the left, exhale and bend to the right. Continue this swaying motion with deep breaths for **3 minutes**. Then inhale straight. *Relax.*
Note: It is common to want to overextend either by reaching all the way to the ground or allowing the torso to twist forward.
This exercise flexes the spine, distributes the energy over the whole body, and balances the magnetic field.

7) **Meditate.** Sit in a perfect meditative posture with the spine straight. Direct all attention through the Brow Point. Pull the Navel Point in—hold it—apply *mulbandh*. Watch the flow of breath. On the inhale listen to silent *Sat*, on the exhale listen to silent *Naam*. Continue **6 minutes** or longer.
This will take you into a deep self-healing meditation.

COMMENTS:
This *kriya* is named after the energy of the sun—*surya*. When you have a lot of "sun energy" you do not get cold, you are energetic, expressive, extroverted and enthusiastic. It is the energy of purification. It holds the weight down. It aids digestion. It makes the mind clear, analytic and action-oriented. The exercises systematically stimulate the positive pranic force and the kundalini energy itself. This should occasionally be in your regular sadhana practice to build the strength of your body and your ability to focus on many tasks.

This set is from *Sadhana Guidelines*.

Disease Resistance & Heart Helper

1) Sit in Easy Pose. Interlace the fingers of both hands. Press the thumb tips together. Put this hand lock with palms up in the lap. Apply *mulbandh*, by contracting and pulling up the rectum, lifting up the sex organ, and pulling in the Navel Point. Chant:

GOD & ME, ME & GOD ARE ONE

With each cycle of the mantra, pull up the locks a little tighter. Continue for **3 minutes**.
The first exercise improves your health by invigorating the First Chakra and elimination. It promotes calmness and disease resistance.

2) Sit in Easy Pose with the hands in Gyan Mudra, resting on the knees. Inhale deeply, exhale slowly and completely without dropping the rib cage. Hold the breath out and pump the stomach in and out. When you cannot pump anymore, take another breath and continue for **3 minutes**.
The Third Chakra, endurance, and nerve strength are stimulated by Exercise 2.

3) Sit in Easy Pose. Bring the left arm in back of the torso. Bend at the elbow and stretch the left hand toward the right shoulder. The palm faces away from the body. Inhale deeply, exhale completely. Hold the breath out as long as you can. Apply *mulbandh*. Then inhale and repeat the cycle. Continue **3 to 5 minutes**.
Exercise 3 strengthens the heart and increases circulation above the diaphragm.

4) **Meditation.** Sit in any comfortable meditation posture. Meditate on the regular energetic flow of the breath. Feel your radiance and light.

COMMENTS:
Three repetitions of this *kriya* is a very effective practice.

This set is from *Sadhana Guidelines*.

More Great Sets

Exercise Set for the Kidneys

1) **Front Stretch with Straight Spine.** Sit with the legs and arms extended straight in front of you. Tightly fold the fingers onto the pads and point the thumbs up. In this position, inhale, exhale and bend all the way forward from the hips, keeping the arms parallel to the ground, and the spine straight. Inhale back up to the starting position. Use a heavy, powerful breath. The breath must get heavier and heavier as you continue. Do 2 bends evey 5 seconds for **5-6 minutes**.
Note: It is common for the arms to drop on the forward motion and lift on the backward motion. It's also common for the spine to extend back beyond perpendicular as in Stress Set for Adrenals and Kidneys.

2) **Pelvic Lift.** Lying on the back, bend the knees, bringing the soles of the feet flat onto the ground, heels at the buttocks. Grab the ankles. Inhale, lift the pelvis up; exhale down. **1-3 minutes.**
This exercise works on the neck, kidneys, urinary tract, and is helpful for hernia problems. The heavy breath stimulates the pituitary gland to secrete.

3) **Cat-Cow Variation.** Come into a Cat-Cow position supporting yourself on your hands and knees. The knees are about shoulder width apart, with toes touching behind you, and the arms straight. Begin Cat-Cow with a heavy breath, inhaling as you flex your spine downwards as if someone were sitting on your back while your head arches up and back, exhaling as you flex the spine in the opposite direction (a). Continue for **2 minutes**. Then remain in Cow Pose and stretch the left leg back and up (b). Hold for **30 seconds** and switch to the right leg for **30 seconds**. Now switch back to the left leg and kick the left buttock with the heel (c) for **1 minute**. Change and kick the right heel for **30 seconds**.
This exercise works on the kidneys.

4) **Nose to Knees.** Lie on the back. Wrap the arms around the shins and hug the knees to the chest. Tuck the nose up between the knees and hold it there while you relax in this position for **1-2 minutes**. Then maintain this posture and sing *Nobility* for **5-6 minutes** followed by *All Things Come from God* for **2 minutes**, or breathe long and gently for **7-9 minutes**.

Exercise Set for the Kidneys

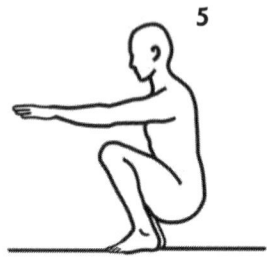

5) **Crow Pose with chanting.** Sit in Crow Pose, a crouching position with the knees drawn into the chest and the soles of the feet flat on the ground. Stretch the arms straight out in front, parallel to the ground, palms facing down, and balance for **1 minute**.

Then begin continuously chanting **Har, Har, Har,** with the tip of the tongue hitting the upper palate with each repetition. Feel the connection between the tip of the tongue and the navel. Chant for **2-3 minutes**.

To end, inhale deeply, tighten the lips and mouth and balance the entire body with the breath. Hold this breath **20 seconds**, feeling that you are in total control, then exhale. Inhale and tighten again, balance your body under your control for **30 seconds.** Exhale and relax.

This exercise totally stimulates the kidneys and urinary tract. If you feel dizzy during the exercise, it is an indication that you need to drink more water.

6) **Kunchun Mudra.** Sit in Easy Pose. Both hands are in Gyan Mudra. The left forearm is held parallel to the ground in front of the chest, palm facing down. The right forearm is held near the side, perpendicular to the ground, elbow bent sharply. The right palm faces up along side of the ear, stretching back as far as possible. Stretch your spine up. Pull up on the muscles of the buttocks, hips and sides, lifting the upper structure till there is no weight on the buttocks. Pull in the abdomen and lift the ribs and diaphragm up, chest out, chin in. Hold **30 seconds**, then let the tension go. Continue for **5 minutes**. Inhale and relax. Now maintain this strong upward pull, and with the tip of the tongue chant

Whaa-hay Guroo, Whaa-hay Guroo, Whaa-hay Guroo, Whaa-hay Jeeo

Keep the waist area drawn up. The eyes will feel heavy and the breath will automatically become very light. Accuracy of the mudra is essential. Continue for **5 minutes**. Then inhale and relax.

This exercise is called Kunchun Mudra. It is very powerful and purifying. It enables total relaxation of the body. When the posture is very accurate, it is equal to exercising 48 hours straight. There is no limit to the length of time you can practice this mudra but make sure to build your time slowly.

This set is from *Kundalini Yoga for Youth & Joy.*

Foundation for Infinity

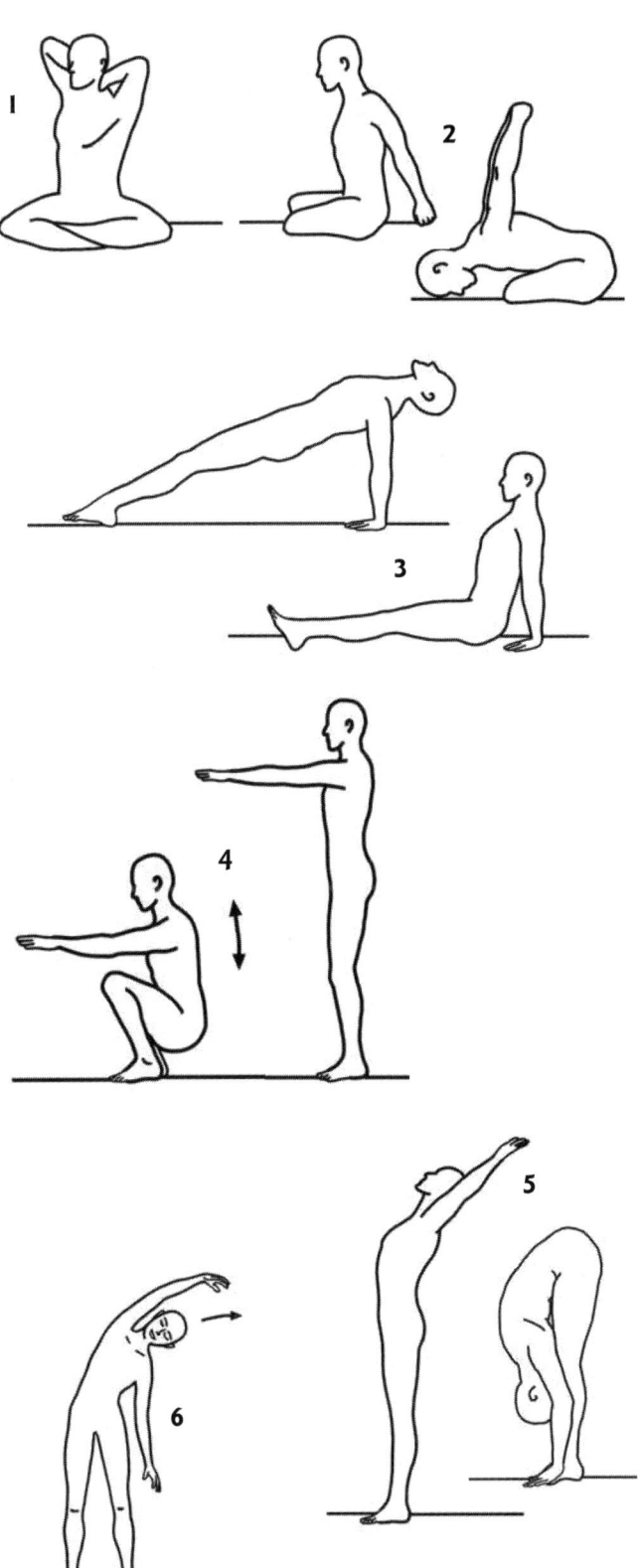

1) **Spinal Twist Variation**. Sit in Easy Pose and interlock the fingers behind the neck at the hairline, beneath any loose hair. Holding the upper arms parallel to the ground, inhale and twist to the left, exhale and twist to the right. Continue at a medium pace for **3 minutes**.
Note: Remind students to keep the Heart Center open, the elbows back, and the spine straight.

2) **Yoga Mudra.** Sit in Easy Pose with the hands interlocked at the base of the spine. Begin Breath of Fire, alternating between this posture and Yoga Mudra for **2 minutes**. Move at a steady pace in coordination with the breath.

3) Come up into **Back Platform Pose** with the head dropped back. Then lower the buttocks to the floor and bring the head straight, in line with the spine. Create a steady rhythm alternating between these two positions with Breath of Fire for **1-1/2 minutes.**
Note: Fingers are pointed forward in this posture. Don't collapse the neck as the head drops back. Head can remain in Neck Lock if discomfort is experienced.
This exercise increases the strength and flexibility of the pelvic area and releases the pelvis if it is locked.

4) Squat in **Crow Pose** and extend the arms straight in front parallel to the floor with the palms facing down. Inhale and stand up, exhale and squat down. Do **26 squats**.

5) **Front Bends.** Stand up with the legs shoulder-width apart. Extend the arms above the head, palms facing forward. Inhale and stretch back as far as possible. Exhale and bend forward to touch the floor. Repeat the cycle **26 times.**

6) **Side Stretch**. Stand up straight and extend the arms above the head. Inhale and bend to the left, then exhale and bend to the right. Bend to each side **26 times.** Then relax the arms.

Foundation for Infinity

7) **Rhythmic Kick**. Remain standing. Place the hands on the waist and kick alternate legs forward keeping the legs straight. With each kick chant **HAR**, placing the tip of the tongue on the palate on the "r" sound. Kick rapdily once per second for **3 minutes.**
Note: Pacing of this exercise is a challenge. Tendency is to kick too quickly and to bend the knee.
The Tantric Har tape works well with this.

8) **Meditation for the Tenth Gate: To Experience Your Boundlessness.**
Sit in Easy Pose with the spine pulled up straight, chin pressed down lightly. Place the hands in the lap, palms facing up, right palm resting in the left, pads of the thumbs touching. Focus the eyes upward, guiding the attention to the top center of the head, the Tenth Gate (Crown Chakra). Mentally say the mantra **HAR HAR** as you pull the Navel Point in. Then, holding the navel in, press the tip of the tongue against the roof of the mouth and mentally say the word **MUKANDAY**. Concentrate deeply and immerse yourself in this meditation to experience the radiance of the *Sahasrara*. Experience your boundlessness. Feel yourself expand beyond time, beyond space, into a realm of total peace and joy. Continue for **11-31 minutes**.
Singh Kaur's Har Har Mukanday from the Crimson Series works well with this.

COMMENTS:
To reach the subtle realm of ether where we are by nature boundless, we must first set a firm foundation on earth. Practicing this *kriya*—which works primarily on the pelvic region—is a means of setting that foundation. Then the meditation launches you into the realms of Infinity. Physiologically the pelvis acts as a foundation, the point of balance, for the torso and the lower foundation on earth. The female pelvis is especially delicate, because the bones aren't fused together, and are therefore easily misaligned. Chronic misalignment, tension and inflexibility will eventually show their effects on physical and emotional well-being through sciatica and menstrual irregularities, and in men, such conditions as impotency.

This set is from *The Inner Workout Manual*.

Healthy Bowel System

1) **Windmill.** Stand with feet slightly wider than shoulder's width apart. Bring the arms straight out to the sides parallel to ground, palms down. Twist to the left and then bend forward from the waist, bringing the right hand to the left foot and the left arm straight up in back. Reverse the motion as you come up. Continue moving up and down for **1 minute**, in a rhythm of about **10 seconds per cycle**. Then switch to the opposite hand and foot and repeat for **1 minute**.
Note: Instruct students to keep head neutral in the forward bend. The head does not turn to look at the upper hand.

2) Continue the same motion but alternating sides and pausing for **5 seconds** as the hand touches the foot. **3 minutes.**

3) Continue the same alternating motion, but pause for **25 seconds** as the hand touches each foot. **2 minutes.**

4) Hold position touching the foot for **2 minutes** on each side.

5) Relax 2-3 minutes.

6) **Side Bends.** Come standing up, with legs hip-width apart, arms parallel to floor and palms down. Bend to the side from the waist, letting the left arm come down the left side as the right arm comes up. Keep the right arm straight. Come back to original position. Then stretch down to the right side and return to original position. 6 seconds per side. Continue for **1 minute.**

7) **Standing Torso Twists.** Start in the position of the previous exercise. Inhale as you twist the torso and arms all the way to the left, exhale back to original position, then inhale as you twist on around to the right and exhale back to the center always keeping the arms in a straight line with each other. 2-3 seconds per complete cycle. Continue for **1 minute.**

8) Relax for 10 minutes.

COMMENT:
These exercises work on the bowel system. Normally when one is becoming sick the bowel movements serve as an early indicator. It is suggested to do these exercises for 30 minutes a day for good health.

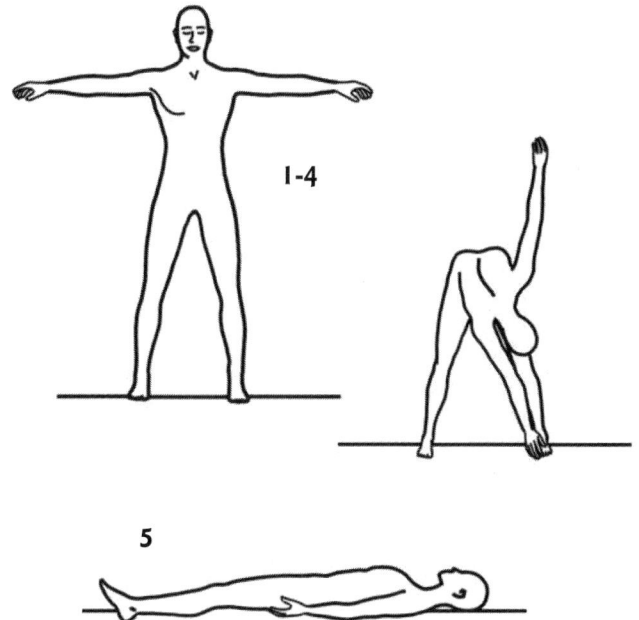
1-4

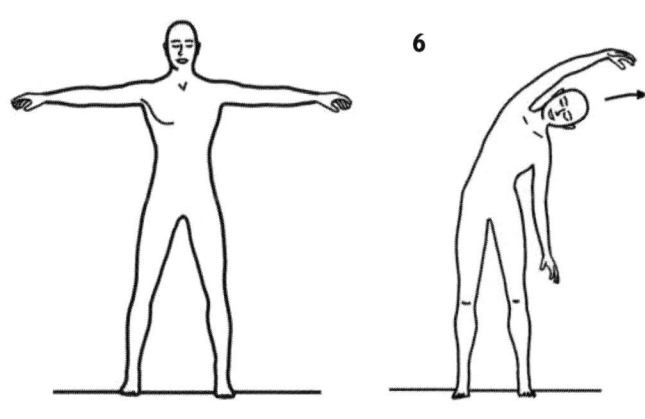
5

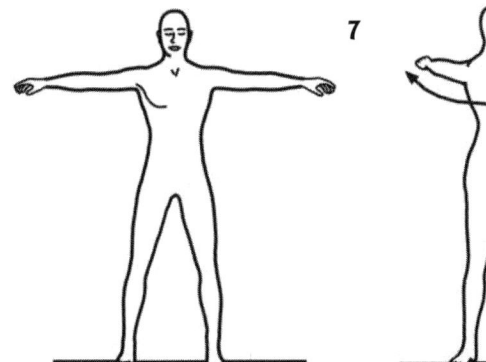
6

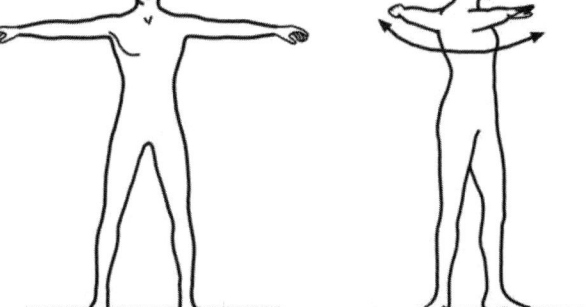
7

This set was originally taught by Yogi Bhajan July 4, 1977, and appeared in *Slim and Trim Yoga*.

Kriya for Disease Resistance 1 of 2

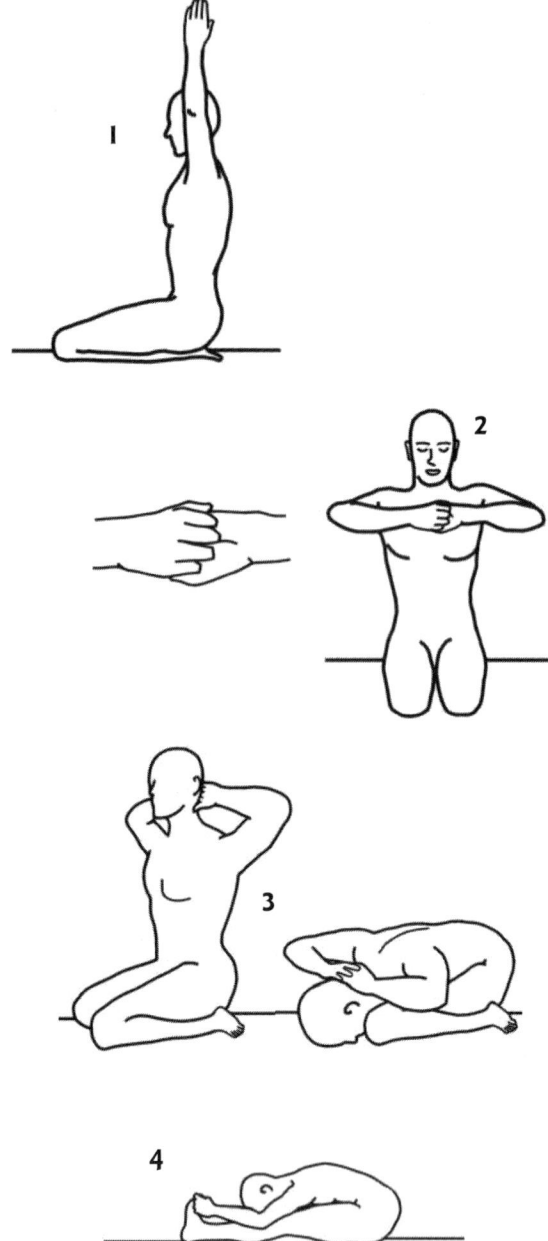

1) **Pumping the Stomach**. Sit on your heels. Stretch the arms straight up over the head with the palms pressed together. Inhale and suspend the breath. Pump the stomach by forcefully drawing the navel in toward the spine and then relaxing it again. Continue rhythmically until you feel the need to exhale. Then exhale. Inhale and begin again. Continue for **1-3 minutes**. then inhale. Exhale and relax. *This exercise stimulates digestion and the kundalini energy in the Third Chakra.*

2) **Bear Grip.** Sit on your heels. Place the hands in Bear Grip at the chest level with the forearms parallel to the ground. Inhale. Suspend the breath and without separating the hands, try to pull the hands apart. Apply maximum force. Exhale. Inhale and pull again. Continue for **1-3 minutes**. Inhale. Exhale and relax. *This exercise opens the Heart Center and stimulates the thymus gland.*

3) **Sitting Bends.** Sit on the heels with your fingers interlocked in Venus Lock behind the neck, beneath any loose hair. Inhale. Exhale and bend forward touching your forehead to the ground. Inhale and sit up again. Continue with powerful breathing for **1-3 minutes.** Inhale, sitting up. Exhale and relax.
This exercise improves digestion and adds flexibility to the spine.

4) **Front Stretch.** Sit with the legs stretched out straight in front. Grab the toes in finger lock. (Index finger and middle finger pull the toe, and the thumb presses the nail of the big toe.) Exhale, and lengthen the core of the spine, bending forward from the navel, continuing to lengthen the spine. The head follows, last. Remain in this position, breathing normally for **1-3 minutes**. Then inhale. Exhale and relax. *This exercise allows the glandular secretions from the previous exercises to circulate though the body and allows the body to deeply relax.*

5) **Neck Rolls.** Sit in Easy Pose. Begin rolling the neck clockwise in a circular motion, bringing the right ear toward the right shoulder, the back of the head toward the back of the neck, the left ear toward the left shoulder and the chin toward the chest. The shoulders remain relaxed and motionless. and the neck should be allowed to gently stretch as the head circles around. Continue for **1-2 minutes**. Then reverse the direction and continue for **1-2 minutes** more. Bring the head to a central position and relax.
This exercise and the two exercises following it combine to open circulation to the brain and to stimulate the higher glands including the pituitary, parathyroid, thyroid, and pineal glands which work together to give harmony to the entire body.

Kriya for Disease Resistance

6) **Cat-Cow.** Come into a position supporting yourself on your hands and knees, with knees shoulder-width apart, heels together, and arms straight. Do not bend the elbows. Inhale and flex the spine downward as if someone were sitting on your back. Stretch the neck and head back. Then exhale and flex the spine up, bringing the chin towards the chest. Continue rhythmically with powerful breathing for **1-3 minutes**. Gradually increase your speed as you feel the spine becoming more flexible. Inhale in the original position. Exhale and relax.
This exercise, in addition to the effects mentioned above, helps to transform the sexual energy of the Second Chakra and the digestive energy of the Third Chakra while stimulating the main nerves that are regulated through the lower cervical vertebra.

7) **Alternate Shoulder Shrugs**. Sit on the heels. Alternately shrug your shoulders as high as possible, keeping the head still. On the inhale, lift the left shoulder, as the right shoulder goes down. On the exhale, life the right shoulder up and the left down. Continue rhythmicaily with powerful breathing for **1-3 minutes**. Inhale, raising both shoulders up. Exhale and relax.

8) **Corpse Pose.** *Deeply relax.* Lie on the back with the arms at the sides, palms facing up, for **5-7 minutes.**

9) **Triangle Pose.** Place the palms of the hands and the soles of the feet flat on the ground. Feet are approximately hip-width apart. Create a straight line between the wrists and the hips, and from the hips to the heels. The chin is pulled in. Roll the arms pits toward each other. Hold this position for **5 minutes**, breathing normally. Then inhale. Exhale and slowly come out of the position and relax.
This exercise aids in digestion, strengthens the entire nervous system and relaxes the major muscle groups of the body.

10) **Elephant Walk.** Stand up. Reach down and grab the ankles. Keeping the knees straight, begin walking around the room. Continue for **1 to 3 minutes**, then return to your place. Sit down and relax.
This exercise aids in elimination and adjusts the magnetic field to prepare you for meditation.

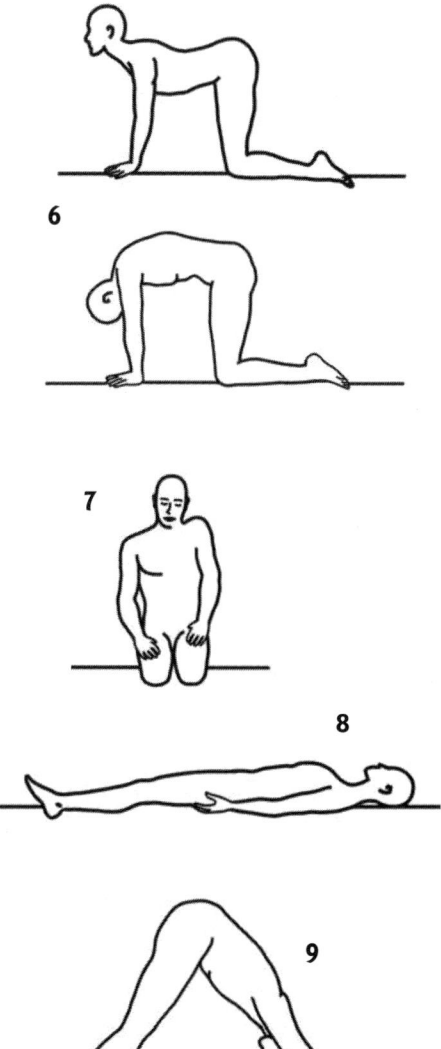

COMMENTS:
To avoid persistent colds and illness, it is essential to keep digestion and elimination functioning well. Add to this a strong metabolic balance and you will have heartiness. This *kriya* develops these capacities. It gives physical strength and builds disease resistance.

Kriya for Morning Sadhana 1 of 4

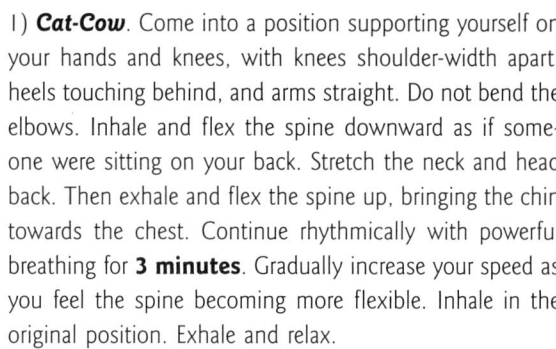

1) **Cat-Cow.** Come into a position supporting yourself on your hands and knees, with knees shoulder-width apart, heels touching behind, and arms straight. Do not bend the elbows. Inhale and flex the spine downward as if someone were sitting on your back. Stretch the neck and head back. Then exhale and flex the spine up, bringing the chin towards the chest. Continue rhythmically with powerful breathing for **3 minutes**. Gradually increase your speed as you feel the spine becoming more flexible. Inhale in the original position. Exhale and relax.
Then inhale into Cow Pose and hold **10 seconds**. Exhale.

2) **Cow Pose Variation.** In Cow Pose, inhale and raise the right leg and the head up as high as possible. Exhale and swing the knee under the body, and bring the head down. Do **30 repetitions**, then inhale and lift the right leg up, exhale and hold the breath for **10 seconds**. Inhale and repeat with the left leg up. Do **30 repetitions**.
Note: Students commonly open their hip in this exercise due to hyper-extension.

3) **Hugging Spinal Bend.** Sit on the heels with knees spread apart. Grasp opposite arms just above the elbows, letting the arms rest against the chest. Bend from side to side in a smooth motion. Inhale center, exhale to each side. **1 minute**. Inhale, hold, exhale.

4) **Spinal Twist variation with Gyan Mudra.** Still sitting on the heels, raise the arms with the elbows bent at 90° and the upper arms parallel to the floor. Hands in Gyan Mudra, focus at the Brow Point, and twist the torso, inhaling left, exhaling right. Powerful breath. **60 repetitions.** Inhale center, hold the breath, focus. Exhale. *Relax.*

5) **Spinal Flex.** Bring the knees together and place the hands palms down on the thighs. Focus at the Brow Point, and flex the spine in rhythm with powerful breaths. Do **108 flexes,** then inhale, pull the locks, hold **10 seconds**. Exhale and sit still. Meditate silently on the breath—inhaling **SAT,** exhaling **NAAM**—for **30 seconds**. Inhale, exhale, *relax.*

Kriya for Morning Sadhana

6) **Front Bend.** Stand up carefully and shake out the legs. Stand with the feet shoulder-width apart. Hook the thumbs together. Inhale, raise the arms over the head with the arms hugging the ears. Stretch back, stretching the ribcage and using the full lung capacity. Relax the head back. Exhale forward and bend down, touching the floor, keeping the knees straight. Repeat **30 times**. Inhale back and hold the stretch a few seconds. Exhale and bend forward at the waist. Let the arms hang down, and completely *relax* for **30 seconds**.

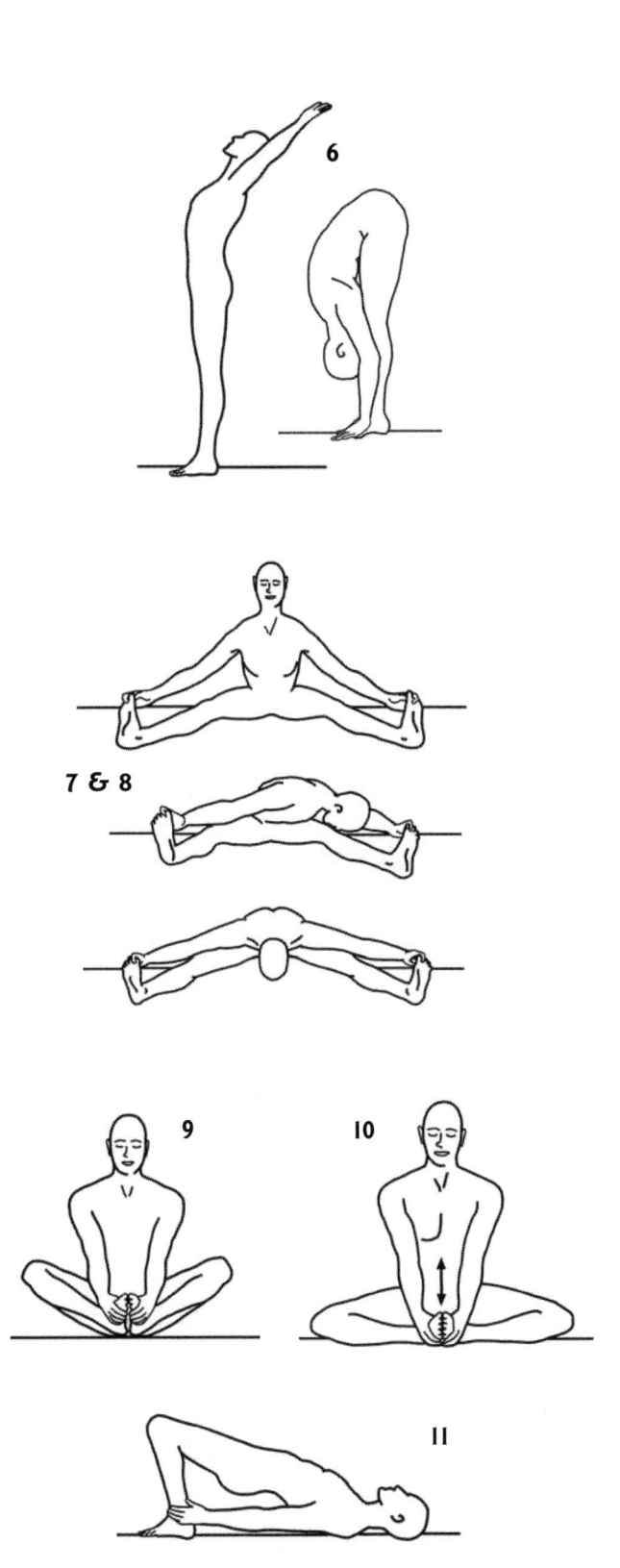

7) **Life Nerve Stretch**. Sit with the legs extended and spread apart. Reach down and grab the toes. Begin stretching, inhaling up to the center, exhaling down to the left. Inhale up to the center, exhale down to the right. Continue **2 minutes**. Keep the knees straight. Spread the legs further apart and continue for **1 more minute**.

8) **Life Nerve Stretch.** Same position, legs wide, continue: inhale up to the center, hold **3 seconds**, then exhale down to the center, then begin stretching down in the center with a continuous pressure and do Long Deep Breathing for **1 minute**. Inhale and stretch down a bit further. Exhale and come up.

9) **Butterfly**. Bring the soles of the feet together and clasp the fingers around the feet. Keep spine and head straight and begin bouncing the knees up and down. Let the knees move vigorously, 10-12 inches, for **1 minute**.

10) **Butterfly Bend.** Hold the same posture, keeping the knees pressed down. Stretch the spine up straight. Inhale up, exhale and bend forward from the waist, bringing the torso down as far as you can. Continue, breathing powerfully for **1 minute**. Inhale up, hold **5 seconds**, exhale stretch down and hold for **5 seconds**. *Relax on the back.*

11) **Pelvic Lift.** Still on the back, bend the knees, place the feet flat on the floor near the buttocks, and grab the ankles. Inhale and lift the hips as high as you can, exhale and lower them down. Inhale up, exhale down **24 times**. To end, inhale, stretch up and hold the breath **10 seconds**. Relax down and extend the legs straight out.

Kriya for Morning Sadhana

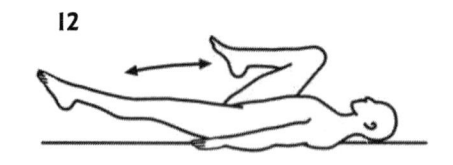

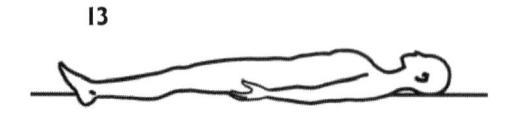

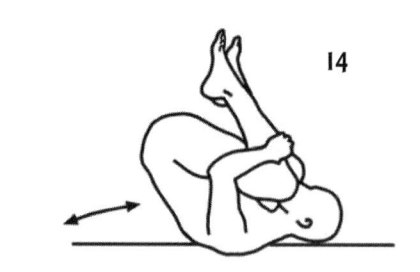

12) Leg Lifts with Piston Motion. Lie on the back and point the toes. Lift both legs to 18 inches. Inhale and draw the left knee to the chest. Exhale as you extend the left leg and simultaneously draw the right knee to the chest, keeping the lower legs parallel to the floor. Continue this push-pull motion with powerful breathing for **2 minutes.** Inhale and hold the legs up, extended out for **10 seconds.** Exhale and relax on the back.

13) Corpse Pose. Relax completely on your back for **1 minute**. Consciously circulate the energy from the navel point all through the body.

14) Back Rolls. Bring the knees to the chest, wrap the arms around them, and begin rocking on the spine forward and back. Massage the whole spine for **1-2 minutes**. Then, rock up, turn around and lie down on the stomach.

15) Cobra Pose. Stretch up into Cobra Pose. Relax your lower back and buttocks. Focus at the Brow Point, and do Breath of Fire. **3 minutes**.
- Inhale, open your eyes, twist left and look at your heels over your left shoulder. Hold **15 seconds**. Exhale center.
- Inhale, twist right and look at the heels over the right shoulder. Hold 15 seconds. Exhale.
- Inhale twist left again. Hold **15 seconds**. Exhale.
- Inhale, twist right again. Hold **15 seconds**. Exhale.
- Inhale center, stretch back and hold **15 seconds**. Exhale.
Relax down.

16) Yoga Mudra. Carefully move into Yoga Mudra. Sitting on your heels, bring your forehead to the floor. Interlace your fingers behind your back and stretch your arms up. Begin Long Deep Breathing. Draw the energy into the upper back. **1 minute**. Inhale, hold, exhale. Relax.

17) Sufi Grind. Sitting in Easy Pose, hold the kneecaps with the hands. Rotate the middle of the body in circles while keeping the head nearly still. Create a pressure at the base of the spine like a grinding wheel. Use the arms for leverage. **1 minute**. Reverse direction and circle for **1 more minute.**

Kriya for Morning Sadhana

18) **Arm Swings**. Sit in Easy Pose. Inhale and draw the elbows back by the sides of the rib cage. Exhale and swing the arms across the chest. Inhale again and draw the elbows back by the sides of the rib cage. Exhale and swing the arms up and back over the head. Repeat with a powerful breath and powerful motion for **1-2 minutes**. Inhale, draw the elbows back, stretch the chest forward. Hold **10 seconds**. Relax.

19) **Shoulder Shrugs.** Sit with the spine straight and hands on the knees with the elbows relaxed. Inhale and squeeze the shoulders up, exhale and drop them down, using a powerful breath. **108 repetitions.**

20) **Neck Rolls.** Gently circle the head, breathing slowly and deeply, keeping the shoulders relaxed. **1 minute.** Change directions. **1 minute**.

21) **Arm Pumps with Venus Lock.** Sit on the heels and focus at the Brow Point. Join the hands in Venus Lock, with elbows straight. Inhale, bring the arms up 60 degrees above the horizontal. Exhale, bring the arms 60 degrees below the horizontal. Continue inhaling up, exhaling down, powerfully. **70 repetitions**.

22) **Arm Stretch with Interlaced fingers**. Still sitting on the heels, bring the arms up overhead. Flip the hands over so the fingers are interlaced with the palms facing up. Roll the eyes up to the Tenth Gate and focus up above the head. Begin powerful Breath of Fire for **1 minute**. Then inhale and hold. Focus at the top of the skull at the Tenth Gate. Hold **15 seconds**. Relax and carefully bring the arms down.

23) **Meditate**. Come into Easy Pose, and sit with a straight spine, one hand on top of the other in your lap, palms up. Meditate silently, inhaling **SAT**, exhaling **NAAM**. Sit completely still and consciously expand your aura. Focus deeply. **1 minute**. Inhale, exhale, relax.

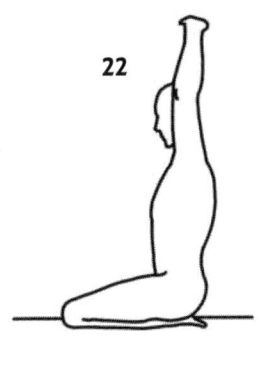

This set was originally taught by Yogi Bhajan in Morning Sadhana in 1971.

Preparatory Exercises for Lungs, Magnetic Field & Deep Meditation 1 OF 2

1) **Whistle Breath.** Sit in Easy Pose. Stretch the arms straight over the head with the palms flat together. Pull the spine up and then tilt it back as far as you can gracefully maintain balance. Breathe consciously through the puckered mouth in a long whistle on the inhale and on the exhale. Continue this for **5 minutes.** *Relax for 30 seconds.*

2) Stay in Easy Pose. Inhale and stretch the arms forward, parallel to each other and parallel to the ground. Interlace the fingers so that the palms face forward. Touch the thumb tips together. Exhale as you bend the elbows and bring the back of the palms near the chest at the level of the Heart Center. Alternate rapidly between these two positions with a strong breath for **2-3 minutes**. Inhale and hold the breath with the arms extended briefly. Relax the breath and maintain the position to begin the next exercise.

3) **Arm Pumps.** With arms extended from the last exercise, inhale, hold the breath in, and pump the arms up over the head and back down parallel to the ground. Then exhale, bringing the hands near the chest. Quickly inhale back into the first position. Continue the sequence in a steady rhythm for **2-3 minutes**. Then inhale with the arms extended and hold briefly for **10-15 seconds.**

4) Immediately extend the arms parallel to the ground at a 60 degree angle to each other. The palms face each other and the elbows are straight. Inhale a deep complete yogic breath. As you inhale, slowly clench the fists. Hold the breath in. Slowly bend the arms and bring the fists toward the chest. Create tremendous tension in all the arm and hand muscles. Pull as if you are dragging a thousand pound weight. When you finally touch the chest, release the breath with an explosive exhale. Repeat this cycle for **3 minutes.** Maintain an emotional and facial posture of anger and determination throughout the exercise.

5) Sitting in Easy Pose, stretch the spine erect. Interlace the fingers and place the hands, palms up, an inch behind the neck. Inhale as you stretch the arms straight up over the head. Keep the fingers interlocked. The thumb tips touch. Exhale back into the first posture. Alternate rapidly, up and down, with a strong smooth breath. Continue for **2-3 minutes**.

Preparatory Exercises for Lungs, Magnetic Field & Deep Meditation

6) **Torso Twists.** Immediately stretch the arms straight over the head with the palms flat together. Hug the ears. Cross the thumbs over each other to lock the hands together. Inhale as you twist the torso and head to the left. Exhale as you turn toward the right. Rotate side to side in a steady quick pace for **2-3 minutes**. Then inhale in the center, hold, and apply *mulbandh*. Exhale.

7) Interlace the fingers and place the hands, palms down, in front of the Heart Center. Inhale as you raise the palms and forearms to the level of the Brow Point. Exhale down into the first position. Create a rapid pumping motion, and a strong steady breath. Continue for **2-3 minutes**. Then inhale and hold **10-15 seconds**. Exhale.

8) **Spinal Twist.** Place the hands on the shoulders with the fingers in front and the thumbs in back. Raise the elbows to shoulder height. Inhale as you twist the torso and head to the left. Exhale as you twist the torso to the right. Create a steady powerful swing. Open the lungs completely. Move with grace as if you rotate around a perfectly balanced and frictionless spinal column. Continue for **2-3 minutes.** Then inhale in the center, apply *mulbandh*, and hold **10-15 seconds**. Exhale.

9) **Shoulder Shrugs.** Sit in Easy Pose. Keep the spine erect and still. Inhale as you raise both shoulders straight up toward the ears. This is a natural motion. Do it without stress or cramping. Exhale as you drop both shoulders down. Create a quick steady pace. Continue for **2-3 minutes.**

10) **Spinal Flex (Camel Ride).** Sit in Easy Pose. Grab the shins in front with both hands. Inhale. Flex the spine forward and rock forward on buttocks. Then exhale, flex the spine backwards and roll back on buttocks. Keep the head level and arms fairly straight and relaxed. Continue for **2-3 minutes.**

11) **Meditate.** Roll the eyes up as far as possible. Concentrate at the top of the head. Meditate for **15 minutes**.

COMMENTS:
This series begins by purifying the blood and expanding the lung capacity. Then the circulatory system is stimulated. The thyroid and parathyroid secretions are added to the increased circulation and the upper magnetic field of the body is enlarged. This is an excellent preparation for beginners who need to learn deep meditation.

This set was originally taught by Yogi Bhajan November 27, 1974.

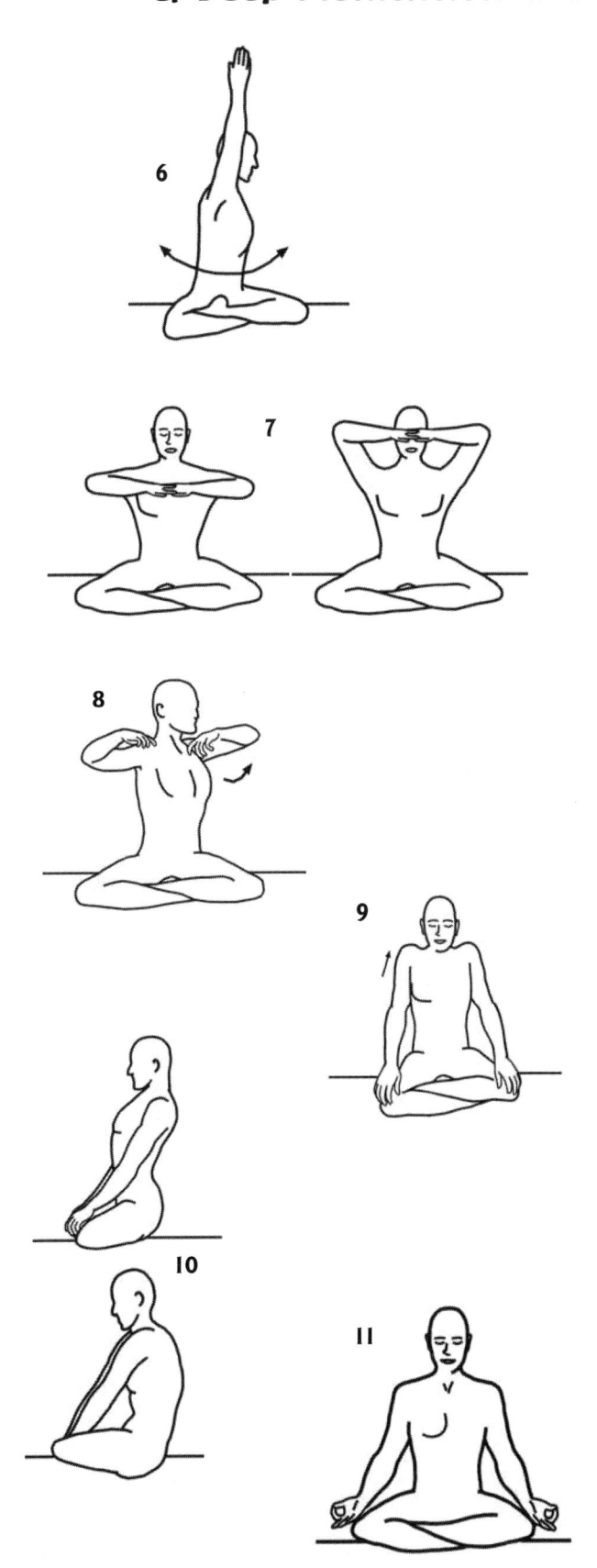

Navel Adjustment Kriya

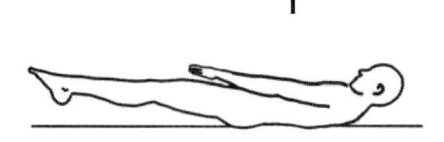

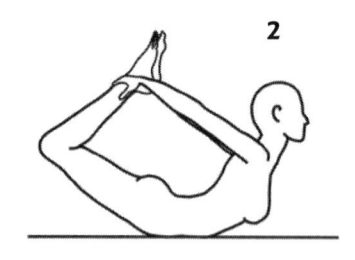

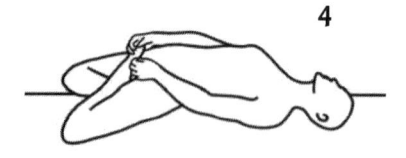

1) **Stretch Pose.** Lying on the back, place the heels together, point toes forward, and lift the heels six inches off the ground. Raise the head to the same height, eyes focused on the toes. Point the fingertips towards the toes. Begin Breath of Fire for **1 minute**. Inhale, hold, exhale, and relax. It is possible to build the time up to **3 minutes**.

2) **Bow Pose.** Roll onto the stomach. Reach back and grab the ankles. Pull up so the navel and sex organs are on the ground with the neck arched back. Begin Breath of Fire for up to **3 minutes**. Then inhale, hold a few seconds, exhale, and apply *mulbandh*. *Slowly relax down onto the stomach.*

3) **Wheel Pose.** On the back, put the palms on the floor above the shoulders. Move the feet flat on the ground by the buttocks. Carefully arch up so the navel is the highest point of the body. Take a few long deep breaths to center the attention so you do not become dizzy, and then do Breath of Fire for **30 seconds to 1 minute**. Inhale, hold a few seconds, exhale, and slowly come down.

4) **Fish Pose.** Cross the legs in lotus and grab the big toes. Put the head on the ground while lying on your back. Arch the neck, back, chest, and the navel up. Do Breath of Fire for **2 to 3 minutes**, then inhale, hold, exhale, and relax.

COMMENTS:
This navel adjustment exercise series can be done in combination with other Nabhi Kriyas, but only if the additional exercises are done prior to this series. When working on adjusting the Navel Point, keep the diet light, especially for the first few days.

Magnetic Field & Heart Center

1) **Heart Center Opener.** Sit in Easy Pose. Hold the arms up at a 60 degree angle with wrists and elbows straight, palms facing up. Begin Breath of Fire for **1 minute**. Then inhale, hold the breath and pump the stomach in and out **16 times**. Exhale, relax the breath. Continue the cycle for **2 to 3 minutes.**
This exercise builds the psycho-electromagnetic field. If the elbows bend, the psycho-electromagnetic field will not be strengthened properly. If the exhale after pumping the stomach is rough or gasping, then the magnetic field is very weak.

2) Immediately sit on the heels with arms parallel to the ground at the sides. Let the hands hang limp from the wrists. Begin Breath of Fire for **3 minutes**. Inhale, hold, exhale, and relax.
The second exercise works directly on the heart.

3) **Stomach Pumps.** Sit on the heels. Spread the knees wide apart and lean back 60 degrees from the ground. Support the body with arms straight down in back. Tilt the neck back, inhale, hold the breath, and pump the stomach in and out until the breath can be held no longer. Exhale. Continue for **1 to 2 minutes**. Then, tilt the spine back further to 30 degrees and continue the breathing cycle for another **1 to 2 minutes**.
This stimulates the thyroid, parathyroid and navel center. If you practice these, you will never need cosmetics. A smooth, radiant complexion and a glow in the eyes and face is a natural by-product of this exercise.

4) **Ong Sohung.** Still sitting on the heels with knees spread, put the forehead on the ground with arms stretched forward and relaxed in Gurpranam. Keep this posture and, after **1 minute**, begin Long Deep Breathing for **2 minutes**. Then for **2 minutes** chant in call and response style:

   Teacher: **ONG, ONG, ONG, ONG**
   Class: **ONG, ONG, ONG, ONG**
   Teacher: **SOHANG, SOHANG, SOHANG, SOHANG**
   Class: **SOHANG, SOHANG, SOHANG, SOHANG**

This feeds the newly-constituted blood into the brain cells and moves the spinal fluid. This helps repair the damage to the brain done by drugs like alcohol and marijuana.

5) **Life Nerve Stretch.** Grab the toes with legs slightly spread. Inhale, exhale and reach down as you lenghten the core of the spine, bending forward from the navel. Head comes down last. Hold for **1 minute**.
This is for balance.

6) **Back Platform.** The body is straight with the heels on the ground and the upper portion of the body held up by straight arms. Drop the head back and begin Breath of Fire. **Back Platform Walk:** After **30 seconds**, begin to "walk" with the legs wider apart until they are spread wide. Walk them back together again and continue "walking" while doing Breath of Fire for **30 more seconds**. Inhale, exhale and move immediately into a front stretch holding the toes for **1 minute**. *Relax on the back for 3 minutes.*
This is for the thyroid, lower back, and heart.

Magnetic Field & Heart Center 2 of 2

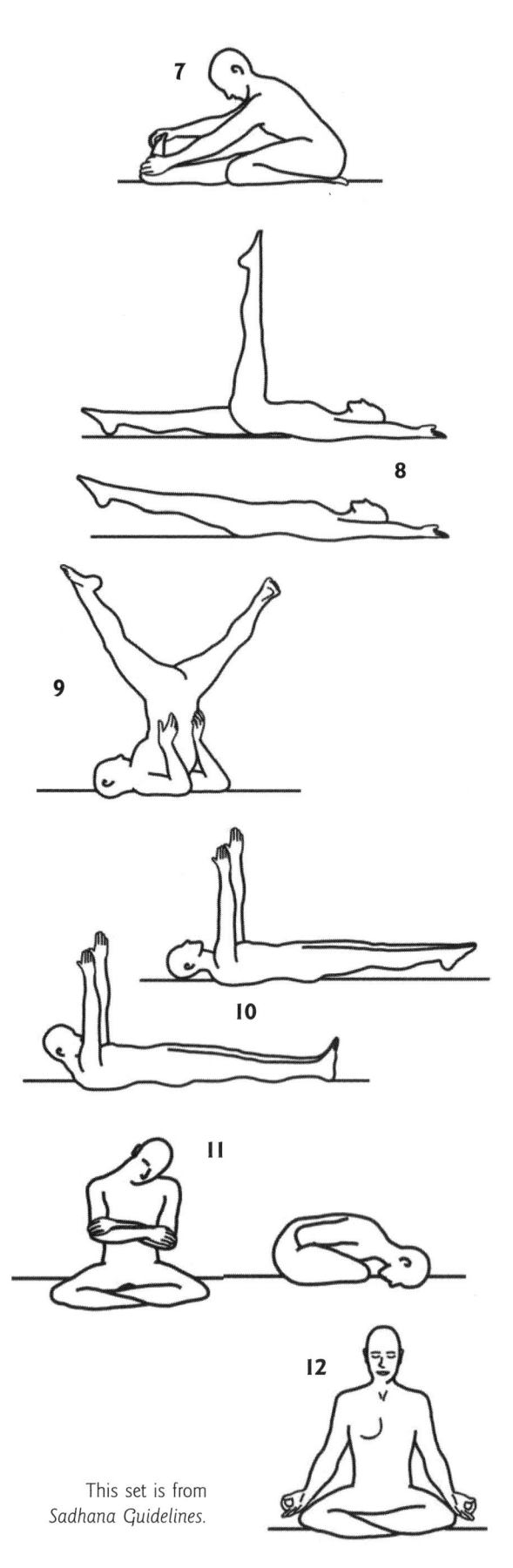

7) **Maha Mudra.** Sit on the left heel, stretch the right leg forward and grab the right big toe with the right middle and index fingers, thumb pressing the big toenail. Pulling back on the toe, grab the foot with the left hand. Keep the chin tucked into the chest, spine straight, and eyes fixed on the big toe. Inhale deeply. Exhale and hold the breath out for **8 seconds** keeping *mulbandh* and Diaphragm Lock tightly pulled. Inhale. Continue for **3 minutes.** *Relax for 5 minutes on the back.*
Maha Mudra is called "the great seal of yoga." Its effects fill pages. This exercise can be practiced by itself.

8) **Alternate Leg Lifts.** Lie on the back. Stretch the arms overhead on the ground. Raise the left leg 90 degrees and begin Breath of Fire for **1 minute**. Switch to the right leg for **1 minute**, continuing Breath of Fire. Then raise both legs 12 inches only and keep up the Breath of Fire for **1 more minute**. *Relax for 2 minutes.*
This balances prana and apana.

9) **Shoulder Stand.** Slowly come into Shoulder Stand. Spread the legs wide and begin Breath of Fire for **3 minutes**. *Relax on the back for 3 minutes.*
This is for the thyroid gland.

10) **Alternate Head & Leg Lifts.** Lie on the back. Inhale and lift both legs **six inches.** Arms should be straight up from the shoulders with the palms facing in. On the exhale let both legs down and bring the head up pressing the chin on the chest. Continue **3 minutes** with long deep breathing. *Relax 2 minutes.*
This is for the Heart Center.

11) **Neck Rolls.** Sit in Easy Pose and hold opposite elbows across the chest. Roll the head in a slow figure 8 for **30 seconds** in one direction, then **30 seconds** in the other direction. Then inhale deeply, and bend forward to the ground. Exhale and rise up as fast as possible. Rise up and down **10 times**.
This is for the Heart Center.

12) Meditate by chanting: **GOD & ME, ME & GOD, ARE ONE.**

GOD & ME   ME & GOD   ARE   ONE

COMMENTS:
This set works on coordination and repair of the nervous system by stimulating the Heart Center. Your normal feeling of happiness, connection, and well-being depend on the balance of your individual psycho-electromagnetic field. If it is strong, your muscles obey the message nerves, and the message nerves give good perception to the brain. Proper maintenance of the nerves depends on the basic elements and hormones in the constitution of the blood. This set will balance the blood. The best results are always obtained if you practice a set until you master it. If you cannot do the exercises for the full time period, do what you can and slowly build up to it. When you can keep up on all the given times and are in a good posture for each exercise, continue the set each day for 40 days as you master the mental poise and meditation of the full set.

This set is from *Sadhana Guidelines.*

New Lungs & Circulation

1) **Arm Swings.** Stand up. Balance equally on both feet. Keep both arms straight with no bend in the elbows. Make *Buddhi Mudra* with each hand (touch the tip of the little finger to the tip of the thumb, the other fingers relaxed but straight). Swing the arms in giant circles up and back over the head, then down in back and forward. The beat is automatic and strong. Concentrate and put all your energy into the exercise. It should be a smooth and continuous swing. Continue for **5 minutes**. Then inhale and stretch the arms straight up briefly. Exhale and relax
This stimulates the lungs, lung meridians, and flushes the upper lymph system.

2) **Reverse Arm Swings.** Still standing up, close the fists of both hands over the thumbs, and reverse the direction of the arm swing. Swing the arms down in front, up in back, and over the head. Keep the arms straight and move them powerfully. Continue for **1-2 minutes**. Then inhale forward with the arms parallel to the ground. Exhale and relax.
This balances the motion of #1 and releases the circulation through the neck and cheeks.

3) **Front Bend Bounce.** Stand up straight. Raise the arms over the head, keeping them straight. Bend forward and place both palms flat on the ground. Strike the ground with the palms **7 times** as you bounce in the bent position. Chant the sound **Har!** with each bounce. Then rise up and clap the hands together over the head as you say **Haree!** Create a steady rhythm with the chant in monotone: *Har, Har, Har, Har, Har, Har, Har, Haree!* Continue for **6-7 minutes**. Inhale and stretch up briefly. Exhale and relax.
This stimulates the Navel Chakra. It releases reserve energy to heal and co-ordinate the body and to improve circulation in the digestive areas. The mantra is an effective trigger for the Navel Point energy. It also frees up emotions like fear and confusion that block the ability to act decisively.

4) **Leg Lifts with Breath of Fire.** Sit down with the legs stretched out in front. Keep the legs and sides of the heels together. Place the palms on the ground next to the hips. With a vigorous motion, lift both legs up to a 60 degree angle, then let them back down. Add a strong Breath of Fire. Coordinate one inhale-exhale of Breath of Fire as you lift the legs up, and another as the legs go back down. Continue for **2 minutes**.
Note to the Teacher: Because the hand position is unspecified, direct your students to find a comfortable position. This pushes circulation below the navel and stimulates the lower colon. It enhances circulation to the lower legs.

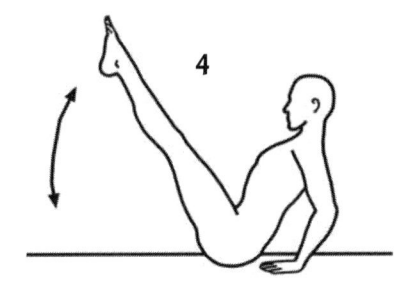

5) **Criss-Cross Legs with Breath of Fire.** Sit with the legs stretched out in front. Place the palms on the ground next to the hips. Lift the legs off the ground 1-1/2 feet. Begin a criss-cross motion of the legs. Spread them comfortably to 45 degrees. Add the Breath of Fire in synchrony with the motion. Continue for **2-3 minutes**, then inhale and hold the legs together briefly, exhale and relax down.
This reinforces the effects of exercise 4, but adds balance to the electromagnetic field. It is also excellent for strengthening the sexual system.

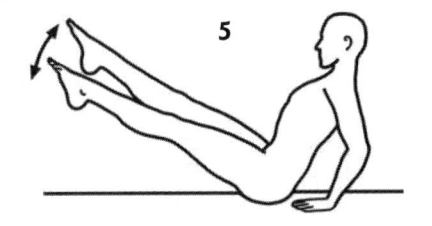

New Lungs & Circulation

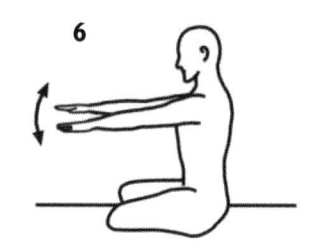

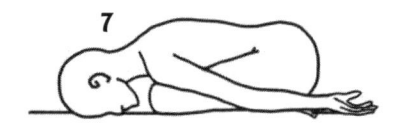

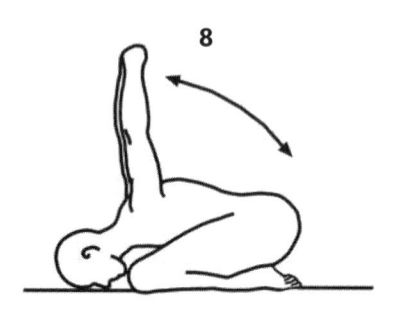

6) **Criss-Cross Arms with Breath of Fire.** Sit in Easy Pose. Extend the arms in front of the torso parallel to the ground and to each other. Palms face down. Begin a criss-cross scissor motion. Alternate the crossing of the arms over each other. When they separate bring them to shoulder width apart. Add to the motion a powerful Breath of Fire. Continue for **30-60 seconds**. Inhale with the arms parallel. Exhale and relax.
This rejuvenates the lungs and synchronizes the electromagnetic field of the heart with the breath rhythm.

7) **Baby Pose with Breath of Fire.** Sit on the heels. Bend forward and place the forehead on the ground. Extend the arms back along the sides on the ground. The palms face up. Concentrate at the Brow Point. Do Breath of Fire. Continue for **30-60 seconds.**
This brings a circulatory flush to the brain, eyes and upper glands.

8) **Moving Yoga Mudra with Breath of Fire.** Still in the same position, lift the arms up and join the hands together behind the back. Interlace the fingers of the two hands in a hammer lock—cross the thumbs over each other to lock the hands firmly. Lift the arms up and then back down. Create a steady, rapid, rhythmical motion. Add Breath of Fire to the motion. Do one Breath of Fire as the arms go up, and one as the arms go down. Continue for **2 minutes**. Inhale, raise the arms up, hold briefly. Exhale and relax.
This affects the very top of the lungs and builds the magnetic field.

9) **Meditate**. Sit in Easy Pose. Become very meditative. Keep the spine straight, chest lifted slightly, with the lower spine tucked gently forward. Elevate your thoughts to the Infinite, the Unlimited and the Vast. Open your heart and give your best personal prayer for empowerment, healing, and awareness. Put your head, heart and soul into it. Continue for **2-3 minutes**.

10) *Relax completely.*

COMMENTS:
You feel full of energy and in control when the lungs and circulation are in excellent shape. The breath and its flow in the body determines your emotional base. This set rebuilds the lungs and improves circulation throughout the body. It is a rhythmical and short kriya for intermediate students or for enthusiastic beginners who are in good condition. In 22 minutes a day you can practice this *kriya* and rebuild your system. It will prepare your lungs for an excellent practice of *pranayam* in Kundalini Yoga.

This set was originally taught by Yogi Bhajan December 7, 1983.

More Great Sets   *Sets & Meditations*

Pituitary Gland Series

1) **Lunge Stretch**. Bend the right knee, with the right foot flat on the floor. Extend the left leg straight back and place the hands on the floor for balance. Arch the head back and hold the position, breathing slowly and deeply for **1 minute**. Then do Breath of Fire for **2 minutes**.

2) **Lunge Stretch Rest**. From position one, bring the right knee down to the floor, and bend the torso to rest over the thigh. Place the forehead on the floor, stretch the left leg all the way back, and rest the arms by the sides, palms up. Breathe slowly and deeply for **3 minutes**.

3) Repeat exercises 1 and 2 with the opposite legs.

4) **Front Bend**. Stand up with the feet about two feet apart. Bend over and touch the fingertips or the palms on the floor. Do Long Deep Breathing for **3 minutes**.

5) **Ego Eradicator.** Stand up again and stretch the arms overhead at a sixty-degree angle, thumbs pointing up, fingers on the palms. Keep your elbows straight as you **breathe long and deep** for **3 minutes**.

6) **Triangle Pose**. Come onto the hands and knees and push up into Triangle Pose. The heels are on the floor and the head and neck relax. Hold for up to **3 minutes**.

7) **Cobra Pose.** Relax on the stomach for **1 minute**. Then bring the heels together, palms flat on the floor under the shoulders. Push up into Cobra Pose. Stretch the head and neck back and begin Long Deep Breathing for **1 minute**. Then turn the head from side to side, inhaling to the left, exhaling to the right. Continue for **2 minutes**. Inhale, exhale, and pull *mulbandh* **3 times**.

8) Sit on the heels in **Rock Pose** and spread the knees far apart. Bring the forehead to the floor with the palms flat on the ground in front of the knees. Inhale and rise up on the knees, stretching the arms up and out like a flower greeting the sun. Exhale and come down bringing the forehead to the floor. Continue for **3 minutes**. *Note to the Teacher: It is common to see students leaning back in the upright position.*

9) **Yoga Mudra**. Sit on the heels again with the knees together and the fingers interlaced at the base of the spine. Bring the forehead to the ground, and lift the arms up straight as far as possible and hold the position for **3 minutes**, with Long Deep Breathing.

COPYRIGHT YOGI BHAJAN 2003

Prana/Apana Balance

1) Sit gracefully in **Celibate Pose** for **2 minutes**, hands are relaxed on thighs. Breath is normal.

2) **Rising up from the Knees.** Place the arms out from the sides, parallel to the ground, with the palms facing up. Inhale for **6 counts** rising up straight from the knees. Hold this position and the breath for **12 counts**. Slowly exhale, taking **6 counts** to lower yourself back down on to the heels. Repeat this cycle **7 times,** on the **8th time** clap the hands over the head.

3) **Push-Pull Pistoning.** Lie on the back with the hands at the sides, raise the legs 1-1/2 feet off the ground. Begin a push-pull motion. The legs stay parallel to the ground. This exercise must always follow the preceding one. Continue for **2-1/2 minutes**.

4) **Leg Lifts 90°.** Immediately inhale and lift the legs to 90 degrees. Hold for **30 seconds**, slowly exhale and lower the legs.

5) **Modified Stretch Pose.** Still on the back, lift the legs **6 inches** and do Breath of Fire for **1 minute.** Inhale, hold, then relax.

6) Now lie on the stomach. Place the hands in Venus Lock at the small of back. Inhale powerfully and arch the spine up from the waist. Be sure to keep your eyes closed as you come up. Hold this position for **30 seconds**. Then exhale powerfully as you open the eyes and lower the torso. Repeat this cycle **10 times.**

7) **Heart Center Pull.** Lie on the back with the arms straight up at **90°**, palms facing each other. Do Breath of Fire for **1 minute**. Inhale. With a great deal of tension in the hands, arms, and chest, and teeth, make the hands into fists, and slowly pull the energy and the fists down to the chest. Exhale. Inhale raising the arms and repeat the above action **1 more time.**

8) *Relax*. Move the mind to the Navel Point and listen to the heartbeat there.

COMMENTS:
Exercises 1, 2, & 3 stimulate the sexual, eliminative, and navel energies so that *prana* and *apana* are properly mixed at the Navel Point, and the power of the Kundalini can be released. Exercises 4, 5, & 6 emphasize the higher chakras and the pranic force at the eyes and heart. If you keep the eyes open when you lift up in Exercise 6, it can cause temporary dizziness as you rebalance. Exercise 7 will allow your heart to dominate and eliminate a lot of pent-up anger that hides in the form of deep muscle tension. When you listen to the heartbeat in exercise 8, feel like you are home, resting at the center of yourself. The heart rhythm is powered by the cosmic creative sound of "*Ong*." This will elevate you and give you mental relaxation and sensitvity.

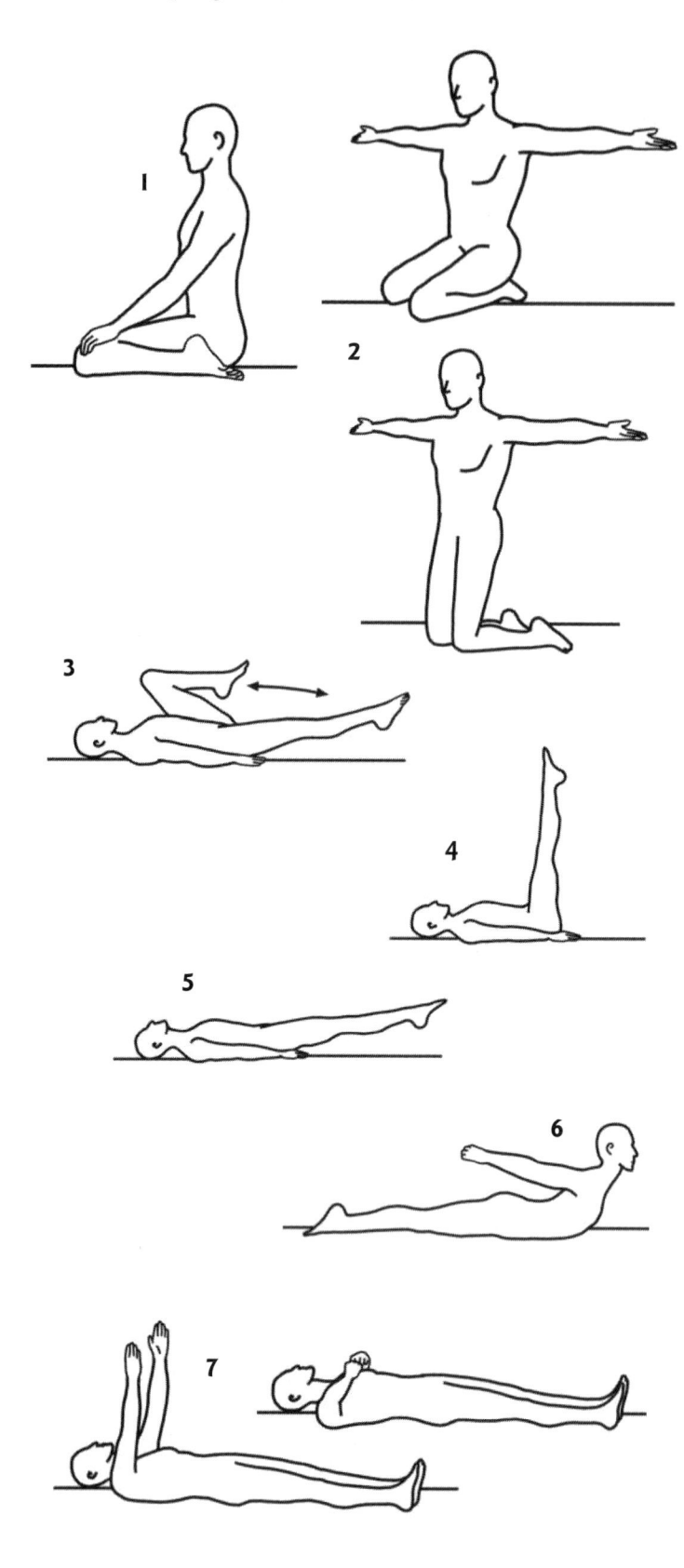

This set was originally taught by Yogi Bhajan in the Spring of 1970.

Releasing Premenstrual Tension & Balancing Sexual Energy

1) Sit on the heels. Extend the left leg straight back along the ground. Bend forward and place the forehead on the ground. Put both arms back along the sides, palms up. Relax all the muscles and relax the breath. Hold for **3 minutes**. Then slowly rise up on the inhale. Bring both legs under, sitting on the heels. Repeat on the other side, also for **3 minutes**.
This exercise is a meditation itself. The time of practice can gradually be increased to 11 minutes on each side. It becomes a self-trance meditation. The pituitary gland is stimulated and the ovaries are relaxed. This posture is also excellent for the eyes.

2) **Throat & Neck Massage**. Sit on the heels. With one hand, gently massage the muscles on each side of the throat and neck. Use a wave-like motion from the collarbone up to the jaw. Continue this rhythmic squeeze for **2 minutes.**
This exercise is for the thyroid and Fifth Chakra.

3) **Ear Massage**. Still on the heels, lift both hands up with the palms facing the ears. Keep the fingers together. Create a slight angle at the wrists so the fingers point away from the skull. Massage the ears and earlobes with the palms. Alternate between circular motion and linear up and down strokes. Continue for **2-3 minutes.** Inhale and gently pull the earlobes downward and away from the body. Hold for **10 seconds** and relax.
This is for lymphatic stimulation and circulation. There are meridian points on the ears that govern all parts of the body. It is a whole body massage using just the ears.

4) **Torso Twists.** Still sitting on the heels, immediately place your hands at the lower back. Interlace the fingers in Venus Lock. Keep the spine straight. Inhale deeply as you twist the torso to the left. Exhale and turn to the right. The motion is moderately slow and complete. Continue for **3 minutes**. To end inhale, pull *mulbandh* and concentrate on the full length of the spine. Imagine energy flowing up the center of the spine rejuvenating and relaxing the whole body. Exhale and relax.
This is for the lumbar spine and relaxation in the pelvis. It is also good for elimination.

5) **Sit-ups with Legs Wide.**
a) **Sit Up to the Center.** Lie on the back. Spread the legs as wide as possible, without strain. Grasp the shoulders with thumbs in back and fingers in front. Move the upper arms out so the elbows rest on the ground. Mentally survey all the muscles in the body. Then, moving very slowly, muscle by muscle, bring the torso gradually forward until you bend all the way up, placing the forehead on the ground. Hold this position with relaxed breaths for **3 minutes**. Inhale deeply as you lie back and relax.
b) **Sit Up to the Left and the Right.** Gradually rise up and forward. This time bend over the left knee. Hold the pose for **1 minute**. Inhale and exhale deeply **3 times**, then inhale deeply as you go back. Repeat the same situp and hold over the right leg. Hold for **1 minute**. Inhale and exhale deeply **3 times**. Then inhale deeply as you lie back.
This is for the sciatic nerve and its branches. It strengthens the abdomen and lets go of tension caused from anxiety.

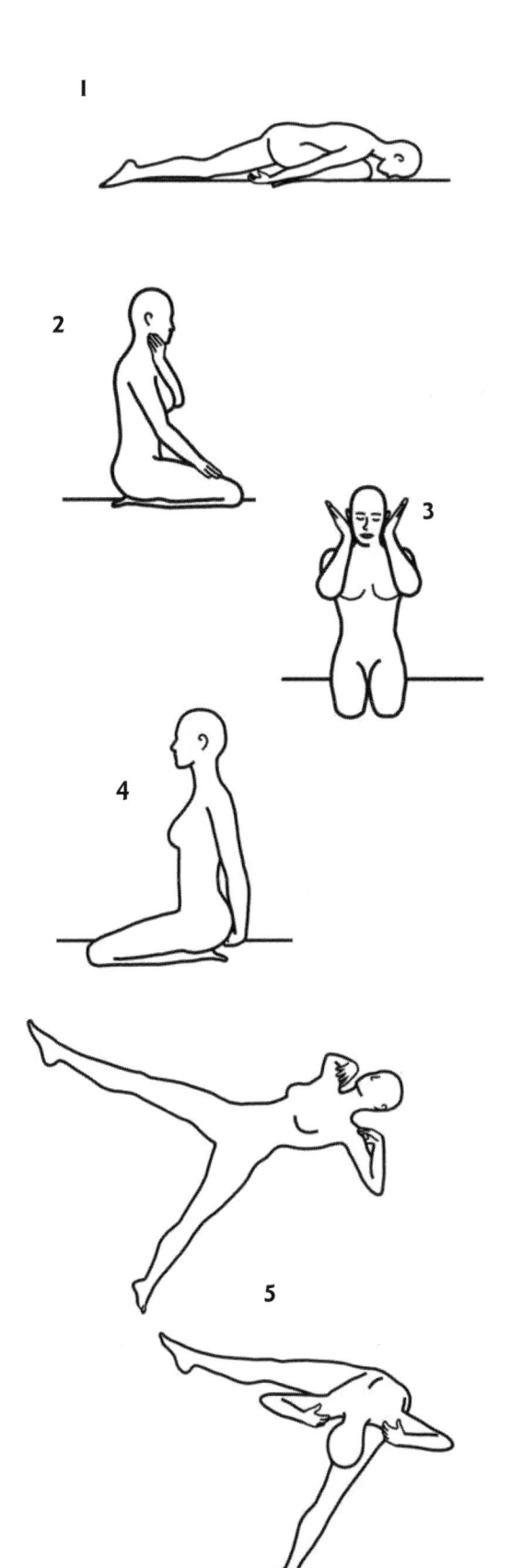

Releasing Premenstrual Tension & Balancing Sexual Energy

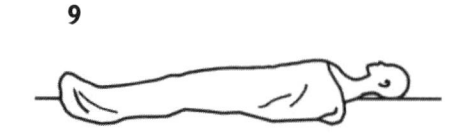

6) **Knee & Elbow Walk.** Start by lying on the stomach. Come up so that you are balancing on the hands and knees. Raise the heels toward the buttocks. Bend the forearms with the hands up by the shoulders. Raise the head so you can see forward. Begin to walk. Continue for **3 minutes.**
Relax completely on the back for **1 minute.**
This promotes circulation, works on the heart and improves the mineral balance.

7) **Lotus Walk.** Sit in Full Lotus Pose. (Lock the feet on the upper thighs with knees near the ground.) Put the hands on the ground beside the knees. Lean forward onto the hands and swing the body ahead. Repeat the motion so you scoot along the ground. Continue for **3 minutes.**
This opens the Navel Point energy, helps headaches and relaxes the sex organs.

8) **Back Platform Pose.** Sit straight with the legs stretched out in front. Put the hands on the ground with the fingers pointed toward the toes, in back and lift the hips up until a platform is formed with the abdomen straight. Raise the head to look forward. Keep the legs straight and begin to "walk" on the heels and hands. Continue for **3 minutes.**
This releases mental anxiety and tension, and strengthens the lower back and hips.

9) **Relax.** Totally relax on the back. Become weightless and float into the blue ethers. Continue for **15 minutes.**

COMMENTS:
This series adjusts the energy in the sex-circulation meridians. It releases the tension in the ovaries and enhances circulation to the pelvic region. It is an excellent set for men: it balances the sexual energy and helps the prostrate.

For women, if you experience chronic problems with tension and/or menstruation, practice this set every day for 40 days. During that time, eat a light diet, drink plenty of water and Yogi Tea. The monthly cycle of menstruation is a major hormonal event. Estrogen levels can change greatly. As the chemical levels vary there are corresponding changes in emotions, a switch in the dominance of the brain hemispheres, and shifts in cognitive abilities—some improve and others lessen. For many women, menstruation is accompanied by cramps and pain. Sometimes this comes from too little exercise and a cumulative build-up of tension. The lack of movement and breathing stops the body from adjusting itself. Tension often builds up and registers in the ovaries, making them rigid and immobile. Normally, the ovaries go through a slow contraction and lifting motion during the month. If the tension is too high, this motion is interrupted. The body attempts to compensate with inappropriate muscles and nerves. This leads to pain and irregularities.

Transforming the Lower Triangle to the Higher Triangle 1 of 2

1) **Camel Pose**. Come into Camel Pose—sit on the heels, grab the ankles, and arch up, lifting the Heart Center upward. Letting the hips follow, lifting them as high as you can. Head is relaxed back. Begin Breath of Fire powerfully. Mentally inhale **Sat**, and exhale **Naam**. Continue for **3 minutes**. Then inhale and hold the breath for **10 seconds**. Now begin chanting **Sat Naam**, as in Sat Kriya. Continue for **3 minutes**.

2) **Knee and Forehead Balance.** Immediately bring the head forward to the ground. Lock hands in Venus Lock on the back. Raise the feet and shins off the ground near the buttocks. Balance on the knees and forehead and meditate at the Brow Point for **3 minutes**.

3) **Knee and Forehead Balance with Buttock Kick**. From Position #2, bring the hands to the ground, and extend the left leg straight back and up to 60 degrees, then bend it towards the buttocks and start kicking the buttocks coordinated with Breath of Fire. Continue for **2 minutes**. Switch legs and repeat **2 minutes**.

4) **Celibate Pose.** Immediately come back into Celibate Pose with buttocks on the ground between the heels. Begin long, deep, and slow breathing for **2 minutes**.

5) **Fish Pose in Celibate Pose.** Sit as above and lie back on the ground. Extend the hands straight up over the head perpendicular to the ground. The palms are flat together. Begin **Sat Kriya** in this position for **3 to 5 minutes**.

6) **Camel Pose.** Come up into Camel Pose. Begin long, deep, and slow breathing for **2 minutes** and then begin Breath of Fire for **2 minutes**. Inhale, hold briefly, and with the exhale, come forward with the head on the ground.

7) **Guru Pranam.** With the head on the ground, extend the arms straight with the palms together. The elbows will hug the ears. Continue for **3 minutes**.

8) **Stretch Pose Sequence.** Lie on the back and come into Stretch Pose. (Head up, and feet 6 inches off the ground, toes pointed, fingers pointing towards the toes.) Begin Breath of Fire for **3 minutes**. Then immediately begin to inhale deeply and lift the knees to the heart. Exhale and put the legs straight on the ground. Continue with long, deep, and slow breathing for **2 minutes**.

9) **Shoulder Stand.** Raise up into Shoulder Stand. Support the spine with the hands with the weight on the elbows. Begin Breath of Fire for **3 minutes**.

10) **Plow Pose.** From Shoulder Stand, lower the legs over the head to the ground in Plow Pose with the arms straight back. Begin Breath of Fire for **3 minutes**. Then raise up to shoulder stand and do Breath of Fire for **3 minutes** again. *Relax on the back afterwards.*

11) **Stretch Pose sequence**. Repeat exercise 8.

12) Roll immediately onto the stomach. Interlace the hands together (palms

Transforming the Lower Triangle to the Higher Triangle

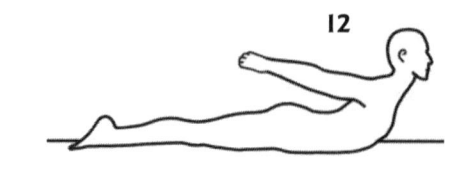

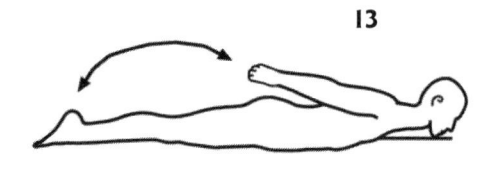

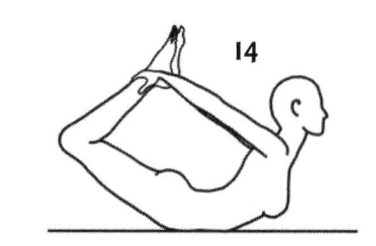

face the head) behind the back and lift the head and shoulders off the ground. Begin Breath of Fire for **3 minutes** and then relax.

13) **Buttock Kicks.** In the same position as Exercise 12, but with the chest relaxed on the ground, begin to kick the buttocks with alternate legs. Continue for **3 minutes.**

14) **Bow Pose.** Reach back, grab the ankles, and arch up into Bow Pose. Rock gently back and forth. Continue for **2 to 3 minutes.**

15) **Cobra Pose.** Come up into Cobra Pose. Begin Breath of Fire for **3 minutes**. Relax.

16) **Butterfly Pose.** Sit up and bring the soles of the feet together. Hold the feet together with both hands. Rock back and forth in rhythm with the chant. Keep the spine straight and aligned rocking forward and back from the hip joint. Movement is subtle and rhythmic.

> *Gobinday Mukanday Udhaaray Apaaray*
> *Hareeang Kareeang Nirnaamay Akaamay*

Continue for **5 to 31 minutes**. *This is a chant of bliss and joy. Put the heart and lungs into it.*

COMMENTS:

If the energy in the lower triangle of chakras is not balanced and allowed to transform to higher energy frequencies, one is totally a slave to hunger, thirst and sexuality, following the whim of the body. This creates great difficulty with any form of discipline. The sexual potency of that person will be sporadic. This set stimulates the energy of the lower triangle: rectum, sex organs, Navel Point, and transforms their energy into the higher brain structures: Pituitary, Pineal, and Memory glands. The relaxation between exercises is short and all breathing should be done with enthusiasm.

Exercises 1 & 6 conquer the rule of hunger, thirst, and poor digestion. Exercises 2 & 3 release energy to the brain and are known as *Adha Shakti Chalnee Kriya*. It gives clarity of thought and clear sparkling eyes. Sciatica can never be a problem. Exercise 4 is for potency and exercise 5 eliminates wet dreams, enabling you to gain sensitivity to the truth in any situation. It creates alliance between your mind and soul so that your mind will never bow before the ego of man. It gives you radiant power. In exercise 6 you will sweat. Any pain that occurs is a result of too much sexual activity or activity with the wrong frame of mind and tension. Exercise 7 is for the upper centers of the head. Exercise 8 is for the Navel Point energy release. Exercise 9 opens the digestion and elimination of the intestines. Exercises 10 through 15 adjust the Navel Point and balance the aura, distributing the sexual energy smoothly. After this *kriya*, meditation becomes automatic.

This set was originally taught by Yogi Bhajan June 11, 1971.

More Great Sets — Sets & Meditations

Sat Kriya Workout

1) **Sat Kriya.** Sit on the heels with the arms overhead and the palms together. Interlace the fingers except for the index fingers, which point straight up. Men cross the right thumb over the left thumb; women cross the left thumb over the right. Begin chanting *Sat Naam* in the rhythm and style of Sat Kriya. Continue for 5 minutes. Then inhale, exhale and apply *mulbandh*. *Relax* on the back for **3 minutes**.

2) **Sat Kriya.** Repeat exercise # 1.

3) **Chest Stretch.** Sit in Easy Pose with an erect spine. Interlace the fingers and place the palms at the back of the neck. Spread the elbows open so they point away from the sides of the torso. Concentrate at the Brow Point. Begin long deep complete breaths. Continue for **3 minutes**. Then inhale and hold the breath briefly. Exhale.

4) **Sat Kriya.** Immediately repeat exercise #1 for **3 minutes**. *Relax* for **2 minutes**.

5) **Frog Pose.** Squat down into the Frog Pose, with the heels together and lifted. Keep them in this position throughout the exercise. Inhale as the buttocks go up and the head goes toward the knees. Exhale as you return to the squat position with the head up. The fingertips stay placed on the ground in front of the feet throughout the motion. Repeat the frog pose **26 times**. *Relax* for **1 minute**.

6) **Sat Kriya.** Repeat exercise #1 for **3 minutes**. *Relax* for **1 minute.**

7) **Frog Pose 10 times.** Immediately go to the next exercise.

8) **Sat Kriya** for **3 minutes**. No rest.

9) **Frog Pose 15 times.** No rest.

10) **Sat Kriya** for **3 minutes**. No rest.

11) **Frog Pose 10 times.** No rest.

12) **Sat Kriya** for **5 minutes**. At the end inhale deeply and hold with *mulbandh* for **30 seconds**. Then exhale completely and hold the breath out with *mahabandh* as long as comfortable. Repeat this breath holding cycle **2 more times**. *Relax* for **15 minutes**.

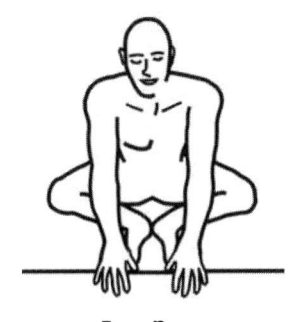

Sat Kriya

Frog Pose

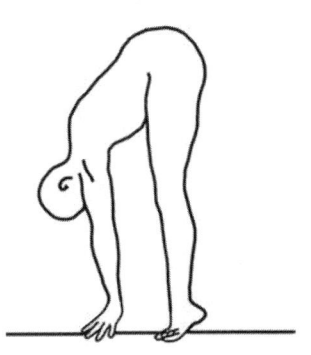

COMMENTS:
This will energize and balance the lower triangle. It is very curative for any digestive or sexual ailments. It gives endurance and breaks fevers. It often produces a pleasant sweat and cleansing of the skin. The first few times the legs may shake or be slightly weak. As the muscles build, you will walk with increased grace and certainty. The transitions bewteen exercises are smooth. So the phrase 'no rest' does not mean leap and jerk. You may need to remind people to concentrate on the centers as they do Sat Kriya. Be sure that the chin is pulled in on Sat Kriya, and that the face is forward in the down position of Frog Pose.

Note to the Teacher: This can be taught for beginners, intermediate, or advanced. As written, it is for intermediate students or students in good physical condition. To adapt it for beginners decrease the exercise times and increase the rests between exercises. For 1, do **3 minutes** of Sat Kriya and **5 minutes** of rest. After exercises 7-11 add **1 minute** of rest, or slightly less depending on the class. As an advanced set that assumes you are warmed up and in good shape, eliminate the rest periods from exercises 4-6.

Sets & Meditations | **More Great Sets**

Wahe Guru Kriya (Trikuti Kriya)

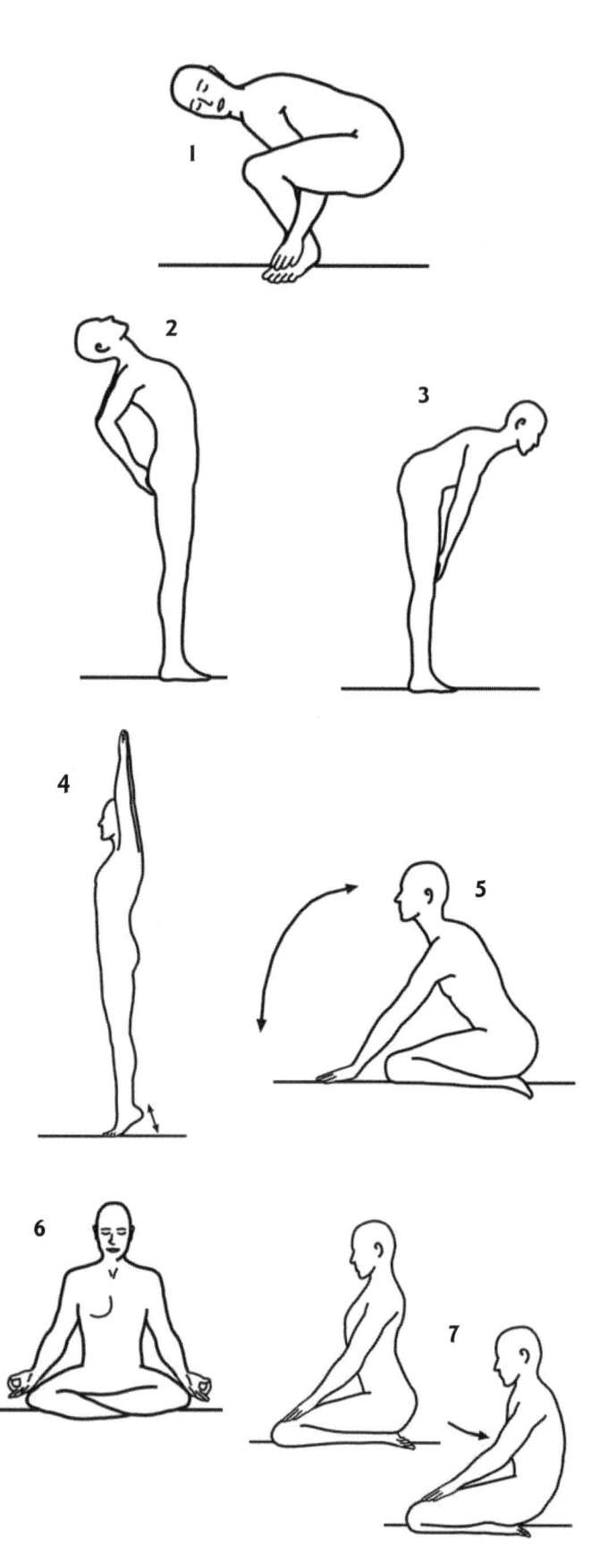

1) Come into **Chair Pose** (knees bent, back parallel to the ground, hands resting flat on the tops of the feet.) Keep the spine straight. The head faces down. Turn the head to the left shoulder and say **WHAA-HAY**. Turn the head to the right shoulder and say **GUROO**. Alternate at a moderate pace to make a continuous sound current: **WHAA-HAY GUROO, WHAA-HAY GUROO, WHAA-HAY GUROO**. Continue for **3 minutes**.

2) Stand up straight. Put hands on the hips and lean backwards. Keep the legs straight. Let the head fall back. Turn head to the left and say **WHAA-HAY**. Turn head to the right and say **GUROO**. Continue for **3 minutes**.

3) Stand up straight. Bend slightly so the hands rest on the knees. Spine is straight but head is up. Chant **WHAA-HAY** while turning the head to the left. Chant **GUROO** while turning the head to the right. Continue for **3 minutes**.

4) **Stand Up Stretch**. Stand up. Stretch arms straight overhead. On **WHAA-HAY**, the feet are flat on the ground. With **GUROO**, rise up on the toes. Continue for **3 minutes**.

5) **Sphinx**. Sit on the heels. Place the palms flat on the floor just in front of the knees. Spine and arms are straight looking like a sphinx. Chant **WHAA-HAY** and then bend forward, touching the forehead to the ground and chant **GUROO**. Continue for **3 minutes**.

6) Sit in Easy Pose. Begin to whisper the *Panj Shabd*:
   SAA-TAA-NAA-MAA.
After **2 minutes**, chant loudly for **2 more minutes**.

7) **Spinal Flex with chanting.** Immediately come on the heels with palms on the thighs. Begin flexing the spine, and with a powerful whisper chant **SAA** forward, **TAA** back, **NAA**, forward, **MAA** back. Continue for **3 minutes**, then meditate.

COMMENTS:
While chanting, on **WHAA** focus at the Naval Point, on **HAY** focus at the chest, and on **GUROO** focus on the pursed lips.
   This *kriya* is known by experiencing it. The set is a total workout for the thyroid, pituitary, and pineal glands. Your whole body will sweat. Meditate after this *kriya* and realize that we are channels for truth and that to maintain grace in the most ungraceful moments is the true human worth.

This set was originally taught by Yogi Bhajan November 27, 1974.

Examples of Sets Focusing on Each Chakra

First Chakra (Mooladhara)
Healthy Bowel System
Flexibility and the Spine
Disease Resistance & Heart Helper

Second Chakra (Svadisthana)
Sat Kriya
Releasing Premenstrual Tension & Balancing Sexual Energy
Sex Energy Transformation* *(from Sadhana Guidelines)*

Third Chakra (Manipura)
Nabhi Kriya
Nabhi Kriya for Prana-Apana

Fourth Chakra (Anahata)
Magnetic Field & Heart Center
The Essence of Self* *(from The Inner Workout Manual)*

Fifth Chakra (Vishuddha)
Wahe Guru Kriya
For Creativity* *(from Physical Wisdom)*

Sixth Chakra (Ajana)
Pituitary Gland Series
Ajna Stimulation* *(from Keeping Up with Kundalini Yoga)*

Seventh Chakra (Sahasrara)
The 7th Chakra is stimulated through concentration and meditation.
Foundation for Infinity

Eighth Chakra (Aura)
Strengthening the Aura
Exercise Set for Balancing the Aura* *(from Kundalini Yoga for Youth and Joy)*
Exercise Set for Electromagnetic Frequency* *(from Kundalini Yoga for Youth and Joy)*

Examples of Appropriate Sets for Beginners
Basic Spinal Energy Series
Awakening Yourself to the Ten Bodies
Kriya for Elevation
Kriya for Morning Sadhana
Exercise Set for the Kidneys
Kriya for Disease Resistance
Surya Kriya

Examples of Good Warm-Up Sets

Some examples of Kundalini Yoga *kriyas* and *pranayam* to use as warm-ups before a more vigorous kriya:

Sun Salutation (*Surya Namaskar*)
Life Nerve Stimulation* *(from Sadhana Guidelines)*
Lungs & Bloodstream* *(from Kundalini Yoga for Youth & Joy)*
Keeping the Body Beautiful* *(from Kundalini Yoga Manual)*
Meditation for the Sunrise* *(from Journal of Science & Consciousness)*
Basic Spinal Energy Series

Pranayam Sequences:
Basic Breath Series (with times shortened)
Nadi Cleansing Breath
4/4 Breath for Energy* *(from Survival Kit Manual)*

---

* not included in this Manual.

CHAPTER 2
Meditations & Pranayams without Mantra

Aerobic Capacity and Efficiency	58
Basic Breath Series	59
Breath Awareness Exercise	60
Breath of Fire with Lion's Paws	61
Caliber for Constant Self-Authority	62
The Caliber of Life Meditation	63
Composite Polarity Mudra Meditation	64
Immune System Booster: The Inner Sun	65
Inner Conflict Resolver Reflex	66
The Liberated Heart Meditation	67
Mahan Gyan Mudra	68
Meditation for a Calm Heart	69
Meditation to Change the Ego	70
Meditation to Conquer Self-Animosity	71
Meditation to Develop the Self-Sensory System	72
Meditation for Emotional Balance – Sunia(n) Antar	73
Meditation to Know the Field	74
Meditation for a Stable Self	75
Nadi Cleansing—"U" Breathing	76
Pranayam Energizer Series	77
Perspective and Emotional Balance	78
Sitali Pranayam	79
Tattva Balance Beyond Stress & Duality	80
Tratakum Meditation	81
Tratakum Meditation Photograph	83

Aerobic Capacity & Efficiency

Sit in an Easy Pose, with a light *jalandhar bandh*.
Hold onto the knees with the hands.

BREATH & MOVEMENT: Inhale completely with a yogic breath. Stretch the rib cage to the maximum capacity. Suspend the breath by lifting the chest and diaphragm. Do not let any air leak in or out during the exercise. Lock the tongue on the roof of the mouth. Press the tongue up, behind the teeth and the most forward point of the roof of the mouth. Begin to flex the spine forward and backward as you hold onto the knees. Flex with a smooth, fairly rapid pace. (Focus on the full flex of the spine, and do not hunch the shoulders forward too much.) When you can no longer hold the breath in comfortably, sit up straight and exhale forcefully. Quickly inhale and continue the spine flex.

TIME: Continue for **11 minutes**.

TO END: Sit straight and inhale deeply. Hold this final breath and concentrate at the Brow Point. Relax.

COMMENTS
This one-exercise kriya has a massive impact on the body and nervous system and builds stamina. It increases the efficiency of the lungs in bringing oxygen into the blood. It pressurizes the heart to regulate itself and adjusts the various heart muscles to co-operate with each other. This kriya also helps the kidney, adrenal, and sex organ systems. Keep water handy. After this exercise you may be very thirsty.

To master this *kriya*, and obtain all its benefits, you must build up your capacity so that you can do the spinal flex with the breath held in for at least 1 full minute at a time. Then build the time of the exercise to 22 minutes once a day. The best way to practice the 22 minutes is to break it up into two 11-minute periods with a 3-5 minute rest between them.

The increased aerobic vitality that results after 40 or more days will makes life richer and more positive, providing a reserve capacity to face challenge. Disease develops when the body gets less oxygen, eliminates less waste, and the brain, organs, and glands decrease their functioning. Eventually the system breaks down. This kriya helps to prevent that breakdown, and maintains your vital capacity as you age.

Meditations without Mantra

Originally taught by Yogi Bhajan in June 1969

Sets & Meditations

Basic Breath Series

EYE FOCUS FOR ALL EXERCISES: Close the eyelids. Press the eyes up gently and focus at the Brow Point (the top of the nose where the eyebrows meet).

1) *Left Nostril Breathing.* Sit in Easy Pose. Rest the left hand in Gyan Mudra (touch the tip of the thumb with the tip of the index finger). The left arm is straight on the left knee. Raise the right hand in front of the face with the palm flat facing to the left. The fingers of the hand are together and point straight up. Press the side of the thumb on the right nostril to gently close it. Begin long, deep, complete yogic breaths through the left nostril. Inhale and exhale only through the left nostril. Continue for **3 minutes**. Inhale and hold comfortably for **10-30 seconds**, exhale and relax.

2) *Right Nostril Breathing.* Sit in Easy Pose. Rest the right hand in Gyan Mudra. Raise the left hand in front of the face with the palm flat facing to the right. The fingers of the hand are together and point straight up. Press the side of the thumb on the left nostril to gently close it. Begin long, deep, complete yogic breaths through the right nostril. Inhale and exhale only through the right nostril. Continue for **3 minutes**. Inhale and hold comfortably for **10-30 seconds**, exhale and relax.

3) *Alternate Nostril Breathing.* Sit in Easy Pose, with the spine relaxed and straight. Make Gyan Mudra with the left hand. Rest the left hand over the left knee. Close the eyelids. Press the eyes up gently and focus at the Brow Point (the top of the nose where the eyebrows meet). Block the right nostril with the thumb. Press just hard enough to close the nostril. Keep the rest of the fingers straight up. Inhale deeply through the left nostril. When the breath is full, bend the right hand into a "U" extending the little fingertip over to press on the left nostril. Close the left nostril and let the right nostril open by releasing the thumb pressure. (You can also use the thumb and index finger.) Exhale smoothly, and completely through the right nostril. When the breath is completely exhaled, begin the cycle again with the inhale through the left nostril. Continue for **3 minutes** with long, deep, regular breaths. Inhale at the end and hold the breath for **10-30 seconds**. Exhale and relax.

4) *Alternate Nostril Breathing.* Repeat exercise #3, except use the left hand to direct the inhale through the right nostril and exhale through the left nostril.

5) *Breath of Fire.* Sit in Easy Pose with both hands in Gyan Mudra. Begin a powerful, regular, and conscious Breath of Fire. Continue for **7 minutes**. Then inhale and hold the breath for **10-60 seconds**. Mentally watch the energy circulate through the entire body. Relax the breath and concentrate on the natural flow of the breath as life force for **3 minutes**. Notice how your mind and emotions have changed.

6) In the same posture, meditate. Inhale deeply and chant Long **SAT NAAM**'s. Continue **3-15 minutes**.

COMMENTS

This set gives you a quick lift in energy, increased clarity, and a sense of balance. If you do the minimum times for each exercise, it only takes 22-25 minutes to completely reset yourself. It is an excellent set for beginners. You learn the relationship to the breath and you observe the differences in emotion and thinking that each type of breathing creates.

Even though breathing is the most natural and essential thing we do, conscious breathing can be quite a challenge. When you alter the breath you begin to oppose and release the habitual patterns of emotion and attention that are coded in the habits of your body and mind. As those patterns begin to alter, you may drift in concentration or interest. If you continue and command the breath, then you will gain a new sense of ease and control where you direct your mind.

This *kriya* is excellent to practice as a preparation for a more strenuous Kundalini Yoga set. It can be practiced in beginning and advanced stages. As a beginner, use the times listed above. For intermediate level practice, do exercises 1 through 4 for five minutes each. For an advanced practice, increase the times of 1 through 4 to a full 10 minutes each.

Breath Awareness Exercise

Sit in an Easy Pose, with a light *jalandhar bandh*.

EYE POSITION: Eyes are closed, pressed gently up, focusing at the Brow Point.

MUDRA: Let your hands rest over the knees in Gyan Mudra or keep them in Prayer Pose at the center of the chest.

BREATH PATTERN & VISUALIZATION: Let your body feel in perfect balance. You can sit in this posture without effort. Let all of your attention gather on the breath. Sense the breath as a quality of motion. How does it move in the different parts of your body as you breathe in a steady and meditative rhythm? What *guna* and elements seem to dominate the quality of your breath as you begin the exercise? How does that change as you continue to meditate?

Bring your attention through the one-inch square (2.5cm^2) area above the root of the nose where the eyebrows meet. Then focus the attention through the brow to the Navel Point area. Concentrate just below the interior of the umbilicus. Feel the motion and life energy of the breath. Visualize the body as luminous. As you inhale, the light increases in brightness, extent, and penetration. Let that breath and light merge with the entire Cosmos. Let the breath breathe you. Experience yourself as a unit and the Cosmos as unlimited. Feel that you are a part of that vastness. The breath is a wave on a much greater ocean of energy of which you are a part.

Notice the motions and changes in the subtle breath, *prana*. Do not try to alter it. Observe it and learn to notice your baseline of *prana*. You are sensitizing your awareness to notice the state of energy and motion in your *prana*. You must calibrate to this baseline to notice and appreciate the effect of various *pranayam* meditation techniques.

TIME: Continue for **3-62 minutes**.

COMMENTS

The character of your thoughts and emotions is reflected in the motion and level of energy in your breath. One of the first habits of a yogi is to notice the state of the breath and *prana*. A disturbance in the subtle *prana* foreshadows what will manifest in the body and emotions. If you learn what your normal state is, then you can notice deviations that are unhealthy as well as healthy enhancements. You can choose certain behaviors and meditations to redirect and shape that inner motion. This short-circuits the cycle of manifestation. You can avoid many illnesses and bad decisions. It also opens your intuition to environmental changes. It increases your awareness of how other people influence you. Meditation on the breath at the Navel Point is the starting point for awareness of *prana*. Yogi Bhajan has had his students meditate in this manner for many hours. He would often add the mantra *Sat Naam* to the flow of the breath.

Practice this meditation in silence and assess your energy state. Establish your zero point internally so you can notice the impact of the various breath combinations.

Breath of Fire with Lion's Paws
Reset the Brain's Electromagnetic Field

Sit in an Easy Pose, with a light *jalandhar bandh*.

MUDRA: Make both hands into Lion's Paws: curl and tighten the fingers of each hand. Keep the tension in the hands throughout the exercise. Extend both arms out to the sides, parallel to the ground with the palms up.

BREATH & MOVEMENT: Bring both arms up over the head so that the hands pass each other over the crown of the head. The elbows bend and the palms face down. Then bring the hands back down as you extend the arms out parallel to the ground again. Start a rhythmic motion in this way. Alternate which wrist is in front when they cross by each other over the head. Create a powerful breath with the motion of the arms. The arm motion is very fast-paced. The breath is an inhale as the arms extend and an exhale as the arms cross over the head. The breath becomes a steady Breath of Fire.

TIME: Continue for **9 minutes**.

TO END: Without breaking the pace of the exercise, stick the tongue out and down all the way. Continue for **15 seconds** more. Then inhale, bring in the tongue and fix the arms at 60 degrees, so that they form an arc around the head with the palms facing down about six inches apart over the head. The hands are still in Lion's Paws. Hold the breath for **15 seconds**. Keep the arms fixed as you exhale and inhale completely. Then hold the breath for **30 seconds**. Relax and let the arms down. Meditate at the Heart Center. Follow the gentle flow of the breath. Chant an inspiring and uplifting song. Continue for **3-5 minutes**.

COMMENTS

This short one-exercise *kriya* has a powerful and immediate effect on the brain and its electromagnetic field. The pressure in the hand position triggers reflexes in the fingertips to each area of the brain. The movement of the arms moves the lymph in the lymphatic system. It also pressurizes the nervous system to change its current state. The Breath of Fire added to the motion enhances functioning of the pituitary and stimulates the pineal gland to increase the radiance and subtle frequency of the brain's projection.

Sets & Meditations
Meditations without Mantra

Caliber for Constant Self-Authority
Originally taught by Yogi Bhajan in March 1979

Sit in an Easy Pose, with a light *jalandhar bandh*.
Keep the torso straight at all times. Do not lean forward or backwards.

MUDRA: Bring the hands in front of the body at the level of the Heart Center. Close the fingers over the thumbs into fists with the thumb tips at the base of the little fingers, if possible. Press the fists together at the first knuckles from the tips of the fingers in such a manner that the base of the palms are together and the backs of the palms face away from the center.

EYE POSITION: Fix the eyes on the tip of the nose. There is no required mantra except the subtle sense of the breath itself.

BREATH: Begin the following steady breathing pattern:
>   *Inhale* deeply through the nose.
>   *Exhale* completely through the mouth with pursed lips.
>   *Inhale* smoothly through the mouth.
>   *Exhale* through the nose.

TIME: Continue for **3 minutes**. Build slowly to a steady **11 minutes**. Build the meditation to a maximum of 22 minutes.

TO END: Inhale and hold the breath as you stretch both hands up over the head. Exhale and continue to stretch for **2 more** deep breaths. Relax.

COMMENTS
Caliber is the ability to maintain the projected status and activity of our committed self. When we become our own directive authority, then the psyche can fulfill the self, and you can be happy. Normally we reject authority and initiate chaos out of an attempt to create individuality by difference rather than through integrity and wholeness.

This meditation enhances your capacity for caliber, to hold and execute self-authority.

The Caliber of Life Meditation

Originally taught by Yogi Bhajan in October 1979

Sit in an Easy Pose, with a light *jalandhar bandh*.

MUDRA: Extend both arms straight forward, and parallel to the ground. Curl the fingers of the right hand into a fist. Extend the thumb straight up. Keep the elbow straight and move the fist to the center of the body. Move the left arm to the center and wrap the fingers of the left hand around the outside of the right hand's fist. Extend the left thumb straight up. Adjust the grip of the hands to that the thumbs can touch along their sides as they point up. The tips of the thumbs will form a little "V" like a gunsight.

EYE POSITION: Focus the eyes on the thumbnails and through the "V." Look through the V like a gunsight, seeing far away and seeing the V.

BREATH PATTERN: Inhale deeply and fill the lungs for **5 seconds**.
Exhale completely and empty the lungs for **5 seconds**. Then suspend the breath out as you stay still for **15 seconds**.

TIME: Continue this breath cycle for **3-5 minutes**. Slowly build up to **11 minutes**. Do not exceed 11 minutes.

COMMENTS

This meditation can form the basis of an extraordinary *sadhana*. It adjusts the projection and command of the breath. It improves the caliber of your capacity to reach excellence in life. It is known to conquer normal depression and discouragement. It builds tremendous strength into the nervous system.

This is the kind of meditation that must be cultivated and built up gradually. Start with 3 to 5 minutes. Be sure that you can do the meditation perfectly for the entire length of time you choose to practice. If not, lessen the time and build up. As you master the practice, you can increase the time that you hold the breath out from 15 seconds up to 60 seconds. Pick a time that is realistic for you. Then build the practice time up to 11 minutes. This is enough time to interrelate the projection of the *prana* throughout the Pranic Body. Do not press this *sadhana* longer.

Remember to keep the elbows straight during the entire meditation. If you feel dizzy or disoriented in this practice, be sure you are doing the suspension of the breath properly, and that you are holding the Neck Lock (*jalandhar bandh*). If you are correct, then have a partner supervise your practice by timing it, having a glass of water handy, and giving you a massage at the end. Then build your nervous system to a new level. When it is strong, you will feel a new stability and trust in yourself.

Composite Polarity Mudra Meditation

Originally taught by Yogi Bhajan in November 1978

Sit in an Easy Pose, with a light *jalandhar bandh*.

EYES: Fix the eyelids 1/10th open.

MUDRA: Relax the arms along the sides. Bend the elbows and raise the hands in front of the chest to the level of the Heart Center. Place both palms facing out from the chest with the fingers of each hand together pointing straight up. Extend the thumbs away from the other fingers toward the center of the chest. Hook the two thumbs together. Turn the right palm forward until the hand is parallel to the ground with the fingers pointing forward. The right wrist is bent at a 90-degree angle. The left palm faces forward and is perpendicular to the back of the right hand. Keep the thumbs locked throughout the meditation.

BREATH PATTERN: Regulate the breath: inhale slowly and deeply. Hold the breath in as long as you comfortably can. Then exhale completely in one slow breath. Hold the breath out as long as possible without gasping. Continue the cycle.

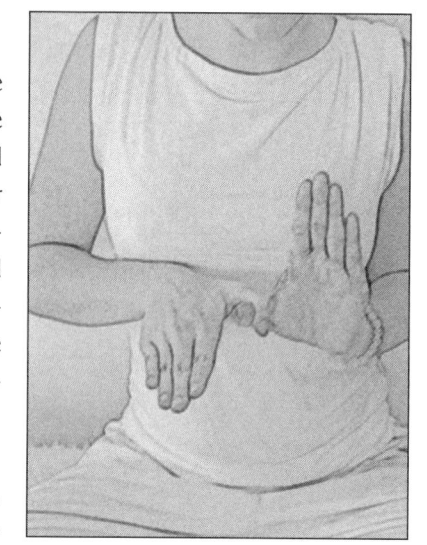

TIME: Meditate for **11 minutes**.

COMMENTS

The Composite Polarity Mudra Meditation teaches you subtlety and command. It is a precise *mudra* that requires fixed attention to maintain it through the *kriya*. It is subtle. The relation between the heartbeat and the repair of the arcline for health requires careful focus. It is the same in any skill. Over time and practice you learn to sense the distinctions that make a difference and that enhance your skill and pleasure in the task. This meditation gets better and better with constant practice. It has dimensions that are difficult at first but which unveil themselves over time.

This is an excellent practice for advanced students. It can be taught to beginners, but do not expect them to notice the finer distinctions that make this meditation so enjoyable and unique.

Immune System Booster: The Inner Sun

Originally taught in April 1986

Sit in an Easy Pose, with a light *jalandhar bandh*, and with head covered.

MUDRA: Bend the left arm and raise the hand up to shoulder level. The palm faces forward. The forearm is perpendicular to the ground. Make Surya Mudra with the left hand (touch the tip of the ring finger to the tip of the thumb). The *mudra* of the left hand may slip during practice—keep it steady. Make a fist of the right hand, pressing the tips of the fingers into the pads at the base of the fingers; extend the index finger. With the extended index finger, gently close off the right nostril. Concentrate at the Brow Point.

BREATH PATTERN: Begin a steady, powerful Breath of Fire. Emphasize the beat at the navel—the navel must move.

MANTRA: Though this is done without mantra, you may want to use a mantra tape for the proper rhythm. Good recordings for the rhythm are Singh Kaur's *Sat Naam Wahe Guroo*, or Sada Sat Kaur's *Angel's Waltz*.

TIME: Continue for **3 minutes**. Very gradually increase the time to **5 minutes**.

TO END: Then inhale deeply and hold the breath. As the breath is held, interlace all the fingers (beginning with the right thumb uppermost) and put the palms in front at a level just below the throat (in front of the thymus), and about 14 inches (35 cm) away from the body. Try to pull the fingers apart with all force. Resist and create a great tension. When you must, exhale. Repeat this sequence **3 more times**. On the last exhale, discharge the breath by blowing through your upturned lips, with the tongue curled back on the roof of the mouth. This will seal the upper palate upward. Then relax.

COMMENTS

This advanced immune therapy hits at viruses and bacteria. The head must be covered, or else you can get a headache. This is a kind of tantric kriya. The immune system interacts with the central nervous system, the glands, and emotions. We are each given the strength to encounter life and life's challenges. We have moral strength, mental strength, emotional strength, and physical strength. All these strengths are inter-connected. We block the flow of that strength when we experience feelings of anger, self-defeat, and blame. To boost the immune system, we must overcome these blocks.

The right hemisphere of the brain stores many of the diffuse negative emotions that lead us to depression and to a lower functioning immune system. This meditation stimulates the sympathetic nervous system and the right hemisphere to adjust themselves. In this process you may go through various emotions as the glands start to shift their balance. That is fine. Relax and keep going until you are through the emotional inertia. Then you will feel light, energized, and hopeful.

With gradual practice you can take the time up to 31 minutes. At that level your whole system is cleaned and rejuvenated. The immune system will have new vigor and will not be blocked by inner conflict. This type of breathing is called the "sun-breath."

Inner Conflict Resolver Reflex

Originally taught by Yogi Bhajan in October 1979

Sit in an Easy Pose, with a light *jalandhar bandh*.

EYE POSITION: Close the eyes 9/10ths of the way.

MUDRA: Place the hands over the chest, with the palms on the torso at the level of the breasts. The fingers point toward each other across the chest.

BREATH: The key to this meditation is attention to the breath.

> **Inhale** deeply and completely for **5 seconds**.
> **Exhale** completely for **5 seconds**.
> **Hold the breath out** for **15 seconds**,
> by suspending the chest motion as you pull in the Navel Point and abdomen.

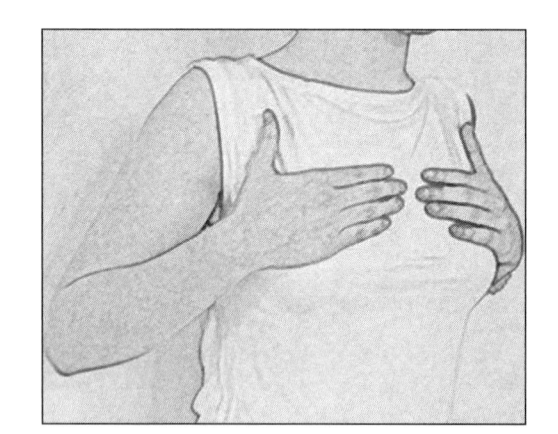

TIME: Begin with **11 minutes**. Build up to **31 or 62 minutes**.

TO END: Inhale deeply and stretch the arms up over the head. Relax the breath and shake the arms and hands for **15-30 seconds**. *Relax*.

COMMENTS

This is a form of ancient therapy. We are often confused and held in deadlock when inner conflict blocks our ability to think and act clearly. In these moments, the mind's *prana*, or energy, is scattered and distributed in a disturbed manner. This breath pattern holds the breath out three times as long as it is held in. So, the body senses a lack of *prana* in vital areas of functioning and asks how it can quickly and optimally reorganize itself to respond to this survival threat. The fibers of the Pranic Body extend and re-channel the *prana* to form a new pattern filled with clarity and action potential. Your built-in computer can calculate your total resources and the level of challenge, then design a strategy to prepare and use the mind and body effectively. This meditation resolves many conflicts and is an automatic reflex for survival. Inner conflict is the result of excess or disturbed *prana*.

The effect is certain, gradual, and simple. Be honest with the breath timing, and the meditation will be honest with you.

The Liberated Heart Meditation
Equanimity, Steadfastness & Immunity

Originally taught by Yogi Bhajan in April 1979

Sit in an Easy Pose, with a light *jalandhar bandh*.

MUDRA: Raise the hands up in front of the face with the palms facing forward. Curl the fingers so that the fingertips press onto the mounds at the base of the fingers. Extend the thumbs out from the hands and press the thumb tips together. The thumbs form a little arc at the level of the lips. The elbows are relaxed, down by the sides of the chest. The hands are held **6 to 8 inches** (15-20 cm) in front of the face.

EYE POSITION: The focus is on the tips of the thumbs.

BREATH PATTERN: Begin to inhale completely in **8 equal strokes**. Then exhale in **8 equal strokes**. One entire breath cycle (16 strokes) takes about **10 seconds**. The only mantra for this meditation is the sound of the breath itself.

TIME: Continue for **11-31 minutes**.

TO END: Inhale deeply, hold the breath as long as comfortable, then exhale. Inhale again and stretch the hands upward. Pull up on the spine as you open and close the fists. Exhale. Repeat the last breath again. Relax.

COMMENTS

The tips of the thumbs touch to form the arched look of the swan's neck. This represents inner grace and the dominance of the neutral mind and the *sattva guna*. You observe all that happens with no anger or enmity. The absence of these reactions makes all the energy of *prana* available to the direction of the mind. The mind has joined with its *prana*. Concentrate on the rhythm of the breath. The 8:8 rhythm will work on the connection between the Heart Chakra and the immune system. The hand position will give you strength.

This is not a beginner's meditation. It should be practiced with respect, and the time should be increased slowly, as your nerves adjust to the psychosomatic changes the meditation initiates.

Mahan Gyan Mudra

Originally taught by Yogi Bhajan in October 1972

Sit in an Easy Pose, with a light *jalandhar bandh*.

EYE POSITION: Focus the concentration at the top of the head.

MUDRA: Make the lower arms perpendicular to the upper arms, with the elbows at shoulder height. Pull the elbows in and the shoulders back, creating a pressure on the spine between the shoulders and the nape of the neck. Place the thumbs over the Sun and Mercury (the third and fourth) fingers. Extend the Jupiter and Saturn (the index and middle) fingers straight upward.

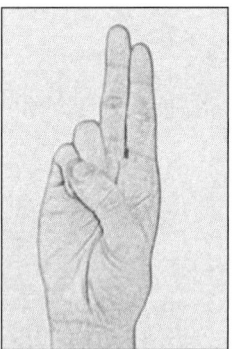

BREATH PATTERN: Breathe long and deep.

TIME: Continue for **11 minutes**.

COMMENTS

Feel that you are very saintly. Don't say that Jesus was great; say that he was a great master who taught the technique to be great. This meditation brings the realm of thoughtlessness quickly. It brings the awareness that redemption is not necessary—we are already redeemed. When calmness is experienced inside, it leads you to the experience of the entire universe, and nature serves you in harmony.

Meditations without Mantra — *Sets & Meditations*

Originally taught by Yogi Bhajan in September 1981

Meditation for a Calm Heart

Sit in an Easy Pose, with a light *jalandhar bandh*.

EYES: Either close the eyes or look straight ahead with the eyes 1/10th open.

MUDRA: Place the left hand on the center of the chest at the Heart Center. The palm is flat against the chest, and the fingers are parallel to the ground, pointing to the right. Make Gyan Mudra with the right hand (touch the tip of the index (Jupiter) finger with the tip of the thumb). Raise the right hand up to the right side as if giving a pledge. The palm faces forward, the three fingers not in Gyan Mudra point up. The elbow is relaxed near the side with the forearm perpendicular to the ground.

BREATH PATTERN & VISUALIZATION: Concentrate on the flow of the breath. Regulate each bit of the breath consciously. Inhale slowly and deeply through both nostrils. Then suspend the breath in and raise the chest. Retain it as long as possible.
Then exhale smoothly, gradually, and completely. When the breath is totally out, lock the breath out for as long as possible.

TIME: Continue this pattern of long, deep breathing for **3-31 minutes**.

TO END: Inhale and exhale strongly **3 times**. Relax.

COMMENTS

The proper home of the subtle force, *prana*, is in the lungs and heart. The left palm is placed at the natural home of *prana*, creating a deep stillness at that point. The right hand that throws you into action and analysis is placed in a receptive, relaxed mudra and put in the position of peace. The entire posture induces the feeling of calmness. It technically creates a still point for the *prana* at the Heart Center.

Emotionally, this meditation adds clear perception to your relationships with yourself and others. If you are upset at work or in a personal relationship, sit in this meditation for 3 to 15 minutes before deciding how to act. Then act with your full heart. Physically, this meditation strengthens the lungs and heart.

This meditation is perfect for beginners. It opens awareness of the breath, and it conditions the lungs. When you hold the breath in or out for "as long as possible," you should not gasp or be under strain when you let the breath move again.

- In a class try it for 3 minutes.
- If you have more time, try it for three periods of 3 minutes each, with one minute rest between them, for a total of 11 minutes.
- For an advanced practice of concentration and rejuvenation, build the meditation up to 31 minutes.

Meditation to Change the Ego

Originally taught by Yogi Bhajan in July 1979

Sit in an Easy Pose, with a light *jalandhar bandh*.

EYE POSITION: Fix the eyes on the knuckles of the thumbs. Narrow the eyelids.

MUDRA: Keep the spine straight and the chest slightly lifted. Relax the arms down at the sides. Raise the hands in front of the center of the chest at the level of the heart. The palms face toward each other. Curl the fingers into a loose fist. Keep the thumbs extended and point them upwards. Bring the hands toward each other until the top segment of the thumbs touch along the side of the thumbs. The rest of the hands stay separated.

BREATH PATTERN: Bring your concentration to the breath.
Create a steady breath rhythm with the following ratio and pathway:
> *Inhale* through the nose slowly. The length is about **8 seconds**.
> *Hold in the breath* for about **8 seconds**.
> *Release the breath* through the nose in **8 equal strokes**.
> *Hold the breath* out for **8 seconds**.

Once this pattern is set, you can gradually increase the time from 8 seconds to as long as you like. If you increase the time, keep the time equal in each section of the *pranayam*.

TIME: Begin this practice gradually. Start with **3 minutes**. Increase the time to **31 minutes** by adding **3-5 minutes** per week of practice.

TO END: At the end of a session, inhale deeply, stretch the hands over the head, and open and close the fists several times. Relax the breath.

COMMENTS
This meditation has many effects. It can be used to combat tension and hypertension. It also creates a deep concentration and a detachment that allows you to observe your attachments. Once you identify your attachments, you can let them go by dis-identifying with them, or by giving the object of attachment to the Infinite, the Cosmos, or God.

Sometimes you will hear strong inner sounds such as drums, bells, whistles, etc. Part of this can be due to pressure adjustments in the skull and eardrums. If the sounds develop in deep meditation, it is a normal adjustment of the neurons in the cortex. This phenomenon will pass quickly and should not distract you from the primary focus and process of the meditation.

Originally taught by Yogi Bhajan in March 1979

Meditation to Conquer Self-Animosity

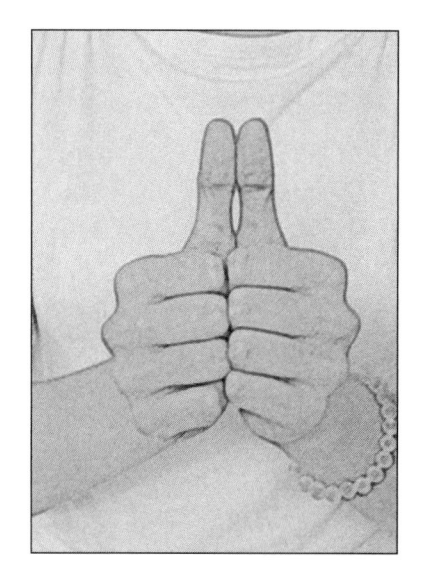

Sit in an Easy Pose, with a light *jalandhar bandh*.
Maintain an alert attitude.

MUDRA: Relax the arms at the sides and raise the forearms up and in toward the chest at the heart level. Draw the hands into fists, and point the thumbs straight up toward the sky. Press the fists together in such a manner that the thumbs and fists are touching. The palms are toward each other. This meditation requires the upper torso to be held straight, without rocking back and forth.

EYE POSITION: Fix the eyes at the tip of the nose.

There is no required mantra other than the subtle sound of the breath.

BREATH: **Inhale** through the nose.
   Exhale completely through the mouth.
   Inhale deeply and smoothly through the mouth.
   Exhale through the nose.

TIME: Continue for **3 minutes**. Gradually build the time to **11 minutes**. Practice daily, but do not exceed 22 minutes in any one session.

TO END: Inhale and stretch the arms up over the head. Keep the stretched position as you take **3 more deep breaths**. Relax.

COMMENTS
There are no enemies. There are challenges to our creativity. The greatest enemy is the self. Self-defeating activity and self-animosity occur where we do not accept ourselves. We instinctively reject self-confirmed continuity. We will oppose our own success and accomplishment just to break with steadiness. That break is the assertion of ego: an attempt at marking and possessing something in Time and Space. This self-animosity distracts us from the real gift of human life: the capacity to confront and experience the self in relationship to the Unknown Infinity of our Self.

This meditation conquers the state of self-animosity and gives you the ability for constant consciousness in support of the core self.

Meditation to Develop the Self-Sensory System

for the Transition from the Piscean to the Aquarian Age

Originally taught by Yogi Bhajan in August 2000

Sit in an Easy Pose, with a light *jalandhar bandh*.

MUDRA: Point the Jupiter finger (forefinger) of the right hand straight up toward the sky, with the thumb and other fingers closed in a fist. The right elbow is bent and relaxed at the side. The left hand is placed flat over the Heart Center (the center of the chest).

FOCUS: Listen to the Self-Sensory System lecture, recorded in your own voice. (*You can find this lecture in Chapter 1 of this Manual.*)

COMMENTS

"Our creativity will be our sensory system. And through this sensory system we will be overflowing with energy, touching the hearts of people, and feeling their feeling, and filling their emptiness. We will act great and our flow will fulfill the gratefulness in the hearts of others. It will be a new relationship. We will create a new humanity which will have the new sensory system, and thus we will establish the Age of Aquarius. This is the fundamental character you have to learn by heart."   —YOGI BHAJAN

Meditation for Emotional Balance
(Sunia(n) Antar)

Originally taught in August 1977

Before practicing this meditation drink a glass of water.

Sit in Easy Pose.

MUDRA: Place the arms across the chest and lock hands under the armpits, with palms open and against the body. Raise the shoulders up tightly against the earlobes, without cramping the neck muscles. Apply Neck Lock.

EYE POSITION: Close the eyes.

BREATH: The breath will automatically become slow.

TIME: Continue for **3 minutes**, gradually increasing to **11 minutes**.

COMMENTS

This meditation is called Sunia(n) Antar. It is very good for women. It is essential at times when one is worried or upset and doesn't know what to do, or when one feels like screaming, yelling, and misbehaving. When out of focus or emotional, attention should be given to the body's water balance and breath rate. Humans are approximately 70 percent water, and behavior depends upon the relation of water and earth, air and ether. Breath, representing air and ether, is the rhythm of life.

Normally we breathe 15 times a minute, but when we are able to rhythmically slow down the breath to only 4 breaths per minute, we have indirect control over our minds. This control eliminates obnoxious behavior, promoting a calm mind regardless of the state of affairs.

When there is a water imbalance in the system, and the kidneys are under pressure, it can cause worry and upset. Drinking water, pulling the shoulders up to the ears and tightly locking the entire upper area creates a solid brake that can be applied to the four sides of the brain. After 2 or 3 minutes, thoughts will still be there, but one does not feel them. This is a very effective method of balancing the functional brain.

Meditation to Know the Field

Originally taught by Yogi Bhajan in 1973

Precede the meditation with a vigorous yoga set which includes *pranayam*.

Sit in Easy Pose with the spine erect.

EYE POSITION: The eyelids are 9/10 shut, with the eyes looking downwards. Concentrate mentally at the Third Eye Point.

MUDRA: Hands in Gyan Mudra.

FOCUS: Keeping the spine straight, begin releasing all the tension from the spine outward. Let each segment of the spine release and each area of the body relax.

TIME: 22 minutes. It will take about **11 minutes** to release your tension. In the second cycle of **11 minutes**, all your intuitional capacities will be aroused.

COMMENTS

This meditation develops a taste for the experience of expanded awareness. It creates sensitivity and the ability to extend the aura out to link with the whole team energy. You will know what is happening to everyone at the same time, and sense where they are, and sense what they are about to do. This sensing includes those opposing you too. You will develop the ability to sense the energy flow in any situation.

This meditation was taught by Yogi Bhajan in Vancouver, B.C. to Canada's Olympic Swim team in 1973.

Meditation for a Stable Self

Originally taught by Yogi Bhajan in September 1979

Sit in an Easy Pose, with a light *jalandhar bandh*.

EYE POSITION: The eyelids are 1/10th open with the eyes focused at the Brow Point.

MUDRA: The hands and arms form a very precise mudra and posture, which is the same for both genders. Hold the right hand 4 to 6 inches (10-15 cm) in front of the body at the level of the throat. Curl the fingers into a fist. Extend the thumb straight up. Hold the left hand directly below the right fist. Curl the fingers of the left hand into a firm fist. Extend the thumb straight up. Adjust the position of the hand so the left thumb tip is about 2 inches from the base of the right fist and the thumbs are aligned with each other. If you do this correctly, the base of the *left* hand to the top of the *right* thumb will cover the space from the level of the diaphragm to the mouth. Hold the elbows so that the forearms are parallel to the ground.

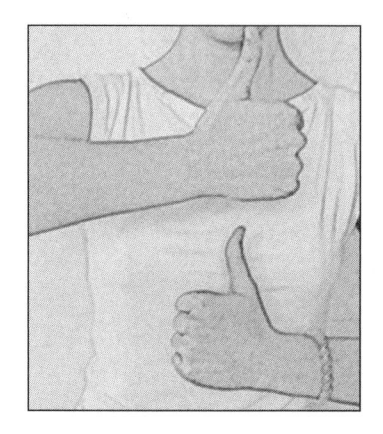

BREATH PATTERN & VISUALIZATION: Regulate the breath into this pattern: inhale deeply and quickly, then exhale immediately, powerfully, and completely. Lock the breath out. Suspend the chest and keep the neck locked. Keep the thumbs stiff and in perfect position. Hold the breath out for a rhythmical **count of 26**. With each count gently apply *mulbandh* and feel the Navel Point squeeze backwards. Visualize as you count: see and feel the energy and awareness going up the spine, vertebra by vertebra. The count of one is the first vertebra at the base of the spine, with the count 26 at the top of the spine into the center of the skull.

TIME: Continue for **3-11 minutes**. 11 minutes is the maximum time for this *kriya*.

COMMENTS:
This meditation is an advanced practice. It requires the student to hold a demanding posture without distraction. You overcome any concern about the body. Then the concentration must be held and the visualization of the energy perfected. It can be cultivated as a *sadhana* when you practice at least 120 days.

The main effect of the meditation is complete stability of the Pranic Body. This means an increase in the sense of self, increased good judgement, and elimination of "normal insanities." We often have conscious or subconscious fears, which make us jumpy and irregular in our judgement and in our trust of the inner self. This meditation removes the reactions to fears and makes you steady.

| Sets & Meditations | Meditations without Mantra |

Nadi Cleansing

Originally taught by Yogi Bhajan in 1969.

Sit in Easy Pose or Lotus Pose with a straight spine. When practicing this *pranayam*, be sure you have an empty stomach or have eaten very lightly.

EYE POSITION: Fix the eyelids 1/10th open and gently roll the eyes upward slightly to enhance your mental focus. Concentrate through the Brow Point. Relax the eyelids so they do not flutter.

MUDRA: Use the right hand to regulate the flow of breath through the nostrils. Block the right nostril with the thumb tip and the left nostril with the index finger. The index and thumb form the "U." This is sometimes referred to as "U-Breathing,"

BREATH PATTERN: The ratio for the length of breathing is **1 (inhale): 4 (hold): 2 (exhale)**. Create the following breathing pattern:

> *Inhale* through the left nostril. **(1)**
> *Hold* the breath in. **(4)**
> *Exhale* through the right nostril. **(2)**
>
> *Inhale* through the right nostril. **(1)**
> *Hold* the breath in. **(4)**
> *Exhale* through the left nostril. **(2)**

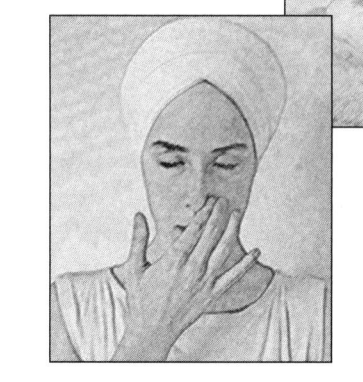

MANTRA: This breath can be done without mantra. But rather than just counting the rhythm or the sound of the breath, mantra helps to maintain the rhythm and adds subtle benefits. You can use the Bij Mantra, *Sat Naam* or the Gur Mantra, *Wha-hay Guroo*. For example, on the inhale, repeat *Sat Naam* **8 times**. Hold as you vibrate, *Sat Naam* **32 times**. Then as you exhale, repeat *Sat Naam* **16 times**. Or you can use *SA TA NA MA*, inhaling to **1 cycle**, holding for **4 cycles**, exhaling for **2 cycles**.

VISUALIZATION: In addition to the breath ratio and the mantra, you can visualize the path of *prana*. Inhale and visualize light flowing down the side of the spine to the base of the spine, on the same side as the breath-in nostril. As you hold the breath in, feel and see the light swirling and growing, with increasing heat, in a cauldron at the base of the spine under the Navel Point. As you exhale, see the light travel up the other side of the spine and out the nostril to the Infinite.

TIME: Continue for **15-62 minutes**.

TO END: Sit in a deep meditation for a **few minutes**.

COMMENTS

This technique was given by Yogi Bhajan in an intensive training in 1969. It is a classical technique, which is referred to in the *Gheranda Samhita* as a "perfect cleanser." Yogi Bhajan explained that this is a purifying practice which, if done as a regular *sadhana*, "burns the karmas" of many lives. The karmas are coded in the structure of the aura, the flow patterns of the subtle *nadis*, and in the deep structure of the mental body. This breath creates a powerful neutral balance of *prana* and *apana* in the system and encourages the flow of kundalini into the central channel of the spine, the *sushmuna*. Every serious student should spend some time perfecting the benefits of this *kriya*.

Pranayam Energizer Series

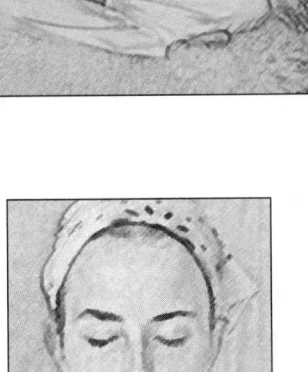

Originally taught by Yogi Bhajan in October 1969

1) **Breath of Fire.** Sit in Easy Pose, with the hands in Gyan Mudra, resting on the knees with the elbows straight. Begin Breath of Fire for **7 minutes**. Then inhale deeply, and hold the breath for **10-30 seconds**. You may apply *mulbandh* as you hold the breath out. This is optional. Exhale and relax.

2) **Long Deep Breathing.** In the same pose, breathe in long, complete, yogic breaths. Breathe deeper than normal so that the entire rib cage is used and lifts several inches on the inhale. Exhale so you pull the Navel Point all the way back. Consciously follow each part of the breath. Continue for **5 minutes**. Then inhale, and hold for **10-15 seconds**. Exhale and relax.

3) Pucker the lips and immediately inhale deeply through them. Exhale through the nose. Continue for **3 minutes**. Then inhale, hold briefly, exhale.

4) **Breath of Fire.** Repeat exercise 1. Make the breath powerful and regular for **2 minutes**. Then inhale deeply and hold, as you focus at the Brow Point. Exhale and relax.

5) **Breath Awareness.** Meditate on the flow of breath as you relax and it settles into a normal rhythm. Feel the subtle pathways of the breath throughout the body. Sense the breath as motion and experience the different kinds of energy flow in every organ and cell.

Sets & Meditations — Meditations without Mantra

Perspective & Emotional Balance
Alternate Nostril Breathing

Originally taught by Yogi Bhajan in 1969

Sit in an Easy Pose, with a light *jalandhar bandh*.

EYES: Eyes are closed, pressed gently up, focusing at the Brow Point.

MUDRA: Use the right thumb and right Mercury finger (pinkie) to close off alternate nostrils.

BREATH PATTERN: Close off the right nostril with the right thumb. Inhale deeply through the left nostril. When the breath is full, close off the left nostril with the Mercury finger (the little finger), and exhale smoothly through the right nostril. The breath is complete, continuous, and smooth. An alternative method of closing off the nostrils is using the thumb and index finger.

MANTRA: Although this can be done without mantra, you can mentally use the Bij Mantra, *Sat Naam*, to help the concentration. Inhale *Sat*, exhale *Naam*.

TIME: Continue with long, deep regular breaths for **3-31 minutes**.

TO END: Inhale, exhale completely, hold the breath out and apply *mulbandh*. Relax completely.

COMMENTS

This is a basic technique in Kundalini Yoga and Hatha Yoga. Every Kundalini Yogi should master this practice. It is excellent to do before bed to let go of the worries of the day.

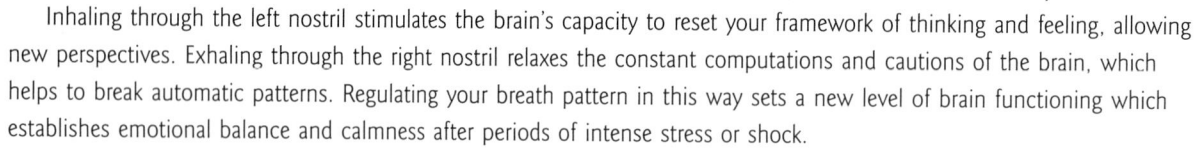

Inhaling through the left nostril stimulates the brain's capacity to reset your framework of thinking and feeling, allowing new perspectives. Exhaling through the right nostril relaxes the constant computations and cautions of the brain, which helps to break automatic patterns. Regulating your breath pattern in this way sets a new level of brain functioning which establishes emotional balance and calmness after periods of intense stress or shock.

The times for practice vary with purpose, skill level, and context:
- **3 minutes** is used if this exercise is added to a set.
- **10 minutes** as a start, if practiced alone.
- **15 minutes** will turn this exercise into a deep meditation.
- **22 minutes** trains the mind to use the state created by this breath as a resource.
- **31 minutes** will cleanse the body and restore the nervous system from the effects of current and past shocks.

Sitali Pranayam

Originally taught in July 1975

Sit in an Easy Pose, with a light *jalandhar bandh*.

Roll the tongue into a "U," with the tip just outside of the lips.

BREATH PATTERN: Inhale deeply through the rolled tongue, exhale through the nose.

TIME: Continue **3 minutes**. Alternatively, you can practice this **26 times** in the morning and **26 times** in the evening. **108 repetitions** is a deep meditation and a powerful healer for the body and digestive system.

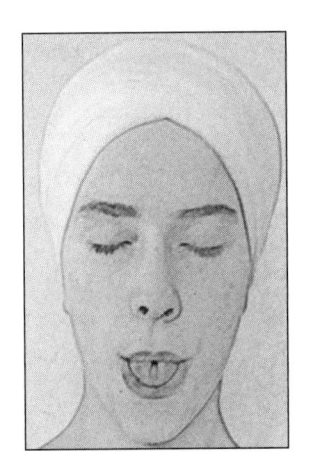

COMMENTS:
This *pranayam* gives power, strength, and vitality. It can have a cooling, cleansing effect. Initially, the tongue tastes bitter, and will eventually become sweet.

Tattva Balance Beyond Stress & Duality

Originally taught by Yogi Bhajan in March 1979

Sit in an Easy Pose, with a light *jalandhar bandh*.

MUDRA: Raise the arms with the elbows bent until the hands meet at the level of the heart in front of the chest. The forearms make a straight line parallel to the ground. Spread the fingers of both hands. Touch the fingertips and thumb tips of opposite hands together. Create enough pressure to join the first segments of each finger. The thumbs are stretched back and point toward the torso. The fingers are bent slightly due to the pressure. The palms are separated.

EYE POSITION: Fix your eyes at the tip of the nose.

BREATH: Create the following breathing pattern:
  Inhale smoothly and deeply through the nose.
  Exhale through the rounded lips in **8 equal emphatic strokes**.
  On each **exhale**, pull the Navel Point in sharply.

TIME: Continue for **3 minutes**. Build the practice slowly to **11 minutes**. Practicing longer is only for the dedicated and serious student.

TO END: Inhale deeply, hold for **10-30 seconds**, and exhale. Inhale again and shake the hands. Relax.

COMMENTS

The five elements are categories of quality that are based in the energetic flow of your life force. If all the elements are strong, in balance, and located in their proper areas of the body, then you can resist stress, trauma, and illness. You also do not get confused in conflicts between the two hemispheres of the brain as they compete for the right to make and direct decisions.

This meditation uses the hand mudra to pressure the 10 points in the fingers that correlate to the zones of the brain in the two hemispheres. The equal pressure causes a kind of communication and coordination between the two sides. The deep inhale gives endurance and calmness. The exhale through the mouth strengthens the parasympathetic nervous system from a control band of reflexes in the ring of the throat. This calms reaction to stress. The strokes of the exhale stimulate the pituitary gland to optimize your clarity, intuition, and decision-making capacities. This meditation resolves many inner conflicts, especially when the conflicts arise from the competition between different levels of your functioning, e.g. spiritual vs. mental vs. physical or survival needs.

Tratakum Meditation

Gazing at a Candle

The use of Tratakum to increase concentration ability is well known. One of the traditional practices for this is to gaze at a candle. To do this properly, select a quiet environment. Sit like a perfect yogi, and cover yourself with a meditation shawl or blanket so your spine does not get cold during the energy changes.

Position a candle about **7 feet away**. The flame should be at the height of the root of the nose. Focus your eyes on the flame and see the corona of light around the flame. See the area just under the hottest tip of the flame where there is a dark spot; light and dark co-exist at this point.

Meditate at the Brow Point with fixed concentration. This will stimulate the frontal lobes of the brain. When looking at the flame, you should see the flame and its light without hallucination. Some people start this practice and try to use the tricks of the eye to see movies in the flame. You should have the capacity to simply see what is and the radiance of what is.

TIME: Meditate on that radiance for at least **31 minutes** with as little blinking as possible.

TO END: Inhale deeply, close the eyelids, and put the image of the radiant light at the Third Eye Point.

Panther Pose

Sit on the heels with the spine straight. Fix the eyes at a point on the horizon (indoors or out), and open them as wide as possible. Raise the arms so the elbows are at a 90° angle. Spread the fingers of the hands wide and arch them like claws.

Begin long deep powerful breaths concentrating on the breath and *pranic* flow through the eyes.

TIME: Continue for **3 minutes.**

TO END: Inhale deep, close the eyes, and meditate on the flow of energy for **20 to 30 seconds**.

Fixate on the Horizon

Sit on the heels with the spine straight. Lean back to a 60° angle from the ground. Raise the arms parallel to the ground, palms facing down. Fix the eyes open at a distant point on the horizon.

Let the breath be slow, long, and deep.

TIME: Continue for between **3 and 31 minutes**.

TO END: Inhale, exhale, and relax.

This exercise develops the pranic energy of the eyes, helps digestion and nerves, and gives you personality control.

Leaning Back & Gazing up

Sit with the legs extending straight. Lean back to 60°. Place the palms on the ground in back as a support, let the head drop back, and pick a point on which to fix the gaze. Begin Breath of Fire.

TIME: Continue for **3 minutes.**

TO END: Inhale, straighten the neck, exhale, and relax.

This is particularly good for cataracts and cloudy vision.

Tratakum Meditation

Guru Yoga

In the yogic scriptures it says, "Even a glance from the eyes of a holy man can cure mental and physical imbalances."

If you identify a new quality in an object of meditation, you have contacted and brought out that quality in yourself. For these reasons, pictures of saints and objects of inspiration have always been subjects of meditation. If you pick a saintly person and meditate to experience his qualities of humility, service, and healing, you learn to express these qualities in yourself. But there is a level beyond this. Not all pictures have the same effect, even if the pictures are of the same person. One picture may show happiness, another sadness, and another contemplation. Meditation on each will provoke those qualities. It is extremely rare for any master to give a photo that shows neutrality and a direct stare from the eyes, which is the only type of picture suitable for Tratakum.

Yogi Bhajan says: "People will enjoy beaming who have meditated on that picture of mine. Not all pictures do something. However weird that particular picture is—sometimes you don't like it—that's the only picture that works. All other pictures can do nothing. That's the only one. What should I do? Some people complain to me, 'Yogiji, your other pictures are more beautiful.' But I say, 'I can't help it. Sometimes non-beautiful things are required, too.'"

In such a photo it is impossible to get stuck on the level of personality. In fact, since it is neutral, the photo will be both impersonal and personal. It will reflect you better than a mirror. In a mirror you can fool yourself with your own face. In the Guru Yoga photo you cannot. In such a photo there must also be a light in the eyes of the teacher. A photo with the direct stare of neutrality can heal and give you the instant ability to contact your own higher guidance.

Teachers are connected by the Golden Chain. You tune into a teacher, he connects with his teacher, who connects with his, and so on until you are linked directly to Infinity. Guru Yoga allows you to ascend the Golden Chain. It is an action done with humility.

We are fortunate to have such a picture of the Mahan Tantric. If it is meditated on properly and seriously, the karmas can be erased and individual destiny expanded. *(A copy of the photo appears on the following page. However, a high quality, glossy 8.5 x 11 print of this photo can be ordered from Ancient Healing Ways.)*

> *Teachers are connected by the Golden Chain. You tune into a teacher, he connects with his teacher, who connects with his, and so on until you are linked directly to Infinity. Guru Yoga allows you to ascend the Golden Chain. It is an action done with humility.*

HOW TO DO IT:

Set the photo about **3-6 feet** (30-60 cm) away. (This meditation picture is best prepared with a colored background. Although there are specific colors which can be used on given days of the week and for their different effects, the color orange is recommended for regular use.)

Set one or two candles in front of the picture so that it can be clearly seen. The rest of the room should be dark.

Sit very straight in an easy meditative posture, and cover your head and body with a shawl or blanket. Sit on a sheepskin or wool blanket to insulate your auric field.

Tune in with the Adi Mantra, humble yourself and tell your mind that the higher Self will guide you across the ocean of individuality, into the peace of the Cosmic Self. Know that you will receive guidance in all matters.

Open the eyes wide, and look eye into eye at the picture. Draw up the lower eyelid slightly. You will feel like you do not need to blink anymore. Completely still the body. The breath will automatically become lighter and lighter. Look at the light in the eyes of the photo and travel mentally through the picture to the source of that light.

TIME: Meditate from **15 minutes up to 4 hours**. A good time is **31 minutes**. You will feel like floating out of the body. Many body changes will occur. Just remember to keep your gaze on the light of guidance in the eyes.

TO END: Close your eyes and picture that face at the Brow Point.

COMMENTS

Nothing else has the value of this meditation. It is a must for any student/teacher of Kundalini Yoga as taught by Yogi Bhajan to have an experience of this. The practice is called "mental beaming." It gives the mind the ability to project to Infinity through the creative power of the imagination.

During the meditation, the picture may begin to move and look three dimensional. Mentally ask a question and listen to the answer.

Try this practice for 40 days in the early morning before sunrise and see what effect it has on you. During this time, eat lightly, and see with new sight during the day. If you like, the *panj shabd* **SA TA NA MA** can be chanted mentally while doing the Tratakum.

Meditations without Mantra

Sets & Meditations
Tratakum Meditation

CHAPTER 3
Meditations with Mantra

Antar Naad Mudra	86
Saa Ray Saa Saa, Saa Ray Saa Saa, Saa Ray Saa Saa Saa Rang	
Har Ray Har Har, Har Ray Har Har, Har Ray Har Har Har Rang	
Adi Mantra for Individual Meditation (Complete)	87
Ong Namo Guroo Dayv Namo Guroo Dayv Namo Guroo Dayvaa	
Awakening the Inner Healer	89
Sushmuna Meditation • Ida Meditation • Pingala Meditation	
Blue Gap Meditation	91
Divine Shield Meditation for Protection & Positivity *Maaaa*	92
Grace of God Meditation	93
I Am the Grace of God	
Ganpati Kriya Meditation I	94
Saa Taa Naa Maa Raa Maa Daa Saa Saa Say So Hang	
Healing Ring of Tantra *Sat Naam, Wha-hay Guroo*	95
Healing with the Siri Gaitri Mantra	96
Raa Maa Daa Saa Saa Say So Hang	
"I am Happy" Meditation for Children	97
I am happy, I am good, Sat Naam ji, Whaa-hay Guroo ji	
Indra Nittri Meditation with the Siri Mantra	98
Ek Ong Kaar Sat Gur Parsaad Sat Gur Parsaad Ek Ong Kaar	
Kirtan Kriya	99
Panj Shabd: Saa Taa Naa Maa	
Laya Yoga Kundalini Mantra	101
Ek Ong Kaar-(uh) Sat Naam-(uh) Siree Whaa-hay Guroo	
Learning to Meditate	102
Bij Mantra: Sat Naam	
Long Chant (Adi Shakti Mantra, or Morning Call)	103
Ek Ong Kaar Sat Naam Siree Whaa-hay Guroo	
Mahan Jaap (Linked Jaap)	104
Panj Shabd: Saa Taa Naa Maa	
Mala Meditation	105
Master's Touch Meditation	106
Aad Such, Jugaad Such, Hai Bhee Such, Naanak Hosee Bhee Such	
Meditation Into Being *I Am, I Am*	107
Meditation on the Divine Mother	108
Kundalini Bhakti Mantra: Aadee Shakti Namo Namo	

Meditation for Healing Addictions	109
Panj Shabd: Saa-Taa-Naa-Maa	
Meditation to Open the Heart *Sat Kartaar*	110
Ek Ong Kaar Sat Gur Parsaad Sat Gur Parsaad Ek Ong Kaar	
Meditation for Projection & Protection from the Heart	111
Mangala Charn Mantra: Aad Guray Nameh	
Meditation for Prosperity I	112
Har Haray Haree Whaa-hay Guroo	
Meditation for Prosperity II	113
Har	
Meditation for Self-Assessment	114
Meditation for Self-Blessing: Guidance by Intuition	115
Panj Shabd: Saa-Taa-Naa-Maa	
Meditation for Stress or Sudden Shock	116
Sat Naam, Sat Naam, Sat Naam, Sat Naam,	
Sat Naam, Sat Naam, Whaa-hay Guroo	
Naad Meditation to Communicate from Totality	117
Whaa Whaa Hay Hay Guroo	
Naad Meditation to Communicate Your Honest Self	118
Saa Ray	
Naad Meditation: Naam Namodam Rasa	119
Aah Ooh Umm	
Parasympathetic Rejuvenation Meditation with the Gong	120
Pran Bandha Mantra Meditation	121
Pavan Pavan Pavan Pavan, Par Paraa, Pavan Guroo	
Pavan Guroo Whaa-hay Guroo, Whaa-hay Guroo Pavan Guroo	
Rejuvenation Meditation	122
Panj Shabd: Saa-Taa-Naa-Maa	
Seven-Wave "Sat Nam" Meditation	123
Sodarshan Chakra Kriya	124
Whaa-hay Guroo	
Tershula Kriya	125
Har Har Whaa-hay Guroo	
Venus Kriyas	126

Sets & Meditations
Meditations with Mantra

Antar Naad Mudra (also called Kabadshe Meditation)

Sit in an Easy Pose, with a light *jalandhar bandh*.

MUDRA: Keep the spine straight. Let the arms extend straight and rest over the knees. Make *Buddhi Mudra* with both hands (touch the thumb tips to the tips of the little fingers). The other fingers are relaxed but straight. Become completely still, physically and mentally, like a calm ocean. If listening to the mantra on a tape, listen to the chant for a minute. Feel its rhythm in every cell. Then join in the mantra.

MANTRA:

SAA RAY SAA SAA, SAA RAY SAA SAA,
SAA RAY SAA SAA, SAA RANG
HAR RAY HAR HAR, HAR RAY HAR HAR,
HAR RAY HAR HAR, HAR RANG

TIME: Continue for 11-31 minutes.

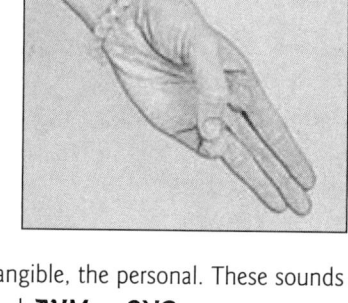

COMMENTS

Antar Naad Mudra is the meditation that opens the chakras for the full effect of any other mantra. It is a sensitizing meditation for the impact of the inner sound current. It is the base of all mantras. The original practice of mastery in mantra required that you master this before any other mantra practice.

The esoteric structure of the mantra is coded in the qualities each of the sounds represent, and the rhythm that weaves them together into a coherent and powerful effect. **SAA** means the Infinite, the totality, God. It is the element of ether. It initiates and contains all other effects. It is subtle and beyond. **HAR** is the creativity of the earth. It is the dense element. It is the power of manifestation, the tangible, the personal. These sounds are woven together then projected through the sound of **ANG** or complete totality, like the original sound **AUM** or **ONG**.

Anyone who practices this meditation is granted prosperity, creativity, and protection against attacks. It gives new power to your words. It brings luck even if you are a scoundrel.

Antar Naad Mudra as a Full Moon Meditation

(*Originally taught in 1993.*)

Put the hands flat together in Prayer Pose at the Navel Point. As the mantra starts with **SA RE SA SA** start to bring the palms up the center front of the torso, about 4-6 inches in front of the body. As you pass the Heart Center, begin to open the hand mudra to make an open lotus, by the time it reaches the level of the Brow Point. The open lotus has the base of the palms together, the little fingertips touch, the thumb tips touch, and the rest of the fingers are spread open.

As the mantra begins **HAR RE HAR HAR** turn the fingers to point down, with the back of the hands touching—it is a reverse Prayer Pose. Slowly bring this mudra down the chakras in rhythm with the music until the fingertips reach the Navel Point on the sounds **HA RANG**. Then turn them around and begin again.

COMMENTS

This cycle of the music and mudra is a key to opening the flow of Kundalini. The new awareness will give you the authority to make the right choices to conquer the ugliness of life. You will be peaceful and secure.

The Complete Adi Mantra for Individual Meditation

Sit in an Easy Pose, with a light *jalandhar bandh*.

EYE POSITION: Focus your eyes on the tip of the nose.

MUDRA: Bring both palms in front of the Heart Center facing upward. Touch the sides of the palms along the little fingers and sides of the hands, as if you will receive something in them. Form Gyan Mudra in each hand.

BREATH PATTERN & MANTRA: Chant the entire mantra **3-5 times** on one breath. Keep the number of repetitions per breath constant. The sound **DAYV** is chanted a minor third higher than the other sounds. The sound of **DAYVAA** carries slightly on the **AA** sound.

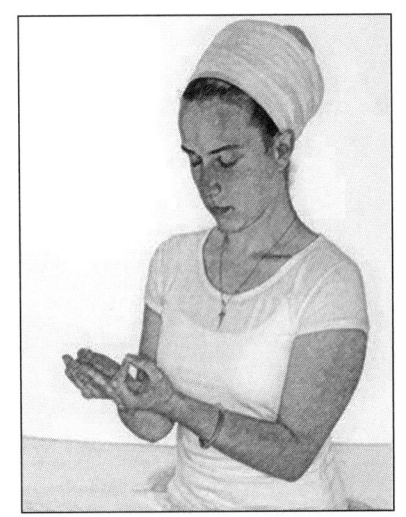

ONG NAMO, GUROO DAYV NAMO, GUROO DAYV NAMO, GUROO DAYVAA

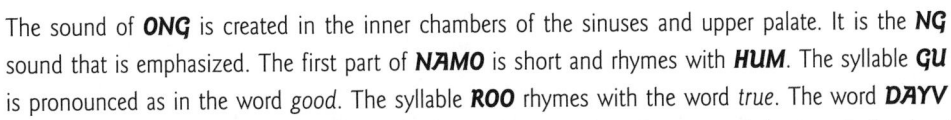

The sound of **ONG** is created in the inner chambers of the sinuses and upper palate. It is the **NG** sound that is emphasized. The first part of **NAMO** is short and rhymes with **HUM**. The syllable **GU** is pronounced as in the word *good*. The syllable **ROO** rhymes with the word *true*. The word **DAYV** rhymes with *save*. The **AA** in **DAYVAA** is chanted with the mouth open and the sound vibrating from an open throat.

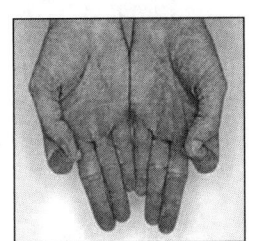

TIME: Continue for **11-31 minutes** for a powerful meditation and guidance. Yogi Bhajan did not restrict longer periods of practice.

COMMENTS

To center before a set of Kundalini Yoga we chant the Adi Mantra, *Ong Namo Guru Dev Namo*, three to five times. Adi means the first or primal; mantra is the creative projection of the mind through sound. This mantra is the first creative action. It centers you into the Higher Self and reminds your lower mind that it is not your ego that will practice or teach Kundalini Yoga. Technically, it links you into the Golden Chain. The Golden Chain is the inner spark of kundalini that is passed from person to person; teacher to student; guru to teacher; cosmos and God to Guru. By chanting this mantra and linking to the Golden Chain, the exercises and meditations that you practice are guided by your higher consciousness and all the teachers that have brought this opportunity to you. It makes you very receptive and sensitive to the message of your body, mind, and intuition. It is used as a link when you teach and as preparation for your personal practice. However, it is not an individual mantra, complete in itself. It is a hook that creates a flow, which you serve. If you need an individual, spiritual link and source of guidance, then there is another form to use: the Complete Adi Mantra.

The complete individual form of the mantra immerses you in awareness and guidance for your personal situation. It establishes a guiding beam between you in your immediate state, and your higher consciousness, that is true through all states. It is very useful if you are entering Shakti Pad in Kundalini Yoga. It is also excellent as a means to gain perspective and direction.

(Continued next page)

The Complete Adi Mantra for Individual Meditation

**ONG NAMO, GUROO DAYV NAMO,
GUROO DAYV NAMO, GUROO DAYVAA**

Yogi Bhajan explained this when he said, "Use this mantra in its complete form anytime you have a lack of faith or any similar thing. Many of you will enter Shakti Pad, or you are in it, this mantra will help. With the grace of Guru Ram Das, when this mantra is chanted five times on one breath, the total spiritual knowledge of all teachers who have ever existed or who will ever exist on this Earth, is beseated in that person."

ONG is the creative energy of the total cosmos and consciousness of the Creator as experienced in this Creation. It has the connotation of energy and activity. It creates involvement without attachment. It generates shakti, the generative force of life. Note that the sound is not **OM**. That sound is for withdrawal and relaxation. **NAMO** means to bow to or to call on. The connotation is one of respect and receptivity. It is the type of bowing that grants dignity through acknowledging a higher consciousness and discipline.

ONG NAMO calls on your consciousness to become subtle and receptive to its own higher resources. It instructs the conscious and the subconscious to let go of the normal restrictions imposed by the limited ego. **GUROO** means wisdom or teacher. It does not mean a personality. Rather, it means the source of the knowledge; not just any knowledge, but the kind of knowledge that transforms you, that alleviates pain, and that increases your awareness. **GUROO** in the spiritual context is the embodiment of the Infinite. The word can be broken into parts: **GU** means darkness or ignorance; **ROO** means light or knowledge; **GUR** means a formula to systematically attain a goal; so a **GUROO** is something which can give you a **GUR** to transform your **GU** to **ROO**!

DAYV means subtle, etheric, divine or belonging to the realms of God. It implies sophistication and wisdom. **GUROO DAYV NAMO** calls on the subtle wisdom that guides you in an impersonally personal manner. It is a wisdom that is stored and transmitted through the subtle and radiant bodies of the aura. It is the realm and guidance of Guru Ram Das.

If the limited individual ego in which we normally live is a small pond, then **ONG NAMO** releases us into a vast and endless ocean. **GUROO DAYV NAMO** gives us the experience of the wisest seaman and all of his charts to guide us to the many ports we are to serve and experience.

Awakening the Inner Healer
Healing Sadhana to Initiate the Healing Zone in You

Originally taught by Yogi Bhajan in November 1985.

The Healing Zone exists everywhere and in all of us. It is reached by refinement of your spiritual channels of energy in the subtle body. This practice is a most sacred knowledge. When the kundalini energy awakens it is called *Shabd Brahm*—the voice of God. It empowers your Word to create in the worlds. During the 10 days, eat a "Tantric Diet." *(See Yogic Diet chapter for recipes.)*

10 DAYS TO INITIATE YOUR HEALING FLOW

DAY 1: Do the **Sushmuna Meditation**

DAY 2: Do the **Ida Meditation**

DAY 3: Do the **Pingala Meditation**

For the remaining **7 days**, chant for **1-1/2 hours** in an ascending scale:

**SAA RAY GAA MAA PAA DAA NEE SAA TAA NAA MAA
RAA MAA DAA SAA SAA SAY SO HANG**

Start at 3 am on the fourth day. Drink nothing but Yogi Tea minus the honey for 20 hours, until 11 pm. From, 11 pm-12:30 am, chant. On the fifth through the 10th days, you can chant any time of the day. An ideal refinement would be to start the next day's chanting where you ended the last: 12:30 am, 2 am, 3:30 am, 5 am, 6:30 am, and 8 am. In this way, you go through and cleanse the zones of the unconscious.

DAY ONE: Sushmuna Meditation

1) Sit in Easy Pose with the spine straight, chin in, and chest out. Form your mouth into a "Leo smile," the lips are pulled wide so that the teeth show. The front teeth are on top of the lower teeth, with a little space in between. Breathe a rapid cannon breath in and out through the teeth. The power of the breath comes from the Navel Point. **5-11 minutes**.

2) Open arms up, 60-degrees, palms up. Visualize a body of water that is wider than the ocean, so vast the horizon is not visible. It is Infinity itself. Feel you are ready to jump in. It is in this space of "just about to" that the power lies. Breathe slowly. **3 minutes**. Comment: In this posture with this perfect mental state, you can transmute your sexual and sensual energy into a very great clarity and purity.

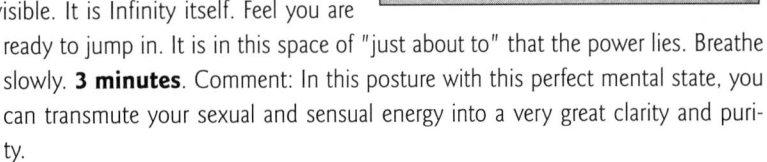

3) Mentally leap into that water keeping the arms up. Go deeper and deeper to touch the bottom with tons of water over you. Penetrate the water inch by inch and mile by mile. **1 minute**.

TO END: Inhale, hold the breath, relax your body and let it float to the top. Give your body the lightness of breath; as the breath is getting shorter, you will come up faster. When you see your head breaking the surface of the water, exhale and relax. Maximum time: **1 minute**.

COMMENTS: Within 2-1/2 hours after you do this set, you will experience the

Awakening the Inner Healer

special energy it produces.

DAY TWO: Ida Meditation

1) Sit in Easy Pose. Extend the left arm up and out to the side at a 45 angle. Relax the hand and fingers and drop the hand at the wrist. Pump the right hand out to the side, parallel to the ground, with the palm forward; then onto the Heart Center, with the palm toward the chest. Use a cannon breath through the rounded mouth, in and out in equal ratio. The breath should come all the way up from the First Chakra. Breathe powerfully. **5-11 minutes.**

2) Bring the hands together at the center of the chest and open them into a lotus. Meditate at the brow on an imaginary screen and see the words

HAR HAR WHAA-HAY GUROO

written as you repeat them mentally. **3 minutes**. Then, focus on the lotus of the hands. Imagine a beautiful woman bedecked with flowers and fine scents. In the ancient tradition it was Lakshmi, the Goddess of Wealth and Prosperity, with two white elephants placing garlands on her, strewing rose petals and spraying nectar water. Be filled with joy. **3 minutes**. Now, combine both images at once. **3 minutes**. Finally, meditate on a beam of pure light projecting from the Brow Point. Listen to the gong and project light with each stroke. **7 minutes**.

3) Repeat exercise 1 for **1-3 minutes**.

4) Put your hands into Prayer Mudra at your Heart Center and meditate there. Concentrate on the palms of your hands and neutralize your energy. Listen to *Naad, the Blessing* by Sangeet Kaur. **4 minutes**.

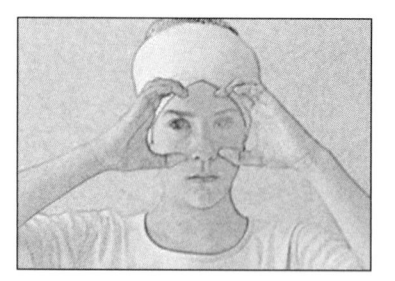

DAY THREE: Pingala Meditation

1) Sit in Easy Pose. Make the hands like a viewer, (look straight ahead through the thumbs and palms) in front of the face. Alternately extend one hand **18 inches**. Do Breath of Fire powerfully, from the navel. Move fast. Rhythmically combine the hand movement, the Breath of Fire, and pumping your navel. Close the eyes for the last 15-20 seconds. **7-11 minutes.**

2) Inhale, extend the arms out to the sides and imagine you are a great eagle, flying in any flight pattern you choose. Breathe slowly and deeply. Go through the heavens. **5-11 minutes**.

3) Inhale deeply and spread your wings as far as you can. Concentrate on the power at the tips of your fingers. Begin to flap the arms up and down quickly as you exhale and inhale powerfully with a hissing breath through the teeth. **2-3 minutes**.

4) Inhale deeply, hold the breath, pull in the navel tightly for **16 counts**, then exhale. Repeat this last breath **2 more times**. Relax, open your eyes. Sing along with some lively music for **5 minutes**.

Blue Gap Meditation

Sit in an Easy Pose, with a light *jalandhar bandh*.

Part I
Make the hands into receptive Gyan Mudra (the index fingertips touch the tips of the thumbs and the other three fingers touch the base of the palms.) The hands are on the knees and the arms are straight.

EYE POSITION: Close the eyes and focus at the Tenth Gate—the fontanel, or soft spot on the top of the head. If you put your chin down into the cavity in the middle of the collarbone, it will give you the power to sense the breath.

MANTRA: Mentally vibrate the sounds:

SAA TAA NAA MAA

Inhale deeply with **SAA**, hold it with **TAA**, exhale with **NAA** and hold it out with **MAA**. Continue in an unbroken moderate to slow rhythm. On the sound **SAA**, the mental concentration should travel to the tip of the nose; on the sound **TAA**, it should rest at the top of the head. On the sound **NAA,** the mental concentration should go out of the top of the head and on the sound **MAA,** it should be totally projected out to Infinity.

TIME: 11-31 minutes.

Part II
Follow Part I by creating a vibratory effect with the following eight rhythmic sounds. Chant aloud, continuously, and at a rhythmic and rapid rate:

SAT NAAM, SAT NAAM, SAT NAAM, SAT NAAM, SAT NAAM, SAT NAAM, WHAA-HAY GUROO

TIME: 11-31 minutes. (In proportion to how long Part I was done).

COMMENTS
You can alter the functional part of the brain with this meditation any time you choose. You'll have this experience when you do the first meditation. Then when you do the eight-rhythm mantra, the energy will start flowing towards your head. You should be able to feel the flow of that energy.

"In our human relativity, in our sensitivity, our mental projection and our mental activity, there's going to be a great change. It is very essential for the human race to be watchful, to be creative and to be equipped with a positive channelizing method for mental energy. There will be new changes and new trends in the human race. It's a fundamental, basic change which is happening. So for certain people like you who are now in your twenties and thirties, in twenty or thirty years when you'll be in your fifties and sixties, it will almost certainly be a very lonely period, because it will be impossible for you to relate to the little ones. There'll be a gap. You will not understand them. About 900 B.C. the humanity had the same problem. It is called the Blue Gap and you will experience it on this Earth again within one hundred years.

"That shall be the coming race, because the sensitivity in man's own self is going to increase, and the mental mind projection is going to be very much activated, whereas the procedure to protect and channelize will be less known to people. If that happens, the net result will be what I have explained to you in a picture. A man is doing his work—he's working, and his pen stops. He'll be paid for those four days, but his pen shall be like this (suspended in midair), because he has projected out. Then he will return in, you see. I have taken you out into the future of the human race just for a couple of minutes. If your mind, your meditation and your sensitivity can be together, and your polarity of the male and female will be very systematic, and your union will create a projective self, which will manifest as your children, then you can be assured. There will be a sensitive race anyway, but that race will sense everything clear, calm and quiet. The potential human disaster has to be avoided. That's what we are talking about."

—YOGI BHAJAN (IN *A MAN CALLED THE SIRI SINGH SAHIB*)

The Divine Shield Meditation for Protection & Positivity

Originally taught by Yogi Bhajan in September, 1971

EYE POSITION: The eyes are closed and focused at the Brow Point.

MUDRA & SITTING POSITION: Raise the right knee up with the right foot flat on the ground, toes pointing straight ahead. Place the sole of the left foot against the arch and ankle of the right foot. The ball of the left foot rests just in front of the ankle bone of the right foot. Make a fist of the left hand and place it on the ground beside the hip. Use this to balance the posture. Bend the right elbow and place it on the top of the right knee. Bring the right hand back along the side of the head with the palm facing the ear. Form a shallow cup of the right palm. Then bring it against the skull so that it contacts the skull below the ear but stays open above the ear. It is as if you formed a cup of the hand to amplify a faint sound that you want to hear.

MANTRA: Inhale deeply and chant the mantra in a long, full, smooth sound. Project the sound as if someone is listening to you. As you chant, listen to the sound and let it vibrate through your whole body. If you chant in a group, hear the overtones that develop and let those tones vibrate all around you and in every cell of your body. The mantra is:

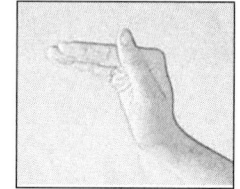

MAAAAAAAAAAAAAAAAAAA

Chant it at a comfortable high pitch. When you have exhaled completely, take another deep breath and continue. In a group you may all inhale at different times. The group sound will seem continuous.

TIME: Continue for **11-31 minutes**. Then change the legs and ear to the other side. Continue for an equal amount of time. Start slowly. Learn to hold the concentration into the sound. Build the meditation on each side to total 62 minutes.

COMMENTS

It is difficult to focus on your higher feelings and sensitivity if you feel fearful and unprotected. If the universe seems hostile, uncaring, and non-responsive it is easy to become filled with cynicism, despair, and hopelessness. In that depressed state it is impossible to sense the fullness and possibilities of life. It is very difficult to solve the very problems that upset you.

Those feelings occur when the aura that surrounds the body is weak and small. The human aura can extend out to nine feet in all directions. If it drops below four feet, we tend to become depressed. We cannot fight off negative thoughts from within or from the environment. If we can extend the aura, the outer arc of the aura acts as a filter and a connector to the universal magnetic field. It is that outer circumvent field that preserves the integrity of the aura, the furiously active blend of thoughts and feelings that emanate from our body and mind.

The aura can be temporarily expanded. One way is to connect your aura with the universal field by using an inner seed sound that activates the power of the Heart Center. The compassion of the universe uplifts and expands you. It provides a Divine Shield to accompany you through your trials and tribulations. This meditation does exactly that. If you make it a regular practice, you will become positive, fearless, and happy. Nothing will stop you as you pursue your goals. It will eliminate the feeling of loneliness and separation from your soul.

The sound of **MAAA** calls on compassion and protection. It is the sound that a baby uses to call on the mother. Here, your soul is the child, and the universe becomes the Mother. If you call, She will come to your aid and comfort. When this shield is strong, it is easy to sense the tide of the universe, the Tao. You become spontaneous and vital as you move in rhythm with the greater reality, of which you are a part.

When the shield is strong you are protected from the impact of your own past actions. You are like a great ship that turns toward God and reality and then must cross the waves of your own wake that you created by your past actions. The shield keeps you alert and awake to the real task of your life.

Meditations with Mantra   Sets & Meditations

Grace of God Meditation

Part I
Lie on the back, fully relaxing the face and body. The eyes are closed.

MANTRA:

I AM GRACE OF GOD
(If a man practices this, he says "I am IN the Grace of God.")

- **Inhale** deeply, hold the breath in while silently repeating **10 times**. You can tense your fingers one at a time to keep count
- **Exhale** all the air out, hold it out and repeat the mantra **10 times**.
- Continue this process of repeating the mantra **10 times** on each inhale and **10 times** on each exhale, for a total of **5 inhalations** and **5 exhalations**. This totals **100 silent repetitions**.

Part II
Relax your breath, and with eyes still closed, slowly come sitting up into Easy Pose. Bring the right hand into Gyan Mudra. The left hand is held up by the left shoulder, palm flat and facing forward, as if you are taking an oath. This is called the "vow" position. Keep the breath relaxed and normal. Tense only one finger of the left hand at a time, keeping the other fingers straight but relaxed. Meditate on the governing energy of each finger *(see table below)*, then repeat the mantra aloud **5 times**.

Continue this sequence for each of the remaining fingers, finishing with the thumb.

TO END: Relax and meditate silently for a few minutes.

COMMENTS
It is said that when a woman practices this meditation for one year, her aura will become tipped with gold or silver, and great strength and God's healing powers will flow through her.

The technique of positive affirmation has been around for thousands of years. It is nothing new. Words increase in power through repetition, and when you are repeating truth, the impact is enormous. Yogi Bhajan gave us this meditation, which is one of the most powerful affirmations a woman can do. The fact is, woman IS the Grace of God. Woman is shakti. The problem is, she doesn't know it.

This meditation is designed to evoke and manifest the inner grace, strength, and radiance of each woman. It helps her to tune in directly with the Adi Shakti, the Primal Power within her own being. It empowers a woman to channel her emotions in a positive direction, strengthen her weaknesses, develop mental clarity and effective communication, and gives her the patience to go through the tests of her own karma. It enables her to merge the limited ego into Divine Will, as well as to improve her physical health.

By practicing this meditation, a woman's thoughts, behavior, personality, and projection become aligned with the Infinite beauty and nobility unveiled by the mantra. It balances the five elements. The amazing thing is, this is such an easy meditation to do! You might pass it over because it is so simple, and not realize what a profound effect it can have on your life.

Practice it faithfully, **twice a day for 40 days**.

It is recommended for women going through menopause to practice it **5 times a day**.

Practice it on an empty stomach.

Little Finger	Mercury	power to relate & communicate, subconscious communication with self	WATER
Ring Finger	Sun & Venus	physical health, vitality, grace, and beauty	FIRE
Middle Finger	Saturn	channel emotion to devotion & patience	AIR
Index Finger	Jupiter	wisdom and expansion, open space for change	ETHER
Thumb		positive ego	EARTH

Sets & Meditations
Meditations with Mantra

Ganpati Kriya Meditation

Originally taught by Yogi Bhajan November 2, 1988

Sit in an Easy Pose, with a *light jalandhar bandh*.

EYE POSITION: The eyes are 1/10th open. Concentrate at the Third Eye Point.

MUDRA: Place the wrists over the knees, hands in Gyan Mudra, with the arms and elbows straight.

MANTRA:

SAA-TAA-NAA-MAA
RAA-MAA-DAA-SAA
SAA-SAY-SO-HANG

Part I
Chant the mantra on a single breath, as you press the fingertips sequentially with each syllable. Use a monotone voice in the Tibetan form or use the same melody you would use for Kirtan Kriya.

MUSIC: Gong was played throughout Part 1 of the meditation.

TIME: Continue for **11-62 minutes**.

Part II
Inhale deeply and hold the breath. Move the body, twist and stretch. Move each muscle of the body. Move the head, torso, arms, back, belly and hands. Then exhale powerfully. Repeat this **3-5 times**.

Part III
Immediately sit straight. Look at the Lotus Point, the tip of the nose. Become totally calm, absolutely still. Meditate for **2-3 minutes**.

COMMENTS
This beautiful and powerful meditation has a history in its name. The ancient symbol for this was the Hindu God of Knowledge and Happiness, Ganesha. The other name for Ganesha is *Gunpati*. Ganesha was depicted as a rotund man with the head of an elephant. This huge body balances and rides on a rat, conveying the message that even the impossible can be done with this meditation. The rat represents the quality of penetration. A rat can get in almost any place. So Ganesha can know anything and can get past any blockages. Wisdom and wise choices grant you happiness in your life.

The impact of this meditation is to clear the blocks from your own karma. Each of us has three regions of life to conquer: The past which is recorded in our *samskaras* and which brings us the challenges and blessings of fate are balanced by these sounds; the present which must be mastered by karma yoga, the practice of action with integrity in the moment; and the future, recorded in the ether and, which at its best and most fulfilled, is called dharma. This *kriya* allows you to let go of the attachments to the mind and to the impact of past actions so you can create and live a fulfilled life and a perfect future.

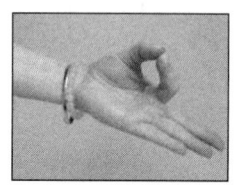

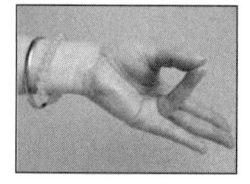

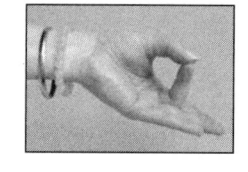

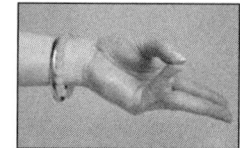

Healing Ring of Tantra

Eleven or more people sit in a circle, in any comfortable, cross-legged position. Form an unbroken circle by holding hands.*

EYE POSITION: The eyes are closed.

MANTRA: The mantra goes around the circle, with each person taking a turn to powerfully call out the mantra in a monotone, answered by all the members of the circle:

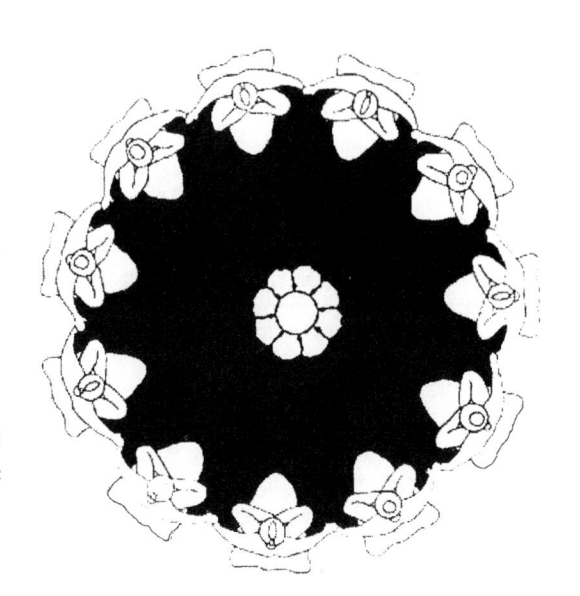

WHAA-HAY GUROO

WHAA and **HAY** each have **1 beat**, and **GUROO** has **2 beats**. The caller then says **SAT NAAM** softly, and the person sitting to the left of the caller becomes the next caller. The chant continues in a clockwise direction around the circle. Maintain a constant rhythm.

BREATH PATTERN: Inhale as the mantra is being chanted by a caller; exhale as you chant the mantra in response.

TIME: Practice for at least **11 minutes**, and not longer than **31 minutes**.

COMMENTS

The healing ring can be used to generate and direct tremendous healing energy towards any person: a member of the circle, someone at a far distance, or someone located in the center of the circle. The participants should focus their minds to listen, and let themselves be filled with the sound, acutely tuning into the call, and then answering.

SPIRAL FORMAT. Another way to do this meditation is with the participants seated in a spiral. Participants join hands, alternately facing in opposite directions. (The left hand of one person will hold the left hand of the person to their left; right hand to right hand of person to their right.) If there are people of both genders, the seating in the spiral should alternate between male and female. Same gender individuals can complete the outer tail of the spiral. The person seated in the center of the spiral, if possible, should be a woman. The person seated in the center and the one in the outermost position of the spiral should hold the palms of each of their free hands facing up, to connect with the Infinite.

The chanting begins with the person seated in the center, and proceeds to the next person in the spiral, until the outermost person chants. Then the chanting proceeds back to the center person.

Note: This meditation in either format is only to be done on the days of the Full Moon, New Moon, and eleventh day of the New Moon, with a minimum of eleven people. During the meditation, the ring must never be broken for any reason.

Sets & Meditations — Meditations with Mantra

Healing with the Siri Gaitri Mantra

Originally taught by Yogi Bhajan in Summer 1973.

Sit in an Easy Pose, with a light *jalandhar bandh*.

MUDRA: Have the elbows tucked comfortably against the ribs. Extend the forearms out at a 45-degree angle out from the center of the body. The palms are flat, facing up, the wrists pulled back, fingers together, thumbs spread. Consciously keep the palms flat during the meditation.

MANTRA: The mantra consists of eight basic sounds:

RAA   MAA   DAA   SAA,   SAA   SAY   SO   HANG

Pull in the Navel Point powerfully on the first **SAA** and **HANG**. Note that **HANG** is not long and drawn out. Clip it off forcefully as you pull in the navel. Chant one complete cycle of the entire mantra, and then inhale deeply and repeat. To chant this mantra properly, remember to move the mouth fully with each sound. Feel the resonance in the mouth and the sinus areas. Let your mind concentrate on the qualities that are evoked by the combination of sounds.

TIME: Chant powerfully for **11-31 minutes**.

TO END: Inhale deeply and hold the breath as you offer a healing prayer, visualizing the person you wish to heal (including yourself) as being totally healthy, radiant, and strong. Imagine the person completely engulfed in healing white light, completely healed. Then exhale and inhale deeply again, hold the breath and offer your prayer. Then, lift your arms up high and vigorously shake out your hands and fingers.

COMMENTS

Certain mantras are to be cherished like the most rare and beautiful gem. The Siri Gaitri Mantra (this is also a Siri Mantra and a *Sushmuna* Mantra) is just such a find. It is unique, and it captures the radiant healing energy of the Cosmos as a gem captures the light of the sun. Like a gem it can be put into many settings for different purposes and occasions. When Yogi Bhajan shared this technology he gave a series of meditations that use the inner dynamics of this mantra. If you master any of these practices you will be rewarded with healing and awareness.

The mantra is called a *Sushmuna* Mantra. It has eight sounds that stimulate the kundalini to flow in the central channel of the spine and in the chakras. As this happens there is usually a huge metabolic adjustment to the new level of energy in the body. The brain is also involved. The sounds balance the five zones of the left and right hemispheres of the brain to activate the Neutral Mind.

The mantra uses a sound current. The sounds create a juxtaposition of energies.

RAA means the energy of the Sun: strong, bright, and hot. It energizes and purifies.

MAA is the energy of the Moon. It is a quality of receptivity, coolness, and nurturing.

DAA is the energy of Earth. It is secure, personal, and the ground of action.

SAA is the impersonal Infinity. The cosmos in all of its open dimensions and totality is **SAA**. Then the mantra repeats the sound; this repetition is a turning point. The first part of the mantra is ascending and expands into the Infinite. The second part of the mantra pivots those qualities of the highest and most subtle ether, and brings them back down. It interweaves the ether with the earth! **SAA** is the impersonal Infinity. Then comes

SAY, which is the totality of experience and is personal. It is the feeling of a sacred "Thou." It is the embodiment of **SAA**.

SO is the personal sense of merger and Identity.

HANG is the Infinite, vibrating and real. The two qualities together (**SO** and **HANG**) mean, "I am Thou."

As you chant this mantra you complete a cycle of energy and go through a circuit of the chakras. You grow toward the Infinite, then you convert the linkage of finite and Infinite at **SAA**. Then you revert back to an embodiment and blend of purity.

"I am Happy" Meditation for Children

Sit in Easy Pose.

MANTRA: The mantra is:

*I AM HAPPY, I AM GOOD,
I AM HAPPY, I AM GOOD.*

*SAT NAAM SAT NAAM SAT NAAM JEE
WHAA-HAY GUROO WHAA-HAY GUROO
WHAA-HAY GUROO JEE*

MUDRA: In the rhythm of the mantra, the children shake their index fingers up and down (like their parents might sometimes do when they are reproaching the child).

COMMENTS

Yogi Bhajan gave this meditation specifically for children to use in times when their parents are fighting and going through a crisis—to give them the experience of remaining stable and unaffected. Of course, the meditation can be done anytime!

Children, especially under the age of six, have a much shorter attention span than adults. All meditations with movement and variation work well. They like simple celestial communication.

Indra Nittri Meditation

Sit in Easy Pose, with a light *jalandhar bandh*.

EYES: The eyes are closed or 1/10th open.

MUDRA: Grasp the knees firmly with the hands. Keep the chest and spine lightly lifted.

MANTRA: Meditate through the Brow Point on the movements of the tongue as you chant the *Siri Mantra* in a steady rhythm:

EK ONG KAAR, SAT GUR PARSAAD
SAT GUR PARSAAD, EK ONG KAAR

Pull the Navel Point in on **EK**.
Release the Navel Point on **KAAR**.
Lift the Diaphragm Lock with **SAT** and **GUR**.
Release the lock on the sound of **PARSAAD**.
This will create a wave-like motion of tension and relaxation in the torso. It will release great heat in the body.

TIME: Continue for **11-62 minutes**.

TO END: Inhale, hold the breath comfortably, and relax.

COMMENTS

This meditation was taught by Guru Nanak to his second son, Baba Siri Chand. His son became a great *baal* yogi. That is a yogi who does not age, who still looks like a young boy, even in his old age. It is said Baba Siri Chand lived over 160 years. He was acknowledged by all the schools of Siddhi Yoga to be a great yogi. Under his guidance all the heads of the schools of yoga came and bowed to Guru Ram Das to seal for the future the lineage of the royal throne of Raj Yoga to his guidance and to his Radiant Body. The yogis who practiced with him were called *udasis*.

This mantra—the Siri Mantra—contains the essence of the wisdom of the Siri Guru Granth Sahib. It brings great intuition to the practitioner. The title above means the eyes of Indra. It connotes the feeling that every pore of the body becomes an all-seeing eye. It represents knowledge that comes through the soul and intuition. The body is a temple through which you can experience the consciousness of the Infinite. As that happens all knowledge and bliss flow through you.

After you chant this mantra do not say anything negative for some time. It is a very creative chant. Anything you say will be amplified and created with great force. When you are in this state give your prayers and most positive projections for health, happiness, and holiness.

Meditations with Mantra *Sets & Meditations*

Kirtan Kriya

This *kriya* is one of three that Yogi Bhajan mentioned would carry us through the Aquarian Age, even if all other teachings were lost. There are four principle components to practicing Kirtan Kriya correctly: Mantra, Mudra, Voice, and Visualization.

EYE POSITION: Meditate at the Brow Point.

MANTRA: This *kriya* uses the five primal sounds, or the Panj Shabd— S, T, N, M, A— in the original *bij* form of the word *Sat Nam*:
- **SAA:** Infinity, cosmos, beginning
- **TAA:** Life, existence
- **NAA:** Death, change, transformation
- **MAA:** Rebirth

This is the cycle of creation. From the Infinite comes life and individual existence. From life comes death or change. From death comes the rebirth of consciousness. From rebirth comes the joy of the Infinite through which compassion leads back to life. Chant the 'A' as if you were pronouncing 'mom,' in the following manner:

SAA TAA NAA MAA

MUDRA: Each repetition of the entire mantra takes **3 to 4 seconds**. The elbows are straight while chanting, hands in Gyan Mudra. Each finger touches, in turn, the tip of the thumb with a firm but gentle pressure.
- **SAA** — the index or Jupiter finger touches the thumb;
- **TAA** — the middle or Saturn finger and thumb;
- **NAA** — the ring or Sun finger and thumb;
- **MAA** — the pinkie or Mercury finger and thumb;

then begin again with the index finger.

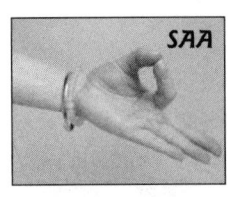

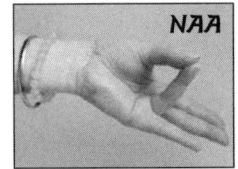

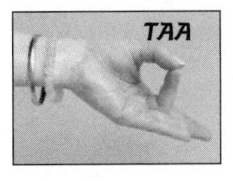

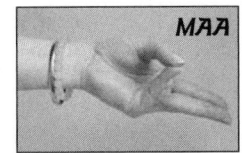

VISUALIZATION

You must meditate on the primal sounds in the "L" form. This means that when you meditate you feel there is a constant inflow of cosmic energy into your solar center, or Tenth Gate (the Crown Chakra). As the energy enters the top of the head, you place Sa, Ta, Na, or Ma there. As you chant **SAA** for example, the "S" starts at the top of your head and the "A" moves down and out through the Brow Point, projected to Infinity. This energy flow follows the energy pathway called the golden cord—the connection between the pineal and pituitary gland. Some people may occasionally experience headaches from practicing Kirtan Kriya if they do not use this "L" form. The most common reason for this is improper circulation of *prana* in the solar centers.

VOICE

The mantra is chanted in the three languages of consciousness:
- **Aloud** (the voice of the human) — awareness of the things of the world
- **Whisper** (the voice of the lover) — experiencing the longing to belong
- **Silent** (the voice of the divine) — meditate on Infinity or mentally vibrate

TO BEGIN THE PRACTICE

Sit straight in Easy Pose and meditate at the Brow Point.
Chant aloud for **5 minutes**.
Then whisper for **5 minutes**.
Then go deeply into silence, mentally vibrating the sound for **10 minutes**.
Then whisper for **5 minutes.**
Then chant aloud for **5 minutes**.

TO END: Close the meditation with a deep inhale and suspend the breath as long as comfortable—up to a minute—relaxing it smoothly to complete 1 minute of absolute stillness and silence. Then, stretch the hands up as far as possible and spread the fingers wide. Stretch the spine and take several deep breaths. Relax.

(Continued next page)

Kirtan Kriya 2 of 2

COMMENTS

Each time the mudra is closed by joining the thumb with a finger, the ego "seals" the effect of that mudra in the consciousness. The effects are as follows:

SIGN	FINGER	NAME	EFFECT
Jupiter	Index	Gyan Mudra	Knowledge
Saturn	Middle	Shuni Mudra	Wisdom, intelligence, patience
Sun	Ring	Surya Mudra	Vitality, energy of life
Mercury	Pinkie	Buddhi Mudra	Ability to communicate

Practicing this meditation brings a total mental balance to the individual psyche. As you vibrate on each fingertip, you alternate your electrical polarities. The index and ring fingers are electrically negative, relative to the other fingers. This causes a balance in the electro-magnetic projection of the aura. If during the silent part of the meditation your mind wanders uncontrollably, go back to a whisper, to a loud voice, to a whisper and back into silence.

Do this as often as necessary to stay alert. Practicing this meditation is both a science and an art. It is an art in the way it molds consciousness and the refinement of sensation and insight it produces. It is a science in the tested certainty of the results it produces. Each meditation is based on the tested experience of many people, in many conditions, over many years. It is based on the structure of the psyche and the laws of action and reaction that accompany each sound, movement and posture. The meditations as *kriyas* code this science into specific formulas we can practice to get specific results. Because it is so effective and exact, it can also lead to problems if not done properly. Chanting the *Panj Shabd*—the primal or nuclear form of *Sat Nam*—has profound energy within it because we are breaking the *bij* (seed or atom) of the sound, *Sat Nam*, into its primary elements.

You may use this chant in any position as long as you adhere to the following requirements:
 1. Keep the spine straight.
 2. Focus at the Brow Point.
 3. Use the "L" form of meditation.
 4. Vibrate the Panj Shabd in all three languages— human, lover, and divine.
 5. Use common sense without fanaticism.

The timing can be decreased or increased as long as you maintain the ratio of spoken, whispered, and silent chanting—always end with 1 minute of complete stillness and silence. Yogi Bhajan said, at the Winter Solstice of 1972, that a person who wears pure white and meditates on this sound current for 2-1/2 hours a day for one year, will know the unknown and see the unseen. Through this constant practice, the mind awakens to the infinite capacity of the soul for sacrifice, service, and creation.

Meditations with Mantra — Sets & Meditations

Laya Yoga Kundalini Mantra

Sit in an Easy Pose, with a light *jalandhar bandh*.

EYE POSITION: Focus through the Brow Point.

MUDRA: Put the palms together in Prayer Pose at the center of the chest, or in Gyan Mudra with the wrists on the knees.

MANTRA & VISUALIZATION:

EK ONG KAAR-(UH)	One Creator Creation
SAA TAA NAA MAA-(UH)	True Identity
SIREE WHAA-(UH) HAY GU-ROO	Great Indescribable Wisdom

The chant is very precise. On **EK** the navel will naturally lightly pull in. On each final "**UH**" lift the diaphragm up firmly. The "**UH**" sound is more a result of the powerful movement of the diagphragm than a pronounced purposeful projected sound. Relax the navel and abdomen on **HAY GUROO.** The sound has a "spin" to it. It is a **3-1/2 cycle rhythm**. As you chant, imagine energy and sound spiraling up and around the spinal cord in a right-handed helix, in a clockwise direction, looking from the top of the spine down to the base. Start at the base of the spine as you initiate the energy from the navel. End with the focus over the head to the Cosmos on **HAY GUROO**.

TIME: Continue for **31 minutes**. Practice for **40-120 days**.

COMMENTS

This extraordinary Laya Yoga chant brings the soul and destiny present. It suspends you above conflicts attracted by success and the activity of the Positive Mind. It lets your activity serve your purpose. It makes you creative and focused on your real priorities and helps you sacrifice what is needed to accomplish them.

The word *Laya* refers to suspension from the ordinary world. Laya Yoga fixes your attention and energy on your essence and higher consciousness without normal distractions and attachments having power over your reactive awareness.

This mantra opens the secret book of Laya Yoga. It enables you to consciously remember and experience the link between you and the Creator. Practice the mantra for 40-120 days. It will etch into the subconscious the memory and experience of your true identity.

This mantra was guarded like a secret gem. It is the key to the inner doors of *naad*, the realm of creative sound. If you listen to the sound of the mantra and then concentrate into its subtle sounds, you will become absorbed into the unlimited domain of your higher Self. The mantra has a structure of 3-1/2 cycles in its spin. Each **UH** sound lifts the diaphragm which commutes the energy of *prana* and *apana* across the heart area. That transformation is one cycle. The 3-1/2 cycle is the pulse rhythm of the kundalini itself. This is why the kundalini is often represented as coiled 3-1/2 times.

As with all other genuine mantras, it is discovered by the seer who travels in the subtle realms of consciousness. It has been confirmed by countless practitioners who adapted the discipline of the meditation. The inner sounds can be heard at different levels of subtlety. The vibrations of *naad* have different octaves of creative impact.

This mantra takes you to the most subtle realm of creativity. It awakens the kundalini force that energizes the whole Creation. It awakens your awareness and empowers the sense of the Subtle Body of the Aura. The practice of the meditation gives intuition and the ability to heal.

When you practice this *kriya* earnestly, be conscious and graceful with each word you speak. Do not listen to negative or coarse speech from others. Remember that the sins of the past are of the past, and that some of the greatest saints were sinners first. If you have the opportunity to learn and to practice this technology of elevation, you have earned it and you deserve it. So do not hesitate to use it and to strive for progress and expansion. Feel that the Infinite Will and yours act together. Strong actions combined with non-attachment make life a dance with much creativity and gratitude.

Learning to Meditate

Sit in an Easy Pose, with a light *jalandhar bandh*.

EYE POSITION: Focus the lightly closed eyes at the Third Eye Point (between the eyebrows.)

MANTRA:

SAT NAAM

MUDRA: With the four fingers of the right hand, feel the pulse on the left wrist. Place the fingers in a straight line, lightly, so that you can feel the pulse in each fingertip. On each beat of the heart, mentally hear the sound **SAT NAAM**.

TIME: Continue for **11 minutes**. Build to **31 minutes**.

COMMENTS

This is a good meditation for someone who doesn't know how to meditate, or wants to develop the ability of concentration in action. It allows you to control reaction to any situation and can bring sweetness and one-pointedness to the most outrageous and scattered mind.

Long Chant (Adi Shakti Mantra or Morning Call)

Sit in an Easy Pose with *jalandhar bandh*.

MUDRA: Have the hands in Gyan Mudra, or resting in Buddha Mudra in the lap. Maintain a strong Neck Lock (*jalandhar bandh*).

MANTRA: Chant the Adi Shakti Mantra,

EK ONG KAAR SAT NAAM SIREE WHAA-HAY GUROO
*One Creator created this Creation. Truth is His Name.
Great beyond description is His infinite wisdom.*

in a 2-1/2 breath cycle, in the following manner:

Inhale deeply and as you pull in the navel abruptly, chant **EK**. Then **ONG KAAR** is drawn out. Give equal time to **Ong** and **Kaar**.

Inhale deeply and as you pull in the navel abruptly, chant **SAT**. Then **NAAM** is drawn out. Then, just as you get to the end of the breath, add a quick **SIREE**. (pronounced **S'REE.**)

Inhale *half* a breath, pull in the navel abruptly, chant **WHAA**. Then **HAY GUROO** (**HAY** should be relatively short, **GUROO** is pronounced **G'ROO** and is drawn out, but not too long.)
The **Ong Kaar** and **Naam Siree** are equal in length. The **Whaa-hay Guroo** is equal in length to **Ong**. Try not to let the pitch fall.

TIME: This can be done for as little as **3 minutes**, or **11 minutes**. It is done in Aquarian morning *sadhana* for **7 minutes**. For a powerful experience of this meditation, do **31 minutes**, or **2-1/2 hours**.

Let the sound resonate in the upper cavity of the head, by closing the back of the throat and vibrating the upper palate, and allowing the sound to come through the nose.

COMMENTS
Yogi Bhajan speaks about this mantra: "This mantra is known as the Ashtang Mantra for the Aquarian Age. It has eight vibrations, and describes the glory of God. Thus said the Master, 'In the time period two-and-a-half hours before the rising of the Sun, when the channels are most clear, if the Mantra is sung in sweet harmony, you will be one with the Lord.' This will open the solar plexus, which in turn will charge the solar centers. The person will get connected with the Cosmic Energy, and thus will be liberated from the cycle of time and karma. Those who meditate on this mantra in silence will charge their solar centers and be one with the Divine. That is why I speak to you of why we should meditate and recite this mantra.

"All mantras are good, and are for the awakening of the Divine. But this mantra is effective, and is the mantra for this time. So my lovely student, at the will of my Master I teach you the greatest Divine key. It has eight levers, and can open the lock of the time, which is also of the vibration of eight. Therefore, when this mantra is sung with the Neck Lock, at the point where *prana* and *apana* meet *sushmuna*, this vibration opens the lock, and thus one becomes one with the Divine."

This mantra is used as the cornerstone of morning *sadhana*, and is also called Long Ek Ong Kaar's or just Long Chant. It has also been referred to as Morning Call. This mantra initiates the kundalini, initiating the relationship between the soul and the Universal Soul. It balances all of the chakras. Though it is part of morning *sadhana*, it can be chanted at any time.

Sets & Meditations — Meditations with Mantra

Mahan Jaap

Originally taught by Yogi Bhajan in January 1975

Sit attentively and meditate at the Brow Point, with eyes closed. It is not necessary for the group to sit in a circle, though they may.

MANTRA: The group begins chanting the *punj shabd* all together for a few minutes.

SAA TAA NAA MAA

Inhale, exhale. Then, the teacher begins the first cycle alone. Best to maintain a brisk rhythm, making each cycle: **2-1/2 to 3 seconds.** Someone else immediately picks up the chant as the first person ends. Maintain the rhythm. Anyone can pick up the chant at any time; it does not move in a sequential order, nor does it move around the circle.

TO END: The teacher instructs the group to chant all together for a few minutes.

COMMENTS

The individual will become sensitized on a new level so that he or she will respond to the energy in the group. Each person is a part of the greater energy balance. Chanting will happen in response to the shift of the total group energy. Ultimately, the individual activity merges with the group activity, with no difference between them, since it is the energy focus of the group that shifts and causes someone to chant. Some may chant more than one time, while others may not chant at all.

A very delicate and sublime sensitivity will be developed in this process. The effect of the chant is that you are multiplied by the total number of people participating plus twice the number squared. This number times each *japa*, or meditative repetition, equals the effect. This means the effect of a few hundred thousand repetitions can be achieved in a moderate size group in a short time. It requires a very perfect concentration, and it would be best if the group has already exercised and achieved a meditative state before starting a *Mahan Jap*.

Mala Meditation

A mala is a simple, effective meditative tool, which can help to reduce stress and enhance wisdom, patience, and health. A mala consists of 108, 54, or 27 beads, traditionally strung on silk thread with one larger bead, called the Guru bead, from which a tassel hangs. The tassel symbolises a thousand lotus petals.

The use of different fingers with the mala: Each finger you use, while meditating with the help of the mala, relates to a different part of the brain. By running the mala over the meridian point of the desired finger, you create a different result. The meridian point is located on the side of each finger, between the tip of the finger and the first knuckle:

- Index finger (Jupiter): wisdom, knowledge, and prosperity.
- Middle finger (Saturn): enhances patience.
- Ring finger (Sun): promotes health, vitality, and strengthens the nervous system.
- Little finger (Mercury): communication skill, and intelligence.

How to use a mala: A mala can be used with either hand. Always start with the bead next to the Guru bead. As you repeat the mantra, move each bead with the thumb, towards the body over the meridian point. Thus, the Guru bead descends and eventually ascends to be the last bead of your meditation. As you hold the Guru bead, repeat your mantra and make a prayer. To begin again turn the mala around without the help of the other hand. Move the beads towards you and continue your mantra.

Using your mala with a mantra: When reciting the mantra **SAT NAAM** move only one bead for both words. With the mantra **WHAA-HAY GUROO**, move only one bead for the two words. You may also use the mantra **SAT NAAM WHAA-HAY GUROO**, saying them both with the movement of one bead. You may use any affirmation or mantra of your choice. The recitation of your mantra may be done silently, in a whisper, or out loud.

Some sample Mala Meditations:

- *To improve your health:* Use a carnelian, coral (red or pink), lapis or turquoise mala. Move the mala over the Sun (ring) finger with either the mantra **SAT NAAM**, or **WHAA-HAY GUROO**, or **SAT NAAM WHA-HAY GUROO**, or a personal healing affirmation.
- *To reduce stress and anxiety:* Use either a lapis, or a coral (red or pink) mala. Move it over the Jupiter (index) finger for wisdom or the Saturn (middle) finger for patience. Use either the **HAR** or **WHAA-HAY GUROO** mantra or a personal affirmation for stress reduction.
- *For prosperity:* Use a carnelian or garnet mala. Move it over the Jupiter (index) finger for wisdom, knowledge and prosperity; or the Mercury (pinkie) finger for enhanced communication skills. Recite the mantras **HAR** or **WHAA-HAY GUROO**.

    Prosperity can also be measured in nonmaterialistic terms. To have the ability to sacrifice, to be tolerant, to be giving, to be compassionate, and to have peace of mind are also states of prosperity. These are attributes which cannot be bought. They are gems in a nonmaterialistic form. A coral mala can be used to enhance a state of neutrality, a jade mala for peace, or a lapis mala to enhance your power of prayer.
- *For saintly virtues:* Use a malachite mala. Move it over your desired finger for wisdom, patience, health, or communication and use the mantra **SAT NAAM**.
- Or, make up your own meditation for the desired effect you want to achieve.

A few pointers on doing these meditations: You can do them casually as you go about your day, or in a deeper meditative state. Sit either in a crosslegged position on the floor or sit in a chair with feet on the ground. Sit with your spine straight, chest out, and chin in. You can focus the eyes on the Third Eye Point. Recite your mantra using your mala as previously described for **11, 31, or 62 minutes**. Remember to listen to your mantra, use the Navel Point, and stimulate the meridians with your tongue.

Malas are sacred meditative tools. If you are not wearing or using your mala, keep it in a silk or satin pouch, or on your altar to enhance, protect, and keep the integrity of the gemstones' vibrations.

Excerpted from Mala Meditation, Gum Kirn Kaur Khalsa

Sets & Meditations — Meditations with Mantra

Master's Touch Meditation

Originally taught by Yogi Bhajan in July 13, 2000

Sit in an Easy Pose, with a light *jalandhar bandh*. Sit very saintly, like you are the greatest incarnation of Lord Buddha.

EYE POSITION: The eyes are slightly open, focused at the tip of the nose.

MUDRA: Maha Gyan Mudra. Place the pad (finger print) of the right index finger (Jupiter finger) on the pad of the left index finger, right palm facing out from the body, left palm facing in towards the body, forming a 45 degree angle of the fingers pointing upwards. Other fingers are curled into the palms with thumbs over. Hold the mudra at the Heart Center, shoulders relaxed.

MANTRA: From the navel sing:

AAD SACH, JUGAAD SACH, HAI BHEE SACH, NAANAK HOSEE BHEE SACH

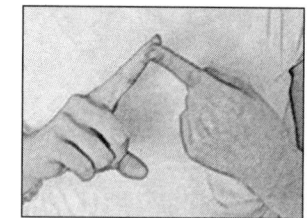

You may sing or chant the mantra, but it must be done in a monotone. The "*suchhh*" sound is emphasized as you pull the navel in on each repetition of the word. As you chant aloud, listen with your inner ear. Let the inner ear vibrate. Tune your inner ear so that the hammering of the hammer bones enables your brain to analyze the sound as you hear it.

TIME: Continue for **2-1/2 hours**.

TO END: Inhale, hold the breath. Exhale, relax the mudra and the breath. Close your eyes and rest for 2 minutes.

COMMENTS

The mantra translates as: Primal Truth, True for all Time, True at This Instant, Oh Nanak, Forever True. These are the four stages of truth that must prevail through one touch. It is recorded in the scriptures that this meditation is to be practiced for 2 1/2 hours. However, it is up to you how long you practice. This is a personal *sadhana* and does not replace group *sadhana* in the Amrit Vela.

Yogi Bhajan says about this meditation, "In this *kriya* that I am giving you, you have to tune your ears. Not the outer ear—it will not help you—it is the inner ear. It has two bones on the side and the hammer, and if the hammer and the bones have a proper hammering, then your brain can analyze and understand at the same time you are hearing. The mudra allows the Infinite energy to come through. Chanting the mantra stimulates the upper palate with the tip of the tongue, tuning the thalamus and hypothalamus. Focusing on the tip of the nose causes the frontal lobe, which controls the personality, to become like lead. At one point the pain can become so unbearable, you cannot stand it. Then it 'breaks,' and you have found what you are looking for, and that is forever. Nobody can take it away. To grow roots, you must open yourself up.

"As an apprentice to this process, you offer yourself in surrender to receive the Master's Touch. You stand on the root of the tree like a little bear, who reaches up to hold the trunk and climbs to the top-most branch to get to the beehive, unaware of bee stings—intent on getting the honey. He drinks the honey, is satisfied, and descends to the ground, falling through the branches which break his fall. After stretching and nurturing himself, the little bear remembers the taste of honey and the sense of achievement. He goes up the tree again and again, reaching that achievement in ecstasy, and nothing else matters.

"Life is a lie if you do not achieve your Self for yourself. That is your honey, your sweetness. You must achieve Infinity where your identity is such a non-identity that it merges in Everything. Once you are that, you bless everybody. You are honored and in bliss—limitless, with no confinement, no territory, no demands, no requests.

"In this process, you provoke, offer, surrender, achieve, and descend. Provoke, because everything is provocation, either to control or to receive. Offer, because you must decide how to offer, or present yourself. Surrender, because when you surrender, your working self becomes zero, *shuniya*. Surrender is the highest power to gain all that you want to gain. Achieve, because once you have a sense of achievement and say, 'My God!,' if you convert that 'My God!' into 'My Soul!' you have already found God. You have a soul—achieve it! When you find your soul or yourself you are complete. Descend, because like a forklift, you may descend, go into the dirt and move up. This descent is in the highest state of mind and spirit.

"When the Age of Aquarius comes and people seek you out, you will have no time but to touch them and say, 'Bless you!' to bring the entire psyche and being of a person into balance. That touch will create a state of *Aad Such, Jugaad Such, Hai Bhee Such, Naanak Hosee Bhee Such. Original Truth, Truth through time, Truth now, and forever Truth*. These must prevail through one touch. This mantra will give you the power of the Master's Touch. And when you perfect this mudra with the Jupiter fingers touching, chant the mantra in one sitting for 2-1/2 hours—one tenth of your day—it will bring you this Touch. There is no power or magic on this planet that can stop it. It has a permutation, combination, projection and power which brings the entire *Prakirti*, the Existence, into the being of *Purkha*, the Divinity. All will be grateful to you; you will find grace, respect, love, and satisfaction that you are serving the creation of God. Then you will see God in everybody, in yourself, and in every facet of life. It will come true: 'If you don't see God in all, you don't see God at all.' You will see God."

Meditation Into Being: "I Am, I Am"

Originally taught by Yogi Bhajan in April 1972

Sit in an Easy Pose, with a light *jalandhar bandh*.

EYE POSITION: Fix the eyelids at 1/10th open. The eyes look straight ahead through the eyelids.

MUDRA: Keep the spine straight. Place the right hand over the right knee. Keep the elbow straight and the hand relaxed in Gyan Mudra (the index finger tip on the tip of the thumb). Raise the left hand in front of the Heart Center. The palm is flat and faces toward the chest. The fingers point to the right.

MANTRA:

I AM, I AM

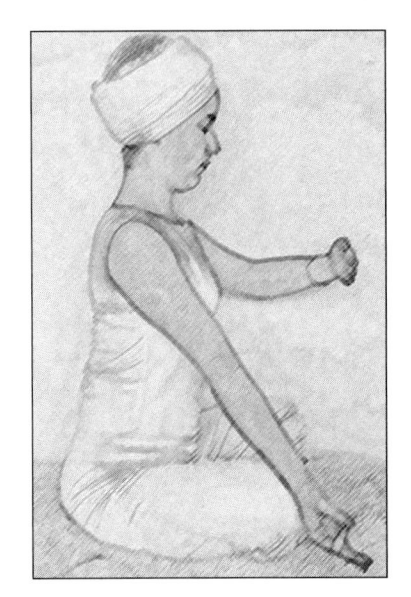

BREATH & MOVEMENT: Start with the left hand **6 inches** (15 cm) from the chest. Chant out loud *I AM* as you draw the hand closer to the chest to a distance of about **4 inches** (10 cm). Then chant *I AM* as you extend the palm straight away from the front of the chest to a distance of about **12 inches** (30 cm). Then take a short breath through the nose as you draw the hand back to the original position of 6 inches (15 cm) from the chest. Create a steady rhythm with the mantra and the breath.

TIME: Continue for **11-31 minutes**.

TO END: Inhale deeply, hold, and relax completely.

COMMENTS

This mantra connects the finite and Infinite identities. The first "*I Am*" that emphasizes the "*I*" is the personal and finite sense of self. The second "*I Am*" that emphasizes slightly the "*Am*" is the impersonal and transcendent sense of the Self. All real mantras blend this polarity of the Infinite and finite in their internal structure and design.

If you only say the first "*I Am,*" the mind will automatically try to answer, "*I am what?*" This sends the mind on a search through all the categories and roles that hold the finite identities. If you immediately say the second part of the mantra, "*I Am*" the thought becomes "*I Am what I Am.*" To be what you are is the essence of truth and will lead you to the nature of Reality. The hand and the breath move in rhythm and strengthen your ability to maintain a sense of self as your awareness expands.

A yogi cultivates the relationship between the finite sense of the self and the infinite sense of the Self. The mind often forgets this relationship when it becomes attached to a particular emotion or object that it wants to keep. One of the important habits the yogi instills in the mind is the ability to break that trance of attachment by a shift to the perspective of Infinity. This is also the perspective of Being. You exist before the objects you collect and even before the body that you use. It is very powerful and effective to remind the mind of your true identity with your Infinite Being. Without this awareness, then philosophy, ethics, and spirituality will reduce to ritual participation in the "good." What the yogi seeks is to participate in life with authenticity and wholeness.

Meditation on the Divine Mother

Originally taught by Yogi Bhajan in November 1973

Part I
Sit in Easy Pose with the eyes closed, and the hands in Gyan Mudra. Meditate on the Infinite energy coming from the primal womb, in an unending spiral, without beginning or end, going to Infinity.

Part II
With the eyes closed, cup the hands with palms **4-6 inches** (10-15 cm) apart, and in front of the face. Beam a mental light through them to the Infinite Light. Watch with mental eyes, through the hands, and see a beam of light going to Infinity.

This is very mind-curing, and you will fall in love with it. Meditate with Long Deep Breathing.

Part III
Chant **SAA-TAA-NAA-MAA**

Go deeper into meditation. Guide your reason to go through the powerful imaginative circle you've created with your hands, like a huge beam of light from a torch. Keep the hands fixed in place.

Part IV
Maintain your position and concentration. Put your mind into that Infinite Light of its own ecstasy and chant the Kundalini Bhakti Mantra:

AADEE SHAKTEE, AADEE SHAKTEE, AADEE SHAKTEE, NAMO, NAMO
SARAB SHAKTEE, SARAB SHAKTEE, SARAB SHAKTEE, NAMO, NAMO
PRITHAM BHAGVATEE, PRITHAM BHAGVATEE, PRITHAM BHAGVATEE, NAMO, NAMO
KUNDALINEE MAATA SHAKTEE, MAATA SHAKTEE, NAMO, NAMO

TIME: All four parts of this meditation should be done for equal lengths of time. They can be practiced for **11, 31, or 62 minutes.**

COMMENTS
This meditation gives concentration and mental beaming. It tunes into the frequency of the Divine Mother—the primal, protective, generating energy. It eliminates fears and fulfills desires. It gives power of action by removing blocks of insecurity.

Meditation for Healing Addictions

Sit in an Easy Pose, with a light *jalandhar bandh*. Straighten the spine and make sure the first six lower vertebrae are locked forward.

EYE POSITION: Keep the eyes closed and focus at the Brow Point.

MANTRA:

SAA-TAA-NAA-MAA

MUDRA: Make fists of both hands and extend the thumbs straight. Place the thumbs on the temples and find the niche where the thumbs just fit. This is the lower anterior portion of the frontal bone above the temporal-sphenoidal suture. Lock the back molars together and keep the lips closed. Keeping the teeth pressed together throughout, alternately squeeze the molars tightly and then release the pressure. A muscle will move in rhythm under the thumbs. Feel it massage the thumbs and apply a firm pressure with the hands.

Silently vibrate the five primal sounds—the *Panj Shabd*—**SAA-TAA-NAA-MAA**, at the brow.

TIME: Continue for **5-7 minutes**. With practice the time can be increased to **20 minutes** and ultimately to **31 minutes**.

COMMENTS

This meditation is one of a class of meditations that will become well known to the future medical society. Meditation will be used to alleviate all kinds of mental and physical afflictions. But it may be as many as 500 years, however, before the new medical science will understand the effects of this kind of meditation well enough to delineate and measure all its parameters.

The pressure exerted by the thumbs triggers a rhythmic reflex current into the central brain. This current activates the brain area directly underneath the stem of the pineal gland. It is an imbalance in this area that makes mental and physical addictions seemingly unbreakable.

In modern culture, this imbalance is pandemic. If we are not addicted to smoking, eating, drinking, or drugs, then we are addicted subconsciously to acceptance, advancement, rejection, emotional love, etc. All of these lead us to insecure and neurotic behavior patterns.

Imbalance in this pineal area upsets the radiance of the pineal gland itself. It is this pulsating radiance that regulates the pituitary gland. Since the pituitary regulates the rest of the glandular system, the entire body and mind go out of balance. This meditation corrects the problem. It is excellent for everyone but particularly effective for rehabilitation efforts in drug dependence, mental illness, and phobic conditions.

Meditation to Open the Heart

Originally taught by Yogi Bhajan in 1971

Sit in an Easy Pose, with a light *jalandhar bandh*.

EYE POSITION: The eyes closed, looking up, focusing at the Brow Point.

MANTRA:

SAT KARTAAR

As you say **SAT**, the hands are pressed together in Prayer Pose at the center of the chest.

As you say **KAR**, the hands are extended out from the shoulders, half-way towards the final position. Fingers are pointing straight up.

As you say **TAAR**, the arms are fully extended out to the sides and parallel to the floor, fingers pointing up.

Make the transition from step to step a flowing movement.

TIME: No specified time.

COMMENTS
If you feel your heart is closed and there is no flow of love, and you want to open your heart, do this meditation.

Meditations with Mantra

Originally taught by Yogi Bhajan in February 1975

Meditation for Projection & Protection from the Heart

Sit in an Easy Pose, with a light *jalandhar bandh*.

MUDRA: Place the palms together at the Heart Center in Prayer Pose. The thumbs are crossed.

MANTRA, BREATH & MOVEMENT: Chant the Mangala Charn Mantra:

Chant:

AAD GURAY NAMEH
As you extend your arms as shown in picture.

The arms return to the Heart Center as you chant:

JUGAAD GURAY NAMEH

and again extend the arms up, as you chant:

SAT GURAY NAMEH
Returning the hands again to Prayer Pose at the Heart Center, chant:

SIREE GUROO DAYVAY NAMEH

Project the mind out as you chant. The full extension of the arms is timed to the chant.

TIME: Continue for **11 minutes**, adding **5 minutes** per day up to **31 minutes**, until you perfect it.

COMMENTS
This meditation gives you an enchanting, magnetic personality, with many unexpected friends. The Mangala Charn Mantra surrounds the magnetic field with protective light. It means:

AAD GURAY NAMEH	*I bow to the Primal Wisdom*
JUGAAD GURAY NAMEH	*I bow to the wisdom through the Ages*
SAT GURAY NAMEH	*I bow to the True Wisdom*
SIREE GUROO DAYVAY NAMEH	*I bow to the great, unseen Wisdom.*

Meditation for Prosperity I

Sit in an Easy Pose, with a light *jalandhar bandh*.

EYE POSITION: The eyes are closed, looking up, focusing at the Brow Point. Alternatively, you may have the eyes open, looking down at the tip of the nose.

MUDRA: Put the elbows by the sides, with the forearms parallel to the ground. The hands are pointing forward, with the palms facing up, wrists straight. Touch the thumbs to the tips of the index fingers. Chant the mantra in a steady cadence.

MANTRA:

HAR HA-RAY HA-REE WHAA-HAY GU-ROO

This mantra uses the three qualities of **HAR**—seed, flow, and completion—unto the ecstatic Infinity of God.

TIME: Continue for **11-31 minutes**.

COMMENTS

This meditation provides guidance, and the way through any block. The future is clear, without anxiety. Every cause has an impact and an orbit of effect. This meditation allows you to use the Neutral Mind to intuit all the expected and unexpected impacts of the mental thoughts you feel now, or that were a part of you in the past. If this part of you is unbalanced, people will distance themselves socially out of subconscious fear of your perception, bluntness, and truth. When balanced, you gain wisdom and self-guidance to hold in trust all that comes to you. You are never swayed by abundance and hold closely to the path.

Meditation for Prosperity II

Originally taught by Yogi Bhajan in 1996

This exercise is part of Subagh Kriya, and can also be practised as a stand-along meditation.

Sit in Easy Pose, with a light *jalandhar bandh*.

EYE POSITION: Focus at the tip of the nose, through eyes 9/10th closed.

MUDRA: Elbows are by the sides, forearms angled up and outward with the fingers at the level of the throat. The exercise begins with the palms facing down.

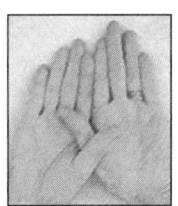

Alternately hit the sides of the hands together. The Mercury (pinky) fingers and the Moon Mounds (located on the bottom of the palms) hit when the palms face up. When the palms hit facing down, the sides of the Jupiter (index) fingers touch, and the thumbs cross below the hands, **with the right thumb under the left**.
Yogi Bhajan said that the thumbs crossing this way is the key to the meditation.

MANTRA: The *Tantric Har* tape is perfect for this meditation.

HAR HAR

Chant continuously from the navel, using the tip of the tongue.

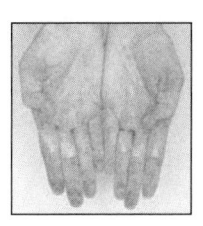

TIME: Continue for **3-11 minutes**.
Yogi Bhajan has said about the timing: "This meditation can be done for up to 11 minutes. It is so powerful in bringing prosperity that more than 11 minutes would be greedy."

COMMENTS
"This meditation stimulates the mind, the moon center and Jupiter. When Jupiter and the moon come together, there is no way in the world you will not create wealth."

- YOGI BHAJAN

Meditation for Self-Assessment

Originally taught by Yogi Bhajan in October 1972

Sit straight, in an Easy Pose, hands in Gyan Mudra.

While the teacher speaks these words, the student listens with eyes closed, then repeats the words aloud. Listen carefully:

I am an individual.
Very graceful.
Totally pious.
Absolutely perfect.
Unmistakably beautiful.
There is nothing the word can describe.
I am absolutely righteous.
A living truth.
In my conversation with friends.
In my conversation with enemies.
In my political life.
In my social life.
In my material life.
In my individual life.
In my private life.
I am absolutely correct.
Righteous.
Wise.
And totally good.
I understand.
Everything.
Absolutely I am perfect in knowledge.
I created God.
He never created me.
I am not kidding—it is the truth.
I am talking about it.
Therefore, I am the Creator.
I can create the word "God."
By writing it on the wall.
By speaking it with my tongue.
By communicating with people.
I made the radio.
Television.
I print the newspaper.
I spread everything which I know to do.
I am master and owner of this whole universe.

Open your eyes. Assess in your consciousness what percentage of what was said you totally agreed to in consciousness?

TO END: Chant **ONG** long and powerfully. If there is a class, have the women start and the men join, so that there is an overlapping of the sound with separate starting times. This is the sound of creativity of the word. Chant **3-11 minutes**. Then inhale deeply, hold the breath, and exhale.

COMMENTS

"In the beginning there was the Word, the Word was with God and the Word was GOD." We always make a basic mistake: we do not recognize the power of the word in creating our world. There is no energy more potent than the word. Because we are unaware of the effect of what we say on consciousness, we say whatever we want and do whatever we feel. There develops a duality between word and action. This duality creates confusion, inconstancy, lack of will and radiance. It is essential for the human life to coordinate our actions with the channel of creative energy of our words. When we say "yes," we should mean exactly that.

Observe how much your mind is behind what you say, or how phoney you are. This meditation causes you to assess how well you have coordinated actions and words. If you have not done this, there will be a duality in personality that you will experience as conflict. We need to assess ourselves in this manner all the time, until the mind is trained to say only what is true. Then you can know the depth of the self and the unlimited creativity of the finite in relation to the Infinite in the personality and existence of the human being.

Meditation for Self-Blessing Guidance by Intuition

Originally taught by Yogi Bhajan in October 1979

Sit in an Easy Pose, with a light *jalandhar bandh*.

EYE POSITION: Fix the eyes 1/10th open.

MUDRA: Extend the arms up in a circular arc so the palms and fingers of each hand face down about **6 or 8 inches** over the crown of the head. The hands are separated by about **12 inches.** The thumbs separate from the fingers and hang loosely.

BREATH: Breathe in a three-part pattern:
- *Inhale* in **8 equal strokes**.
- *Exhale* completely in **8 equal strokes**.
- *Suspend the breath* out for **16 beats** in the same rhythm.

MANTRA: Mentally repeat the mantra,

SAA-TAA-NAA-MAA **8 times** with each full cycle of the breath.

TIME: Continue in this pattern for **11 minutes**. Begin with 11 minutes, increase to 22 and then slowly increase it to 31 minutes.

TO END: Inhale deeply, and raise the arms high up over the head. Stretch the arms backwards and upwards. Drop the head back and look up. Stretch with all your strength to extend the lower back and the neck. Then exhale and let the arms down. Repeat this final breath **2 more times**. Relax.

COMMENTS

This meditation requires some endurance and practice to perfect it. The arms will seem comfortable at first, but they often become painful after a period of time. When that occurs, become very calm and draw your focus onto the breath and the mental mantra. Let the images and sensations of the arms fade.

The arms trace out the upper arcline in the aura that shines around the body. This increases the flow of *prana* through the Crown Chakra, the upper solar center. This in turn releases a powerful stimulant to the pineal and pituitary glands. The result is an increase in intuition. Intuition is a perceptual function of the entire brain and the whole mind.

Intuition corrects the often mistaken judgements from the psychic realms. Most psychics read fragments of the subconscious. They use these pieces of the psyche for their own purposes. This meditation gives you the blessing to be still and to discriminate the real from the unreal, the dharmic from the karmic, fantasy from creative imagination. It gives you guidance and relentless dedication to your vision.

Meditation for Stress or Sudden Shock

Originally taught by Yogi Bhajan in January 1979

Sit in an Easy Pose, with a light *jalandhar bandh*.

MUDRA: Relax the arms down with the elbows bent. Draw the forearms in toward each other until the hands meet in front of the body about **1 inch** (2.5 cm) above the navel. Place the palms up, and rest the right hand in the palm of the left hand. Place the thumbtips together, and pull the thumbs toward the body.

EYE POSITION: Look at the tip of the nose, the Lotus Point.

BREATH: Deeply inhale and completely exhale as you chant the mantra.

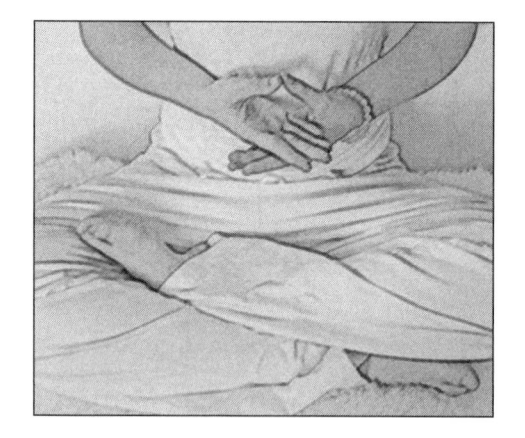

MANTRA: Chant the mantra **3 times**. The entire mantra must be chanted on only one breath. Use the tip of the tongue to pronounce each word exactly, and chant in a monotone. The rhythm must also be exact.

> **SAT NAAM SAT NAAM SAT NAAM SAT NAAM**
> **SAT NAAM SAT NAAM WHAA-HAY GUROO**

TIME: Begin with **11 minutes** and slowly build up to **31 minutes**.

TO END: Inhale and completely exhale **5 times**. Then deeply inhale, hold the breath and stretch the arms up over the head as high as possible. Stretch with every ounce that you can muster. Exhale and relax down. **Repeat twice.**

COMMENTS

This meditation balances the left hemisphere of the brain with the base of the right hemisphere. This enables the brain to maintain its equilibrium under stress or the weight of a sudden shock. It also keeps the nerves from being shattered under those circumstances.

Originally taught by Yogi Bhajan in September 1983

Naad Meditation to Communicate from Totality

Part I
Sit in Easy Pose.

EYES: Close the eyes or keep them 1/10th open.

MUDRA & MOVEMENT: Bring the hands next to the shoulders with the palms forward, the fingers pointing up, the wrists straight, and the elbows relaxed along the sides of the torso. Make Gyan Mudra with each hand (touch the thumb tips to the tips of the index fingers). Move both hands at the same time as if throwing darts. They move forward about **12 to 18 inches** (30-45 cm) as you chant each syllable of the mantra:

**WHAA WHAA HAY HAY
WHAA WHAA HAY HAY
WHAA WHAA HAY HAY GUROO**

This mantra is spoken in monotone. Each beat is spoken distinctly like a dart of sound.

TIME: Continue for **31 minutes**.

TO END: Inhale deeply and hold the breath. Relax.

Part II - with a Partner
Immediately turn to a partner and discuss the question:
"How do I create trust and distrust in my relationships with my communication?"

TIME: Continue for **3 minutes**.

Part III
Immediately sit straight and place the hands on top of the head. Interlace the fingers. Create a mild pressure on top of the head. Twist smoothly side to side. Inhale left, exhale right.

TIME: Continue for **3 minutes.**

TO END: Inhale to the center and hold the breath as you concentrate on the crown of the head. Then relax.

COMMENTS
This meditation lets you merge into the feeling of totality. When you speak from that feeling you create trust. With trust you establish strong relationships.

In the beginning of this tradition of *Naad Vidya*, the practice was only given to families and to children from royal lineages. The families had to be worthy of the training for seven generations or the applicant was not accepted. There were two places of study. The Guru would send the student to a *gurusala* to learn discipline from a teacher, or to a *dharmasala* to learn the ways to live and behave. Over time these were combined into ashrams.

The gift of these practices is the power of *vak siddhi*, which lets you have sensitivity to the subtle roots and to the impact of sound. You learn the sound of things and the subtle sound of consciousness that allows all other sounds to be.

Naad Meditation to Communicate Your Honest Self

Originally taught by Yogi Bhajan in September 1983

Part I

Sit in an Easy Pose, with a light *jalandhar bandh*.

EYES: The eyes are closed. Concentrate at the Brow Point.

MUDRA: Bend the arms and raise the hands next to the shoulders. The wrists are straight and the palms face forward. Begin to alternate pressing the thumb tip on the index finger tip and then on the ring finger tip. Press with about 5 pounds of pressure.

MANTRA: As you rhythmically alternate the fingers, chant these sounds:

SAA - pressing the index finger
RAY - pressing the ring finger

The sound of the chant is a monotone. Feel the pulse of the sound and the energy changing in the body.

TIME: Continue in a steady pace for **31 minutes**.

TO END: Inhale and hold as long as it is comfortable. Exhale through the mouth and keep it out with the mouth open. Inhale through the nose again. Hold the breath in for **30 seconds,** exhale through the mouth and keep it open for **20 seconds**. Inhale deeply and hold the breath for **30 seconds** and relax as you exhale through the mouth.

Part II - with Partner

Turn to your partner and discuss honestly the topic: **"Why don't you believe me?"** Discuss this for **3-15 minutes**. Then assess yourself: **"Am I satisfied or disappointed in this communication?"**
Then, use the right hand with the palm open to slap the hand of your partner. You both try to slap the hands. As you do this, look at each other's eyes and speak obnoxiously for **3 minutes**.
Immediately put a giant smile on your face. Keep the smile there. Shake the hand of your partner in a simple friendly rhythm for **3 minutes.** Then thank your partner and relax.

COMMENTS

This meditation changes the chemistry of the brain. All communication is based on the chemistry and interchange within the brain. The fingertips are points of stimulation for the different areas of the brain. The *naad* rhythm opens creativity and sensitivity to speak from the heart.

Good communication expresses the real you. It projects the whole self. It discharges your honest self. Clear communication is fearless and does not need anything from the person to whom you are speaking. When you speak out of neediness you distort the real message of your heart.

This meditation lets you know where your heart is and what is in it.

Meditations with Mantra

Originally taught by Yogi Bhajan in September 1983

Naad Meditation: Naad Namodam Rasa

Sets & Meditations

Part I
Sit in an Easy Pose, with a light *jalandhar bandh*.

EYES: Focus the eyes at the tip of the nose, or at the Third Eye Point.

MUDRA & MANTRA: Let the arms hang by the sides. Bend the elbows to make the forearms parallel to the ground with the palms up and the fingers pointing straight forward, away from the torso. Make Buddhi Mudra with each hand (connect the thumb tip to the tip of the little finger). Start a rhythmical alternation of the forearms. Move the forearms up and down 4 to 6 inches above and below the horizontal. The arms stay parallel. Continue this motion in rhythm with the three sounds of the mantra:

AAH   OOH   UMM

Pronounce each sound from the throat so it vibrates from the diaphragm and the nose. It must have good resonance and timbre.

TIME: Continue in a steady pace for **31 minutes**.

TO END: Inhale deeply and hold for as long as comfortable. Exhale. Immediately move into Part II.

Part II - with Partner
a) Immediately turn to a partner and converse about the topic: **"How well do I do the impossible?"** for **3 to 11 minutes**.

b) Next, use the right hand with the palm open to slap the right hand of your partner. You both try to slap hands. As you do this look at each other's eyes and speak obnoxiously to each other for **3 minutes**.

c) Immediately look at your partner, and while smiling, talk about, **"The blessings of my life and how I overcome challenges."** Keep smiling. Continue for **3 to 11 minutes**.

COMMENTS
This mantra is a Trikuti Mantra. It blends all three *gunas* and neutralizes the *ida* and *pingala* into the central channel of the *sushmana*. In the language of Naad Yoga, the sound AHH is the first primal sound. It is the first finite voice that begins the differentiation of all creation. It means 'come.' The first Infinite voice that moves you back to unity is WHA. The sound OOH means 'Thou.' The sound UMM means 'we.' Taken all together the mantra becomes: 'Come, Thou, into the form of Life.' Chanted in this way it is the Bij Naad of the mantra *OM* or *AUM*.

Your total strength is not in your muscles. Your real strength is in your chemical communication system of the brain. The brain does not connect only through nerve pathways. There are chemical solutions that go between different areas and give you abilities. This was known to the yogis before 100,000 B.C. They could look into areas of the body and view its strength, flow and projection. They developed a science to adjust and circulate those chemicals of the brain. They called the science, *'Naad Namodam Rasa.'* *Naad* means communication, both gross and subtle. *Namodam* means to address someone. *Rasa* means a juice or healing secretion. This was the science of how to adjust the communication through the inner juices.

The tiredness, confusion and ineffectiveness of the brain and life can be corrected with this science. The technology was only taught to select disciples. It has never been openly given before this moment. In the East you had to prove yourself as a student first. The job of the teacher was to give you an impossible task. The job of the student was to do it in order to learn to do the impossible. That is the nature of God who makes everything from nothing! This meditation was not given to a family unless they had given seven generations of service first.

But the time is such that all these techniques must become available and practiced if we are to go to the next stage of our maturity on Earth. We must know how to adjust ourselves and how to be potent and conscious in our communication.

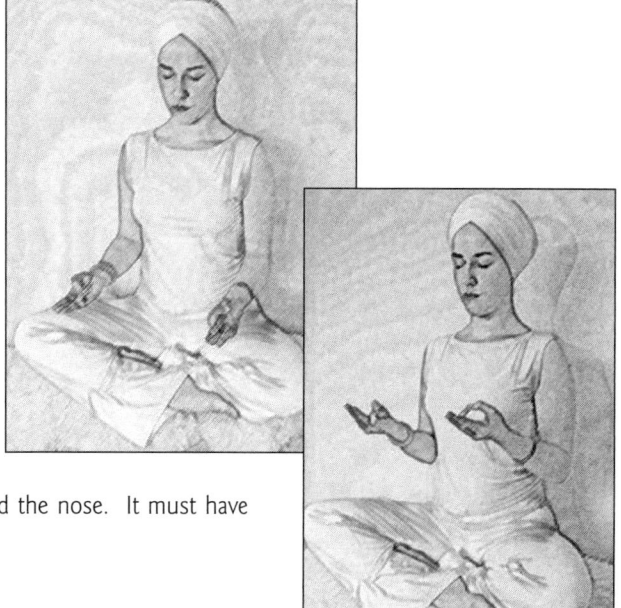

… Sets & Meditations … Meditations with Mantra

Parasympathetic Rejuvenation Meditation with the Gong

Sit in an Easy Pose, with a light *jalandhar bandh*.

EYE POSITION: Close the eyes completely. Press the eyes up slightly to focus through the Brow Point. Visualize and sense the entire body simultaneously.

MUDRA: Make the spine erect, straight and comfortable. Equalize the tension in the body so that both sides feel equal. Tuck the lower spine forward, but do not force it. Relax both arms and elbows. Place the hands on the knees with the palms face down.

BREATH & FOCUS: Focus on the flow of breath. Let it become slow, and meditative. Start with even, deep, complete yogic breaths. Then let the breath gradually become lighter and more meditative. It should breathe itself once you fully concentrate and become still.

The teacher of the class will play the gong. It should go through at least three cycles of build-up and release. End the gong with soft final tones and a long die-out, so the gong slowly comes to a natural rest. If there is not a gong or a teacher who knows the art of gong-playing, use a gong tape with good speakers that reproduce most of the tones. A tape can capture up to about 80 percent if the range if the system is very good.

TIME: Continue for **6-31 minutes**.

TO END: Inhale deeply and relax.

COMMENTS
The mantra for this meditation is the sound of the gong. As you listen to the gong's sound, it will penetrate every cell and fiber of your body. At times it can seem frightening or overwhelming. Emotions and thoughts are provoked from the subconscious. The entire nervous system is put under a pressure to adjust and to heal itself. When that pressure builds, totally relax in the deepest meditation possible. Surrender the mind and body. The sound will carry you beyond all fears. The pressure will release the nervous system of many illnesses. Feel yourself ride the sound into the Infinite itself. If you play or listen to the gong 11 minutes or longer, do not drink any water for a half hour after the meditation.

This meditation will clear the nerve-endings and make you very sensitive to the motions of *prana* and to the effects of sound. The restriction on water allows the sympathetic and parasympathetic systems to interact with each other internally rather than turning their energy to another task.

The parasympathetic nervous system is ruled by sound. The sympathetic nervous system is ruled by vision. It is the sympathetic system that needs to be regulated. When it triggers too often and in the wrong regions of the body, you can be greatly weakened. The parasympathetic system regulates the sympathetic. But it is weakened by drugs and by poor health. To regenerate the parasympathetic system, nothing is more powerful than the sound of the gong.

(See Yogi Bhajan's tape on playing gong and Spirit Songs CD from Ancient Healing Ways.)

Pran Bandha Mantra Meditation

Sit in an Easy Pose, with a light *jalandhar bandh*.

EYE POSITION: Focus at the Brow Point, at the screen of the forehead. Roll the eyes up slightly.

MUDRA: Let the hands rest in the lap, right hand into the left palm. Or just sit with both hands in Gyan Mudra. Become completely still, physically and mentally, like a calm ocean. Listen to the chant for a minute. Feel its rhythm in every cell. Then join in the mantra.

MANTRA:

> PAVAN PAVAN PAVAN PAVAN
> PARA PARAA, PAVAN GUROO
> PAVAN GUROO, WHAA-HAY GUROO
> WHAA-HAY GUROO, PAVAN GUROO

TIME: Continue for **11-31 minutes**.

COMMENTS

Pran Bandha Mantra means that mantra, or sound combination, that collects, binds, and commands the life force or prana. In our usual non-liberated state, we are controlled by our attachments. We become attached to our finite identity, or to time, space, and intensity of emotion or experience. This mantra takes you beyond those finite attachments. It opens the door to another dimension of the Self. It merges you into the unlimited sea of *prana* and life.

Mantras are revealed or discovered in higher states of consciousness. The seer is aware of both the subtle and gross aspects of the sound. In the subtle realms of consciousness it is the particular blend of qualities that creates the manifestation of things, thoughts, and feelings into our normal life.

This mantra forges a link between you as a finite unit magnetic field and the universal, creative magnetic field of energy that we call consciousness. The mantra is from Guru Nanak's *Jap-ji*. One who practices this to perfection experiences deathlessness. You can merge into the greater *pranic* body that does not die with the physical body. Prayers and mental desires become much more effective. This meditation can give you the capacity to embody a divine personality, and to become creative and fearless.

Rejuvenation Meditation

Originally taught by Yogi Bhajan in February 1979

Sit in an Easy Pose, with a light *jalandhar bandh*.

EYE POSITION: Focus the eyes past the tip of the nose toward the distant ground and beyond into the depths of the Earth.

MUDRA: Relax the arms down along the sides. Bring the hands in front of the chest with the palms toward the torso. Keep the elbows snug against the side of the ribs. Join the hands along the sides of the palms and the sides of the little fingers. Spread the fingers and thumbs apart. Bend the wrists so the palms face up toward the sky.

BREATH & MANTRA: The breath must be precise. Inhale deeply and slowly through semi-puckered lips. Hold the breath in for **4 seconds** (or the length of one mental cycle of the mantra).

SAA TAA NAA MAA

Then exhale powerfully in **4 equal strokes** through the nose. As you exhale mentally recite the mantra:

SAA TAA NAA MAA

Then hold the breath out for **2 seconds** or the length of one mental **WHAA-HAY GUROO**.

TIME: Continue for **11 minutes**. With practice, increase to **31 minutes**.

COMMENTS

This is a potent meditation for the glandular system. It is a "medical meditation." Its effects are strong enough to help the system fight disease. It does not replace allopathic forms of medicine, but it does open the healing and preventative capacity of your body. The meditation focuses its effects on the glandular system, the guardians of your health.

Be careful to start slowly with this *pranayam*. It can make you very spacey and dreamy. It is best to practice this before going to bed. If you master it, you will know why the yogis and sages always call breath the energy of life.

Seven-Wave "Sat Nam" Meditation

Sit in Easy Pose, with a light *jalandhar bandh*.

EYE POSITION: The eyes are closed, looking up, focusing at the Brow Point.

MUDRA: Place the palms flat together at the center of the chest in Prayer Pose, with thumbs touching the center of the sternum.

MANTRA:

SAT NAAM

BREATH & MANTRA PATTERN: Inhale deeply, concentrating on the breath. With the exhale, chant the mantra in the law of seven (the law of the tides). Vibrate **SAT** in six waves, and let **NAAM** be the seventh. On each wave, thread the sound through the chakras beginning at the base of the spine at the First Chakra. On **NAAM**, let the energy and sound radiate from the Seventh Chakra at the top of the head through the aura, unto Infinity. As the sound penetrates each chakra, gently pull the physical area it corresponds to. The first center is the rectum; the second is the sex organs; the third is the Navel Point; the fourth is the heart; the fifth is the throat' the sixth is the Brow Point; and the seventh is the top of the head.

TIME: Continue for **11-31 minutes**.

COMMENTS

If you can build this meditation to at least 31 minutes per day, the mind will be cleansed just as the ocean waves wash the sandy beach. This is a *bij* (seed) mantra meditation. *Bij* mantras such as *Sat Naam* are sounds which can totally rearrange the habit patterns. We all have habit patterns—we could not function without them. But sometimes the patterns we have created are not wanted. You have changed, so you want the patterns to change. By vibrating the sound current *Sat Naam* in this manner, you activate the energy of the mind that erases and establishes habits.

This meditation is good as an introduction to Kundalini Yoga. It will open the mind to new experience. A long-time student will still meditate in this way, particularly to clear off the effects of a hurried day before beginning another deep meditation. After chanting this mantra, you will feel calm, relaxed, and mellow.

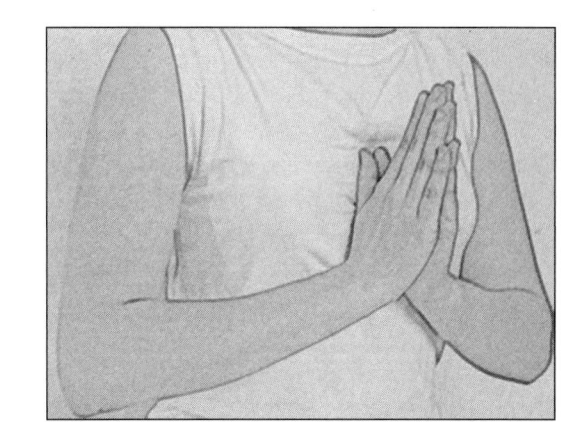

| Sets & Meditations | Meditations with Mantra |

Sodarshan Chakra Kriya

Originally taught by Yogi Bhajan in Demember 1990

Sit in an Easy Pose, with a light *jalandhar bandh*.

EYE POSITION: The eyes are fixed at the tip of the nose. (This meditation is not to be done with the eyes closed.

MANTRA:

WHAA-HAY GUROO

MUDRA & BREATH PATTERN:
a) Block the right nostril with the right thumb. Inhale slowly and deeply through the left nostril. Suspend the breath. Mentally chant the mantra **WHAA-HAY GU-ROO** **16 times**. Pump the Navel Point **3 times** with each repetition, once on **WHAA**; once on **HAY**; and once on **GUROO**, for a total of **48 unbroken pumps**. $1/3$ $1/3$ $1/3$
b) After the **16 repetitions**, unblock the right nostril. Place the right index finger (pinkie finger can also be used) to block off the left nostril, and exhale slowly and deeply through the right nostril.
c) Continue repeating a) & b)

TIME: for **11-31 minutes**. Master practitioners may extend this practice to **62 minutes,** then to **2-1/2 hours** a day.

TO END: Inhale, hold the breath **5-10 seconds,** then exhale. Stretch the arms up and shake every part of your body for **1 minute**, so the energy can spread.

COMMENTS

This is one of the greatest meditations you can practice. It has considerable transformational powers. The personal identity is rebuilt, giving the individual a new perspective on the Self. It retrains the mind. According to the *tantra shastras*, it can purify your past karma and the subconscious impulses that may block you from fulfilling you. It balances all the 27 facets of life and mental projection, and gives you the *pranic* power of health and healing. It establishes inner happiness and a state of flow and ecstasy in life. It opens your inner universe to relate, co-create, and complete the external universe.

This meditation balances the Teacher aspect of the mind. It acts on all the other aspects like a mirror to reveal their true nature and adds corrections. You act as a human being not just a human doing. If the Teacher aspect is too strong, you risk a spiritual ego, which becomes too attached to the ability to detach and to be "above" normal struggles. When the Teacher aspect is too weak, you can mis-use your spiritual and teaching position for personal advantage.

When balanced, the Teacher aspect is impersonally personal. It starts with absolute awareness and a neutral assessment from that awareness. The Teacher uses intuition to know directly what is real and what is a diversion. You respond from the Neutral Mind beyond the positives and negatives. You are clear about the purpose and the laws of each action. A complete Teacher is not an instructor. The Teacher is the expression of Infinity for the benefit of all. You master non-attachment so that you are simultaneously in all your activities and not of them.

Treat the practice with reverence and increase your depth, dimensions, caliber, and happiness. It gives you a new start against all odds.

"Of all the 20 types of yoga, including Kundalini Yoga, this is the highest Kriya. This meditation cuts through all darkness. It will give you a new start. It is the simplest *kriya*, but at the same time the hardest. It cuts through all barriers of the neurotic or psychotic inside-nature. When a person in a very bad state, techniques imposed from the outside will not work. The pressure has to be stimulated from within. The tragedy of life is when the subconscious releases garbage into the conscious mind. This *kriya* invokes the Kundalini to give you the necessary vitality and intuition to combat the negative effects of the subconscious mind.

There is no time, no place, no space, and no condition attached to this mantra. Each garbage point has its own time to clear. If you are going to clean your own garbage, you must estimate and clean it as fast as you can, or as slow as you want. Start practicing slowly—the slower the better. Start with five minutes a day, and gradually build the time to either 31 or 62 minutes. Maximum time is 2-1/2 hours for practice of this meditation."   - YOGI BHAJAN

Tershula Kriya
"Thunderbolt of Shiva"

Sit in an Easy Pose, with a light *jalandhar bandh*.

EYE POSITION: The eyes are closed looking at the back of the eyelids.

MUDRA: Bring the elbows next to the ribs, forearms extended in front of you, with the hands in front of the heart, right over left, palms up. The hands are approximately 10 degrees higher than the elbows. There is no bend in the wrists. The arms from the fingertips to the elbows form a straight line. The thumbs are extended out to the sides of the hands, the fingertips and palms are slightly offset.

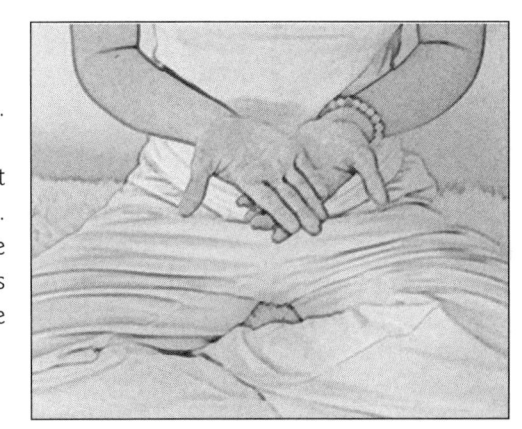

MANTRA: Mentally chant the mantra:

HAR HAR WHAA-HAY GU-ROO

BREATH & VISUALIZATION: Inhale through the nostrils, pull back on the navel, and suspend the breath. Mentally chant the mantra for as long as you are able while retaining the breath. While chanting, visualize your hands surrounded by white light. Exhale through the nostrils and visualize lightning shooting out from your fingertips. When you have completely exhaled, hold the breath out, pull *mulbandh*, and again mentally recite the mantra as long as you are able. Inhale deeply and continue.

TIME: Recommended time of practice is **31-62 minutes**.

COMMENT

Tershula is the thunderbolt of Shiva (one of the Hindu Trinity of gods): Brahma, Vishnu and Shiva, Shiva is the destroyer or regenerator. *Tershula* can activate the self-healing process. This meditation balances the three *gunas*—the three qualities that permeate all creation: *rajas, tamas,* and *sattva*. It brings the three nervous systems together. It gives you the ability to heal at a distance, through your touch or through your projection. Many psychological disorders or imbalances in the personality can be cured through practice of this *kriya*, and it is helpful in getting rid of phobias, especially father phobia.

It is suggested that this meditation be done in a cool room, or at night when the temperature is cooler, since it directly stimulates the kundalini and generates a great deal of heat in the body.

Sets & Meditations | **Meditations with Mantra**

Venus Kriyas

How to Practice Venus Kriyas
Venus Kriyas are Kundalini Yoga exercises done with a partner, usually a partner of the opposite sex. Although Venus Kriyas are less intense than White Tantric Yoga, they fall into the category of a more advanced Kundalini Yoga practice, because they intensify the experience of the exercise through the polarities of the male-female interaction. So, adhere to the following guidelines when teaching or practicing Venus Kriyas:
- Always tune in with the Adi Mantra: Ong Namo Guru Dev Namo before practicing Venus Kriyas.
- Venus Kriyas are not done to sensually or sexually seduce one's partner. They are done from a state of elevation, to elevate the relationship and the polarities to a purity and their highest vibration. If done with the wrong intention, they lose their effectiveness and in fact, it can be more damaging than helpful.
- Limit the exercise to 3 minutes (unless specifically taught otherwise by Yogi Bhajan.)

Teaching Venus Kriyas
If you are a Kundalini Yoga teacher, and are going to teach Venus Kriyas follow these guidelines:
- It is best to reserve Venus Kriyas only for those with Kundalini Yoga experience. Use your judgement to assess when your students have the disicpline to practice Venus Kriyas. In Venus Kriyas, the energetic and sensory connections of the partners are used to elevate the sexual and sensory energy to a connection based on awareness and the capacity to see the sacred in the other.
- Do not line up in lines as in Tantric Yoga. Two people can sit together anywhere. If you line up, then the energy is shared diagonally. That is not the intention of Venus Kriyas. The energy is only intended to be shared between partners.
- Do not create an entire class using Venus Kriyas. Just use one or two along with a Kundalini Yoga kriya. Yogi Bhajan often added a short Venus Kriya to his Friday classes, to honor the ruling planet Venus.

Here are two separate Venus Kriyas.

Heart Lotus
Sit in Easy Pose or Lotus Pose across from your partner. Look into his or her eyes.

Part 1
Form your hands into a lotus: all your fingers are spread with the hands cupped, and only your little fingers will touch. The man suspends his little fingers under the woman's little fingers, but the fingers of the partners DO NOT touch. This makes a heart lotus. Look into the soul, the heart of your partner, through the eyes. Continue for **1-1/2 to 3 minutes.**

Part 2
Now place one hand over the other at the Heart Center. Close your eyes and meditate on the Heart Center. Go deep within, to the center of your being. Continue for **1-1/2 to 3 minutes.**

TO END: Inhale deeply and exhale deeply **3 times,** then relax.

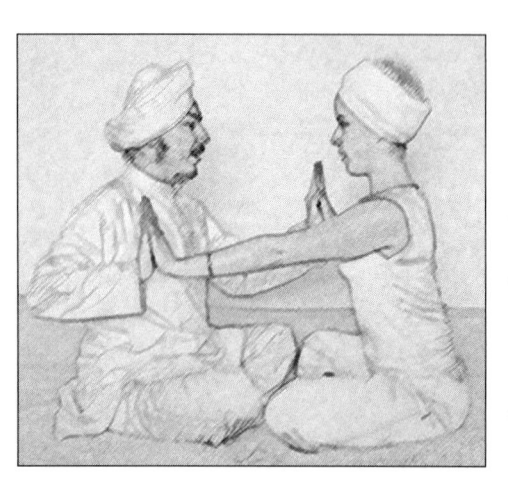

Pushing Palms (Mitna Kriya)
Sit in Easy Pose facing your partner, knees touching. Look into your partner's eyes. Place your palms on your partner's. Begin pushing the palms alternately while rhythmically chanting the Guru Gaitri Mantra:

**GOBINDAY, MUKANDAY, UDAARAY, APAARAY,
HAREEUNG, KAREEUNG, NIRNAAMAY, AKAAMAY**

The woman chants the entire mantra first, then the man.

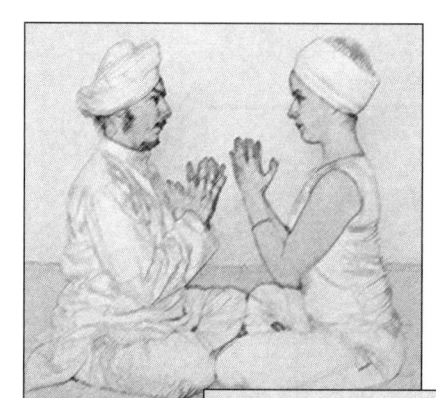

Resources for the Kundalini Yoga Teacher

Includes . . .

Resource Organizations
  Kundalini Research Institute (KRI) • 3HO (Healthy, Happy, Holy Organization)
  3HO International Kundalini Yoga Teachers Association (IKYTA)
  3HO Events • White Tantric Yoga • Spiritual Name Requests • Yogi Bhajan
  Yoga Alliance • Sikh Dharma
Resources for Products & Publications
Publications

Individual consciousness will refine you, group consciousness will expand you, and universal consciousness will redeem you to Infinity.
—YOGI BHAJAN

Resources for the Kundalini Yoga Teacher

Resource Organizations

Kundalini Research Institute (KRI)

The Kundalini Research Institute exists to:
▸ Create global recognition and access to the Teachings of Yogi Bhajan through product development and the Library of teachings.
▸ Uphold the purity, integrity and accuracy of the Teachings of Yogi Bhajan through KRI Review and the KRI Seal of Approval.
▸ Offer support for authors to create and translate products based on the Teachings of Yogi Bhajan.
▸ Create the KRI International Kundalini Yoga Teacher Training certificaiton programs.

For a list of Kundalini Yoga products with the KRI Seal of Approval, please view the KRI website:
www.kundaliniresearchinstitute.org

The KRI Seal of Approval is granted only to products that are approved through KRI review. Look for this seal to guarantee the accuracy and integrity of the science of Kundalini Yoga and 3HO Lifestyle as taught by Yogi Bhajan.

Kundalini Research Institute (KRI)
PO Box 1819, Santa Cruz, NM 87567
(505)629-1048 Fax: (505)753-5982
www.kundaliniresearchinstitute.org
www.yogibhajan.org

3HO Foundation
(Healthy, Happy, Holy Organization)

3HO is an international non-profit organization dedicated to sharing a Healthy, Happy, Holy lifestyle and the science of Kundalini Yoga as taught by Yogi Bhajan, Master of Kundalini Yoga, through education, service, and spirit.

Men and women of varying age, race, ethnicity, religion and cultural background consider themselves part of the worldwide 3HO community. 3HO believes that diversity is a key part of the organization's ability to serve humanity as a whole. What brings people together in association with 3HO is the desire to live a meaningful lifestyle and to be of service to the betterment of humankind.

3HO International
PO Box 1560, Santa Cruz, NM 87567
1-888-346-2420 Fax: (424)731-8348
www.3HO.org

3HO International Kundalini Yoga Teachers Association (IKYTA)

Membership in IKYTA:

All participants enrolled in *The Aquarian Teacher* Level 1 Teacher Training program in the US and Canada automatically become Associate Members of IKYTA. Upon receipt of a KRI Level 1 Teaching Certificate, all newly certified teachers are upgraded to Professional Membership for the remainder of the calendar year. IKYTA membership must be renewed annually. Professional Members receive, in addition to Associate membership benefits, referrals from IKYTA, personalized listings in the annual Kundalini Yoga Teachers Directory online and in *Aquarian Times* magazine, and more! Please view the IKYTA membership form online at www.ikyta.org for current membership benefits.

The goals of IKYTA are:
1) To create unity among Kundalini Yoga Teachers.
2) To create communication among all 3HO Kundalini Yoga Teacher Associations worldwide.
3) To maintain an online directory of it's Professional Members, who are KRI Certified Teachers, for referral and networking.
4) To ensure the excellence of all Kundalini Yoga Teachers, classes and Teacher Training systems.
5) To train successful teachers who are knowledgeable about Kundalini Yoga, meditation and 3HO lifestyle, and skillful at marketing to reach the maximum number of people.
6) To promote IKYTA members, and Teacher Training programs worldwide.
7) To gain public recognition for 3HO and Kundalini Yoga among the general public and the yoga community.

3HO International Kundalini Yoga
Teachers Association (IKYTA)
P.O. Box 1560, Santa Cruz, NM 87567
(505)819-0886
www.ikyta.org

Resources for the Kundalini Yoga Teacher
RESOURCE ORGANIZATIONS

3HO Events

3HO Camps & Events
3HO sponsors international yoga-based camps and festivals throughout the year and around the globe. Some of these include:

- Summer Solstice in New Mexico
- Winter Solstice in Florida
- Yoga Festivals throughout Europe, and South America
- Ladies Camp
- The Master's Touch
- Khalsa Youth Camps

These camps are designed to give people the opportunity to experience and practice Kundalini Yoga, meditation, vegetarian diet, and conscious living. They also serve to create a community of people on the path of self-discovery and spiritual consciousness.

3HO Events Information
PO Box 1560, Santa Cruz, NM 87567
1-888-346-2420
www.3HO.org/events

International Peace Prayer Day
Each June people from all walks of life including spiritual leaders, musicians, humanitarians, and politicians of all faiths gather in the Jemez Mountains of northern New Mexico for this day-long 3HO event. This special event includes the awarding of grants to organizations working for peace and honors a Man and Woman of Peace for the year. The day also includes a Sacred Healing Walk, an old Hopi Indian custom which was handed down to us as caretakers of this sacred land.

www.3HO.org
1-888-346-2420 or 505-629-0267

White Tantric Yoga

"The beauty of White Tantric Yoga is that it is subtle, it is exalting, and it works to give you the mastery of life."
—Yogi Bhajan

www.whitetantricyoga.com

Spiritual Name Requests

Receiving a spiritual name reinforces and accelerates your progress on the path to your highest destiny. Yogi Bhajan trained Nirinjan Kaur Khalsa, his Chief of Staff, in his method of determining spiritual names. We are pleased that we can continue to provide this service. Please remember that a spiritual name is a powerful vibratory blessing, and should be sought only if you sincerely plan to use it with reverence.

Request a spiritual name online at the 3HO website:
www.3HO.org/spiritual-names
Or send written requests to:
Spiritual Names Office
1A Ram Das Guru Place
Española, NM 87532

Offerings: Yogi Bhajan taught that in accordance with cosmic law, it is customary to give in order to receive. We humbly suggest that you include an offering with your spiritual name request. You can make your check or money order payable to: '3HO Offering.'

Yoga Alliance

IKYTA is a founding member of the Yoga Alliance, a national alliance of diverse yoga organizations. It's purpose is to provide support services to yoga professionals, and to establish standards for the field. It provides a registry of teachers who meet the national standards created for Yoga Teacher Training in the United States. Once you become a KRI certified teacher, you will be eligible to join the Yoga Alliance, and become part of the registry with rights to use the YA logo on promotional materials.

1-888-921-9642
info@yogaalliance.org   www.yogaalliance.org

Sikh Dharma

For more information on the Sikh way of life, including music, Yogi Bhajan's lectures, and Prosperity yoga sets and meditations, visit:

www.sikhdharma.org
www.sikhnet.com, www.dasvandh.org

Sikh Dharma International
PO Box 2213
Espanola, New Mexico 87532 USA
(505) 629-1562

Resources for the Kundalini Yoga Teacher
RESOURCES FOR PRODUCTS & PUBLICATIONS

Resources for Products & Publications

To order Kundalini Yoga books, manuals, audio and videotapes and CDs, we recommend the following resources:

▸ KUNDALINI RESEARCH INSTITUTE
Buy from The Source.
www.kundaliniresearchinstitute.org

THE SOURCE, KRI's online bookstore:
www.thesource.kriteachings.org
customerservice@kriteachings.org

▸ ANCIENT HEALING WAYS
Distributors of Kundalini Yoga products, including books, videos, tapes, CDs, Yogi Bhajan live lectures.
International Contact info:

www.a-healing.com
1-877-753-5351 or (505)753-5351
PO Box 459, Española, NM 87532
sirirams@windstream.net

IKYTA members receive a 10% discount on all retail orders.
Wholesale discounts available.

▸ SPIRIT VOYAGE MUSIC

15806 Woodgrove Road, Purcellville VA 20132
www.spiritvoyage.com
1-888-735-4800
info@spiritvoyage.com

15% discount for all IKTYA Members on retail orders.
Wholesale discounts available.

In Europe:
▸ SAT NAM VERSAND

www.satnam.eu
info@satnam.eu
Tel (0049) - (0) 6078 / 78 90 60
Fax (0049) - (0) 6078 / 78 90 65

3HO products, including music, books, videos

Publications

▸ AQUARIAN TIMES NEWSLETTER
Aquarian Times is 3HO's monthly newsletter offering inspiration, support, and resources for staying connected and living the healthy, happy, holy lifestyle.

Subscribe at: www.3HO.org

Index

3 ½ cycle meditation, 12, 101
108 repetitions,
   exercises containing, 13, 26, 36, 39, 79

A

Abdomen, 19, 20-21, 30, 33, 49-50
   toning exercises, 19, 21
Addiction (see also Drugs, Habits),
   meditation to heal, 109
Adho Mukha Svanasana (Triangle Pose), 10, 35, 47
   Triangle Push-Up, 23
Adi Shakti, 93
   mantra (Morning Call), 103
Adrenal glands, exercises for, 24-25, 58
Advanced Students, exercises for, 14-16, 19, 53, 64, 67, 75, 126
Aerobic capacity,
   increase, 58
Aging (see Vitality, Youthfulness)
Aloud (voice), 99
Alternating exercises
   arm stretch,
      forward, 40
      upward, 40
   back platform, 31
   buttock kicks, 20, 52
   head & leg lifts, 44
   leg kicks (Rhythmic Kick), 32
   leg lifts, 19, 25, 44
   plow pose, 15
   shoulder shrugs, 12, 35
   side bends, 14
   toe touches, 15
   windmill, 14, 33
   Yoga Mudra, 31, 46, 47
Alternate Nostril Breathing, 59, 78
Anger (see Emotions)
Anxiety (see Emotions)
Apana, 101, 103
   exercises for, 18, 20-21, 44, 48, 76
Aquarian Age, 72, 99, 103
Archer Pose (*Virabhadrasana*), 14
Arcline, 11, 115
   exercises to repair, 64, 99-100
Arm Pumps, 12, 39-40
Arm Swings,
   seated, 39
   standing, 45
Arm Stretch, 39
   exercises stretching arms, 40, 41, 43, 45, 54
Ashtang Mantra, 103
Assessment,
   of your energy, 60, 114
Attention (see Focus)
Aura,
   balancing, 20, 100
   karma coded in, 76
   linking, 74
   to sense, 18, 101
   to strengthen, 19, 23, 92, 93
Awareness,
   breath, 60, 69, 77
   expanded, 68, 74, 87-88, 107
   Yoga of, v

B

Baby Pose (*Garbhasana*), 46
Back,
   general exercises for, 10, 13, 14-16
   see also Back Rolls, Cat-Cow, Cobra Pose, Shoulder Shrugs, Spinal Flex, Spinal Twist
   strengthen lower back, 20, 43, 50
Back Platform (*Parvottasana*), 31, 43, 50
Back Rolls, 25, 38
Backwards stretch (standing), 14, 54
Balance (see also Chakra(s)),
   exercises to increase, 59
   mineral balance, 50
Beginner Students, sets for, 13, 59, 69
Bhujangasana (Cobra Pose), 10, 18, 38, 47, 52
Body Drops, 24
Bow Pose (*Dhanurasana*), 14, 42, 52
Bowel, exercises for, 33
Bowing,
   seated (moving), 34, 43, 44, 47
   seated (still), 15, 38, 51
   standing (moving), 14, 37, 45
Brain,
   exercises for, 31, 61, 91
   stimulate with Front Platform, 20
   Breath, 77
   awareness, 60, 77
   command of breath, 63
   projection of, 63
Breath of Fire,
   exercises with,
      arm stretch, 39
      baby pose, 46
      back platform, 31, 43
      bow pose, 42
      camel pose, 51
      cobra pose, 18, 38, 52
      criss-cross arms, 46
      criss-cross legs, 45
      ego eradicator, 11, 17
      fish pose, 42
      front platform, 20
      heart center opener, 43
      heart center pull, 48
      knee-forehead balance, 51
      leg lifts, 44, 45
      life nerve stretch, 20
      lion paws, 61
      lunge stretch, 47
      Maha Mudra, 17
      mudra at solar plexus, 24
      nose-to-knees, 11
      plow pose, 51
      shoulder stand, 44, 51
      stretch pose, 11, 42, 48, 51, 52,
      wheel pose, 42
      yoga mudra, 31, 47
   meditations with, 59, 61, 65, 77, 81, 90
Butterfly, 37
   bend, 37
   pose, 52
Buttock Kicks, 20, 51-52

C

Calmness (see Emotions)
Camel Pose (*Ustrasana*), 51
Camel Ride (Spinal Flex), 11, 13, 17, 26, 36, 41, 54, 58
Cannon Breath, 24
Cardiovascular System (see also Circulation, Hypertension),
   sets to strengthen, 10, 22, 58
Cat-Cow (*Marjariasana*) Pose, 16, 25, 29, 35-36
Celibate Pose, sets containing, 11, 48, 51
Chair Pose, 54
Chakra(s),
   balancing all, 17-22, 103
   exercises for, 26-28, 32, 34-35, 45, 49, 52, 55, 67, 86, 90, 96, 115, 123-24
   opening for meditation, 86
   sample sets for each, 55
Chants (See Mantras)
Chaturanga Dandasana (Push-up), 10
Children's Meditation, 97
Circulation (see also Cardiovascular System, Lymphatic System),
   exercises for arm, 17
   exercises to improve general, 10, 17, 41
   exercises for leg, 45
Circulatory Flush,
   baby pose with breath of fire, 46
Clarity (see Mental Clarity)
Cobra Pose (*Bhujangasana*), 10, 18, 38, 47, 52
Commitment,
   exercises to increase, 62
Complexion,
   exercises to improve, 43
Composite Polarity Meditation, 64
Concentration (see Mental Clarity, Focus)
Confusion,
   exercises to eliminate, 13, 45
Consciousness,
   higher consciousness, 71, 87-88, 99-100, 101
   languages of, 99
Corpse Pose (Savasana), 18, 25, 35, 38
Creation, cycle of, 99
Creativity,
   exercises to enhance, 71, 72
   projection, 87
Criss-Cross Arms, 46
Criss-Cross Legs, 45

D

Deathlessness, 121
Depression (see Emotions)
Dhanurasana (Bow Pose), 14, 42, 52
Diaphragm Lock (see also *Uddiyana Bandh*), 44
Digestion (see also Bowel), 10, 22, 34-35, 81
   leg pistoning to aid, 20
   kicking buttocks to aid, 20
   relieve difficult, 20-21, 23
   shoulder stand, 51
Disease (see also Immune System), 58
Dizziness (during exercises),
   breathing, 42, 63
   neck lock, 63
   water, 63
Drugs (see also Addiction),
   detoxification, 14-16
   rehabilitation, 109

Index

E

Ego,
    Eradicator, 11, 17, 47
    spiritual ego, 5, 124
Ek Ong Kar Sat Gur Prasad mantra, 98
Ek Ong Kar Sat Nam Siri Wahe Guru mantra, 101, 103, 105
Electromagnetic Field,
    exercises for, 43-44, 45, 46, 61
Elephant Walk, 35
Elimination (see also Detoxification, Digestion),
    exercises to assist, 17, 28, 35, 49, 52
Emotions,
    exercises for,
        anger, 67, 71
        anxiety, 49, 50
        calmness, 28, 68, 69, 73, 78, 79, 80
        depression, 63, 65, 92
        fear, 45, 75, 92, 108, 109
        happiness, 62, 92
        insecurity, 108
        worry, 73, 78
    release habitual patterns of, 59
Energy (see also Chakra(s), Kundalini),
    exercises to boost, 59
    and breath, 60
    sensing, 18, 74, 101
Eyes (see also Gazing),
    spiritual sight, 98, 99-100
    circulatory flush, 46
    develop pranic energy of, 43, 48, 49, 51, 81-83

F

Fear (see Emotions)
Fish Pose *(Supta Virasana)*, 42, 51
Fingers,
    significance of, 93, 100
Focus (Concentration, see also Mental Clarity),
    exercises to improve, 26-27, 59, 69, 70, 81, 101, 108
Frog Pose, 12, 26, 53
Front Bend *(Uttanasana)*, 10, 19, 31, 37, 45, 47
Front Life Nerve Stretch, 17
Front Platform, 20
Front Stretch, 15, 34, 43
    with Straight Spine, 24, 29
Full Moon
    meditations, 86, 95

G

Garbhasana (Baby Pose), 46
Gazing meditations,
    candle, 81
    horizon, 81
    upwards, 81
Golden Chain, 82, 87
Grace of God, 93
Great Seal of Yoga (see *Maha Mudra*)
Guru Gaitri Mantra, 126
Guru Pranam (Supta Parvatasana), 15, 43, 51
Guidance (also see Mental Clarity),
    exercises to receive, 87-88
Guru Yoga, 82
Gyan Mudra, 12, 59, 69

H

Habits (Habitual Patterns),
    exercise to release, 59, 78, 123
    habits of a yogi, 60, 107

Hands,
    relieving blocked energy in, 21
Happiness (see Emotions)
Harmony,
    exercises to bring, 34, 68, 103
Headache,
    covering the head, 65
    during Kirtan Kriya, 99
    Lotus Walk to relieve, 50
Healers,
    distance healing, 125
    exercises for, 21, 89-90
Healing, 21, 89-90, 95, 96, 109
Hearing (inner) sounds, 70
Heart (see Cardiovascular System)
Heart Center, 21, 31, 34, 43-44
    pull, 48
    still point, 69
Hernia, exercises to alleviate, 29
Hormones,
    balance, 43-44, 49-50
    shoulder shrugs, 18
Hypertension (see also Cardiovascular System)
    exercises to combat, 70

I

Ida Meditation, 90
Immune System,
    exercises to strengthen, 23, 28, 34-35, 65, 67, 122
Index Finger (see Jupiter Finger)
Indra Nittri meditation, 98
Inner Conflict, , 65, 66, 80
Insecurity (see Emotions)
Intuition,
    increase, 60, 80, 87-88, 98, 101, 115, 124
Inverted postures,
    sets containing 12, 14-16, 19, 23, 26, 35, 37

J

Jalandhar Bandh (Neck Lock), 58, 60-73, 75, 78, 79-80, 86-87, 91, 94, 96, 98, 101-103, 106-116, 119-125
Jupiter Finger (Index Finger), 65, 68, 93-94, 99-100, 105, 106, 107, 112, 113, 117, 118

K

Karma,
    cleansing exercises, 76, 82-83, 94, 103, 124
Kicking
    buttocks, 20, 52
    knee-forehead balance with, 51
    cat-cow variation, 29
Kidneys,
    exercises for, 24-25, 29-30, 58
Kirtan Kriya, 99
Knee and Elbow Walk, 50
Knees to Chest, 19
    nose to knees, 11, 29
    back rolls, 25, 38
    with buttock kick, 20
Kunchun Mudra, 30
Kundalini,
    and The Golden Chain, 87
    initiating, 103
    pulse rhythm, 101
    pumping the stomach, 34
    Shabd Brahm, 89
    stimulate, 22, 26-27, 96, 124 125
    to open flow, 18, 76, 86

L

Laya Yoga Meditation, 101
Leg Lifts, 14, 19, 38, 44-45, 48
Leg Pistoning, 20, 38
Life Nerve Stretch,
    front *(Paschimottanasana)*, 17, 43
    left-right *(Upavistha Konasana)*, 11, 15, 18, 37
Linked Jaap, 104
Little Finger (see Mercury Finger)
Long Chant (Long *Ek Ong Kar's*), 103
Locust Pose *(Salabhasana)*, 14
Lotus Point, 116
Lotus Walk, 50
Lungs (see also Respiratory System),
    exercises to strengthen, 10, 40-41, 58, 69
    arm pumps, 12
    arm swings, 45
    moving yoga mudra, 46
    increase efficiency, 58
    open,
        ego eradicator, 11, 17, 47
        life nerve stretch, 20
        spinal twist, 41
    preparatory exercises for praanayam, 45-46
    rebuild, 45-46
    rejuvenate,
        criss-cross arms, 46
    stimulate lung meridians, 45
Lunge Stretch, 47, 49
Lymphatic System,
    exercises for, 39, 61
    arm swings, 45

M

Magnetic Field,
    exercises for,
        criss-cross arms (heart), 46
        ego eradicator, 11, 17, 47
        elephant walk, 35
        knees-to-chest with leg extension, 19
        life nerve stretch, 18, 20
        moving yoga mudra, 46
        sets to strengthen, 40-41, 43-44, 45-46, 121
Maha Gyan mudra, 106
Mahan Jaap, 104
Maha Mudra, 44
    modified, 17
Mala meditation, 105
Mantra (see also Sound Current),
    discovery of, 121
MANTRAS
    Ad Guray Nameh, 111
    Ad Such, 106
    Adi, 87
    Adi Shakti, 108
    Ashtang, 103
    Ek Ong Kar Sat Gur Prasad, 98
    Ek Ong Kar Sat Nam Siri Wahe Guru, 121
    Gobinday Mukunday, 126
    Guru Gaitri, 126
    Har, 113
    Har Har Wahe Guru, 125
    Har Haray Hari Wahe Guru, 112
    Long Chant, 103
    Mangala Charn, 111
    Morning Call, 103
    Ong Namo Guru Dev Namo, 87
    Pran Bandha, 121

Index

Pavan Guru, 121
Ra Ma Da Sa, 96
Sa Re Sa Sa, 86
Sat Naam, 102, 116, 123
Sa Ta Na Ma, 99, 104, 109, 115
Siri Gaitri, 96
Sushmuna, 96
Wahe Guru, 116, 124
Marjariasana (Cat-Cow), 16, 25, 29, 35-36
Massage,
  ear, throat, 49
  organs, 10, 22
Meditation,
  preparing for,
    elephant walk, 35
  sets explicitly ending with, 21, 27, 28, 39, 41, 46, 76
  using the gong for, 120
  using the Mala for, 105
MEDITATIONS
  Adi Mantra (complete), 87-88
  Adi Shakti Mantra (Long Chant), 103
  Antar Naad Mudra, 86
  Awakening the Inner Healer, 89
  Blue Gap, 91
  Caliber of Life, 63
  Composite Polarity, 64
  Divine Shield, 92
  Divine Mother, 108
  Ego, to Change, 70
  Emotional Balance, 73
  For a Calm Heart, 69
  For a Stable Self, 75
  Grace of God, 93
  Gunpati Kriya, 94
  Healing Addictions, 109
  Healing Ring of Tantra, 95
  I am Happy, 97
  Ida, 90
  Inner Conflict Resolver, 66
  Indra Nittri, 98
  Laya Yoga, 12
  Liberated Heart, 67
  Mahan Jaap, 104
  Mala, 105
  Master's Touch, 106
  Naad to Communicate Honest Self, 118
  Naad to Communicate Totality, 117
  Naad: Naam Namodam Rasa, 119
  Open the Heart, 110
  Parasympathetic Rejuvenation with Gong, 120
  Pingala, 90
  Pran Bandha Mantra, 121
  Projection & Protection from the Heart, 111
  Prosperity I, 112
  Prosperity II, 113
  Rejuvenation, 122
  Self-Animosity, to Conquer, 71
  Self-Assessment, 114
  Self-Authority, 62
  Self-Blessing Guidance, 115
  Self-Sensory System, 72
  Seven-Wave, 123
  Stable Self, 75
  Stress or Sudden Shock, 116
  Sushmuna, 89
  Tratakum (Gazing), 81, 82
  Tattva Balance, 80
  Venus Kriya, 126
Memory, exercises to improve, 13

Menstrual problems, 49-50
Mental Clarity, 13, 59, 66, 69, 80, 89
Mental Illness, 109
Mentally Vibrate, 99
Mercury Finger, 24, 68, 78, 93, 99-100, 105, 113
Moon Mounds, 113
Morning Call, 103
Moving Yoga Mudra, 46
MUDRAS
  Brahma, 62
  Buddha (also Buddhi), 45, 99-100, 103, 119
  Gyan, 12, 26, 28, 30, 36, 59, 69, 87, 91, 93, 94, 99-100, 107, 108, 112, 114, 117, 118, 121
  Kunchun, 30
  Lion's Paws, 61
  Lotus, 24
    modified, 122
  Maha Gyan, 106
  Maha, 44
    modified, 17
  Prayer, 90, 101, 111, 123
  Shuni, 99-100
  Surya, 99-100, 118
  Yoga Mudra, 38, 47
    moving, 31, 46
Mulbandh (Root Lock), 13-15, 17-20, 22, 26-28, 41-42, 44, 47, 49, 51, 53, 75, 77-78, 125

N

Navel Center,
  exercises for the, 20, 42, 45
  Har mantra for, 45
  open navel energy (Lotus Walk), 50
  reset with Stretch Pose, 20
Neck Lock (see Jalandhar Bandh)
Neck Rolls, 13, 18, 34, 39, 44
Neck Turns, 12, 26
Nervous System,
  exercises to strengthen, 28, 35, 43-44, 61, 63, 123
  recovery from shock, 78, 116
Nose, tip (see Lotus Point)
Nose to Knees, 11, 29

O

Ong Namo Guru Dev Namo mantra
  (see also *Adi Mantra*), 87
Oxygen efficiency (see Respiratory System)

P

Parathyroid,
  exercises for, 43
Pelvic,
  circulation, 50
  relaxation, 49
  release, 31
Pineal Gland,
  exercises to balance, 61, 109
Pingala meditation, 90
Pinky Finger (see Mercury Finger)
Pituitary Gland,
  exercises to stimulate, 29, 61, 80
Platform Pose, back (*Parvottanasana*), 31, 43, 50
Platform Pose front, 20
Plow Pose (*Halasana*), 15, 51
Polarity Meditation, 64

POSTURES
  Adho Mukha Svanasana (Triangle Pose), 10, 23, 35, 47
  Alternate Head & Leg Lifts, 44
  Alternate Leg Lifts, 19, 44
  Alternate Shoulder Shrugs, 12, 35
  Archer, 14
  Arm Pumps, 12, 39-40, 46
  Arm Stretch, 39
  Arm Swings, 39, 45
  Baby Pose (*Garbhasana*), 46
  Back Platform (*Purvottanasana*), 31, 43, 50
  Back Rolls, 25
  Baddha Konasana (Butterfly Pose), 37, 52
  Bear Grip, 13, 34
  Bhujangasana (Cobra Pose), 10, 18, 38, 47, 52
  Body Drops, 24
  Bow Pose (*Dhanurasana*), 14, 42, 52
  Butterfly Pose (*Baddha Konasana*), 37, 52
  Buttock Kicks, 20, 51, 52
  Camel Pose (*Ustrasana*), 51
  Camel Ride (Spinal Flex), 11, 13, 17, 26, 36, 41, 54, 58
  Cat-Cow (*Marjariasana*), 16, 25, 29, 35-36
  Celibate Pose, 11, 48, 51
  Chair Pose, 54
  Chaturanga Dandasana (Push Up), 10
  Chest Stretch, 53
  Cobra Pose (*Bhugangasana*), 10, 18, 38, 47, 52
  Corpse Pose (*Savasana*), 18, 25, 35, 38
  Criss-Cross Arms, 46
  Criss-Cross Legs, 45
  Crow Pose, 30, 31
  Dhanurasana (Bow Pose), 14, 42, 52
  Ear Massage, 49
  Ego Eradicator, 11, 17, 47
  Elephant Walk, 35
  Fish Pose (*Supta Virasana*), 42, 51
  Frog Pose, 12, 26, 53
  Front Bends (*Uttanasana*), 10, 19, 31, 37, 45, 47
  Front Bend Bounce, 45
  Front Life Nerve Stretch, 17
  Front Platform, 20
  Front Stretch with Straight Spine, 24, 29
  Garbhasana (Baby Pose), 46
  Guru Pranam (*Supta Parvatasana*), 15, 43, 51
  Halasana (Plow Pose), 15, 51
  Heart Center Pull, 48
  Heart Center Stretch, 21
  Hugging Spinal Bend, 36
  Kandharasana (Pelvic Lifts), 29, 37
  Kicking Buttocks, 20
  Knee & Elbow Walk, 36, 50
  Knees to Chest, 19
  Leg Lifts, 14, 19, 38, 44-45, 48
  Leg Pistoning, 20, 38
  Life Nerve Stretch,
    front (*Paschimottanasana*), 15, 43
    left and right (*Upavistha Konasana*), 11, 15, 18, 37
  Locust Pose (*Salabhasana*), 14
  Lotus Walk, 50
  Lunge Stretch, 47, 49
  Marjariasana (Cat-Cow), 16, 25, 29, 35-36
  Mountain Pose (Standing Straight), 10
  Moving Yoga Mudra, 46
  Neck Rolls, 13, 18, 34, 39, 44
  Neck Turns, 12, 26
  Nose to Knees, 11, 29
  Paschimottanasana (Life Nerve Stretch, front), 26, 39
  Pelvic Lifts (*Kandharasana*), 29, 37

Index

Platform Pose, back (*Parvottanasana*), 31, 43, 50
Platform Pose, front, 20
Plow Pose (*Halasana*), 15, 51
Pumping the Stomach, 43
Purvottanasana (Back Platform), 31, 43, 50
Rising Up from the Knees, 48
Rock Pose (*Vajrasana*), 47
Salabhasana (Locust Pose), 14
Sat Kriya, 22
    sets containing, 13, 15, 18, 26, 53
Savasana (Corpse Pose), 18, 25, 35, 38
Shoulder Shrugs, 12, 13, 35, 39, 41
Side Bends, 14, 33
Side Stretch, 31
Sit Ups with Legs Wide, 49
Sitting Bends, 27
Spinal Bend, 27
Spinal Flex (Camel Ride), 11, 13, 17, 26, 36, 41, 54, 58
Spinal Twists (Torso Twists), 12, 13, 17, 33, 36, 41
Spinal Twist with Gyan Mudra, 36
Standing Straight, 10
Standing Torso Twists, 33
Stretch Pose, 11, 20, 42, 48, 51
Stretching Backward, 14
Stretching Up, 10
Sufi Grind, 38
Sun Salutation (*Surya Namaskar*), 10, 55
Supta Parvatasana (Guru Pranam), 15, 43, 51
Supta Virasana (Fish Pose), 42, 51
Surya Namaskar (Sun Salutation), 10, 55
Tadasana (Standing Straight), 10
Throat and Neck Massage, 49
Torso Twists (Spinal Twists), 12, 13, 17, 36, 41
Torso Twists (Standing), 33
Triangle Pose (*Adho Mukha Svanasana*), 10, 23, 35, 47
Upavistha Konasana (Life Nerve Stretch Left & Right), 11, 15, 17, 18, 20
Ustrasana (Camel Pose), 51
Uttanasana (Front Bend), 10, 19, 31, 37, 45, 47
Vajrasana (see Rock Pose)
Virabhadrasana (Archer Pose), 14
Wheel Pose (*Urdhva Danurasana*), 42
Windmill, 33
Yoga Mudra, 31, 38, 46-47
Prana (Pranic Flow),
    exercises for, 17, 20-21
Pran Bandha Mantra, 121
Pranic Body, 75
Projection (personality),
    exercises to strengthen, 23, 62, 63, 81, 87, 93
Prostate,
    exercises for, 49-50
Protection, exercises for, 23, 92, 108
Purifying exercises, 30, 76, 89
Push Up (*Chaturanga Dandasana*), 10

R

Ra Ma Da Sa Mantra, 96
Ra Ma Da Sa, Sa Say So Hung Mantra, 96
Radiance (also see Complexion), 32, 43, 93
Relationships,
    for clarity in, 69
Relaxation,
    sets ending with,
        10 minutes, 19, 33
        15 minutes, 13, 14-16, 19, 41, 49-50, 53
        varying time, 12, 16, 19, 22, 46

Respiratory System,
    exercises to strengthen, 58
Ring Finger (see Sun Finger)
Rising Up from the Knees, 48
Rock Pose (*Vajrasana*), 47
    exercises containing (see also Sat Kriya), 12, 13, 26, 38, 39

S

Sa Re Sa Sa, 86
Sa Ta Na Ma, 94, 99, 104, 115
Sabbotage (Self-), 71
Sahasrara, 32
Sat Kriya, 22
    sets containing, 13, 15, 18, 26, 53
Sat Nam, 102, 116, 123
Saturn Finger, 68, 93, 99-100, 105
Samasthiti (Standing Straight), 10
Savasana (Corpse Pose), 18, 25, 35, 38
Sciatic Nerve (exercises for), 17, 49, 51
Sensitivity,
    exercises to heighten, 91
Sexual System,
    balance sexual energy, 49-50, 51-52, 53
    relax sex organs (Lotus walk), 50
    strengthen sex organs, 45, 58
    transform sexual energy, 22, 26, 89
Shock,
    exercises to alleviate, 78, 116
Shoulder Shrugs, 12, 13, 35, 39, 41
Shoulder Stand, 15, 51
Side Bends, 33
Side Stretch, 45
Sight (see Eyes)
Silent (voice), see Mentally Vibrate
Siri Mantra, 96, 98
Sit-ups
    with legs wide, 49
Sound Current (see also Word), 86, 117, 121
Speaking (see Word)
Spinal Flex, 11, 13, 17, 26, 36, 41, 54, 58
    with chanting, 54
Spinal Twists (Torso Twists), 12, 13, 17, 33, 36, 41, 49
    with Gyan Mudra, 36
Spine,
    cervical, 29, 34, 35
    exercises for, 13, 14-16, 17-18
    lumbar, 17, 20, 43, 49, 50
    thoracic (mid-spine), 17
Stable Self Meditation, 75
Stamina,
    exercises to build, 58
Standing Straight (*Samasthiti* or Mountain Pose), 10
Standing Torso Twists, 33
Still Point (see Zero Point)
Stomach (also see Abdomen, digestion), 20
    pumps, 43
Stress (see Emotions, Shock)
Stretch Pose, 11, 20, 42, 48, 51
Stretching Backwards, 14
Stretching Up, 10
Subconscious Mind,
    cleaning, 124
Success, 71
Sufi Grind, 38
Sun Breath, 26, 65
Sun Finger, 65, 68, 93, 99-100, 105

Sun Salutation (*Surya Namaskara*), 10, 55
Supta Virasana (Fish Pose), 42, 51
Surya Namaskara (Sun Salutation), 10, 55
Sushmuna,
    mantra (*Raa Maa Daa Saa*), 96
    meditation, 89

T

Tadasana (Standing Straight), 10
Tattvas,
    to balance, 80, 93
Ten Bodies, 11, 12
Tenth Gate,
    meditation for, 32
Throat and Neck Massage, 49
Thymus,
    exercises for,
        bear grip, 34
        Inner Sun meditation, 65
Thyroid,
    exercises for,
        back platform, 43
        neck turns, 26
        shoulder stand, 44
        massage, 49
Torso Twists (Spinal Twists), 12, 13, 17, 33, 36 41
Torso Twists (Standing), 33
Tratakum,
    meditations, 81-82
    picture, 83
Triangle Pose (*Adho Mukha Svanasana*), 10, 23, 35, 47

U

Upavistha Konasana (Life Nerve Stretch Left & Right), 11, 15, 18
Urdhva Mukha Svanasana (Cobra Pose), 10, 18, 38, 47, 52
Urinary Tract, exercises to improve, 29
Ustrasana (Camel), 51
Uttanasana (Front Bend), 10, 19, 31, 37, 45, 47

V

Venus Kriyas, 126
Venus Lock, 12, 34, 39, 48, 49, 51
Virabhadrasana (Archer Pose), 14
Vitality, 58, 79, 124

W

Warm-up Exercises, 10, 55
Water balance, 73
Wheel Pose (*Urdhva Danurasana*), 42
Whisper (voice), 99
Windmill, 14, 33
Word, 114
    amplify power of, 89, 98
    conscious and graceful speech, 101
    sound of creativity of, 114
Worry (see Emotions)

Y

Yoga Mudra, 31, 38, 46-47
Youthfulness, 13, 29-30, 69

Z

Zero Point,
    for entire system, 60
    for heart center, 69

other books by Sybil MacBeth...

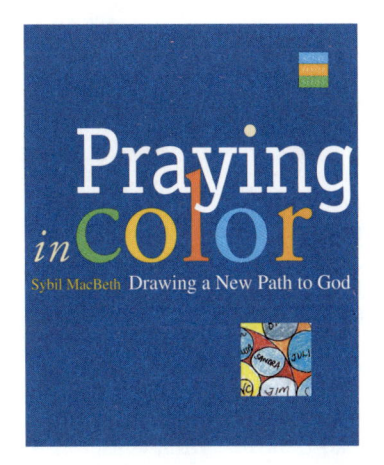

Praying in Color
Drawing a New Path to God
ISBN: 978-1-55725-512-9, $17.99, Paperback

Maybe you hunger to know God better. Maybe you love color. This new prayer form can take as little or as much time as you have or want to commit, from fifteen minutes to a weekend retreat.

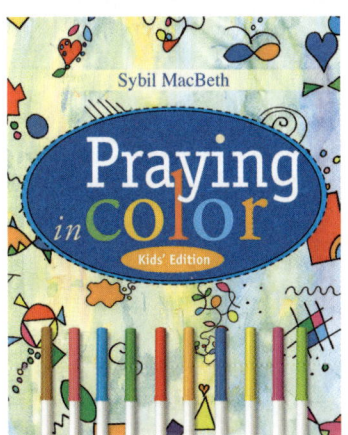

Praying in Color
Kids' Edition
ISBN: 978-1-55725-595-2, $16.99, Paperback

Now kids can pray in color, too! This first-of-its-kind resource will forever change the way kids pray—and how adults try to teach them to do it.

The Season of the Nativity
Confessions and Practices of an Advent, Christmas & Epiphany Extremist
ISBN: 978-1-61261-410-6, $17.99, Paperback

Sybil MacBeth's memoir, front-porch theology, and pages of practices and activities invite individuals and families to enjoy this season in a way that has more peace and more Christ and less chaos and guilt. She offers simple tools for busy people—perhaps to reclaim a joyful and yes, serious Nativity season for the first time.

Available from most booksellers or through Paraclete Press:
www.paracletepress.com; 1-800-451-5006. Try your local bookstore first.

about paraclete press

who we are

Paraclete Press is a publisher of books, recordings, and DVDs on Christian spirituality. Our publishing represents a full expression of Christian belief and practice—from Catholic to Evangelical, from Protestant to Orthodox.

We are the publishing arm of the Community of Jesus, an ecumenical monastic community in the Benedictine tradition. As such, we are uniquely positioned in the marketplace without connection to a large corporation and with informal relationships to many branches and denominations of faith.

what we are doing

Paraclete Press Books | Paraclete publishes books that show the richness and depth of what it means to be Christian. Although Benedictine spirituality is at the heart of who we are and all that we do, we publish books that reflect the Christian experience across many cultures, time periods, and houses of worship. We publish books that nourish the vibrant life of the church and its people.

We have several different series, including the best-selling Paraclete Essentials and Paraclete Giants series of classic texts in contemporary English; Voices from the Monastery—men and women monastics writing about living a spiritual life today; our award-winning Paraclete Poetry series as well as the Mount Tabor Books on the arts; best-selling gift books for children on the occasions of baptism and first communion; and the Active Prayer Series that brings creativity and liveliness to any life of prayer.

Mount Tabor Books | Paraclete's newest series, Mount Tabor Books, focuses on the arts and literature as well as liturgical worship and spirituality, and was created in conjunction with the Mount Tabor Ecumenical Centre for Art and Spirituality in Barga, Italy.

Paraclete Recordings | From Gregorian chant to contemporary American choral works, our recordings celebrate the best of sacred choral music composed through the centuries that create a space for heaven and earth to intersect. Paraclete Recordings is the record label representing the internationally acclaimed choir Gloriæ Dei Cantores, praised for their "rapt and fathomless spiritual intensity" by American Record Guide; the Gloriæ Dei Cantores Schola, specializing in the study and performance of Gregorian chant; and the other instrumental artists of the Gloriæ Dei Artes Foundation.

Paraclete Press is also privileged to be the exclusive North American distributor of the recordings of the Monastic Choir of St. Peter's Abbey in Solesmes, France, long considered to be a leading authority on Gregorian chant.

Paraclete Video | Our DVDs offer spiritual help, healing, and biblical guidance for a broad range of life issues including grief and loss, marriage, forgiveness, facing death, bullying, addictions, Alzheimer's, and spiritual formation.

Learn more about us at our website:
www.paracletepress.com,
or call us toll-free at 1-800-451-5006.